This book comes with access to more content online.

Quiz yourself, study with flashcards, and get certified!

Register your book or ebook at
www.dummies.com/go/getaccess.

Select your product, and then follow the prompts
to validate your purchase.

You'll receive an email with your PIN and instructions.

CCSP®

2nd Edition, with Online Practice

by Arthur J. Deane, CISSP, CCSP

CCSP® For Dummies®, 2nd Edition, with Online Practice

Published by: **John Wiley & Sons, Inc.,** 111 River Street, Hoboken, NJ 07030-5774, www.wiley.com

Copyright © 2024 by John Wiley & Sons, Inc., Hoboken, New Jersey

Media and software compilation copyright © 2021 by John Wiley & Sons, Inc. All rights reserved.

Published simultaneously in Canada

For general information on our other products and services, please contact our Customer Care Department within the US at 877-762-2974, outside the US at 317-572-3993, or fax 317-572-4002. For technical support, please visit https://hub.wiley.com/community/support/dummies.

Wiley publishes in a variety of print and electronic formats and by print-on-demand. Some material included with standard print versions of this book may not be included in e-books or in print-on-demand. If this book refers to media such as a CD or DVD that is not included in the version you purchased, you may download this material at http://booksupport.wiley.com. For more information about Wiley products, visit www.wiley.com.

Library of Congress Control Number: 2023949196

ISBN 978-1-394-21281-1 (pbk); ISBN 978-1-394-21280-4 (ePDF); ISBN 978-1-394-21284-2 (epub)

SKY10060489_112323

Contents at a Glance

Table of Contents

Introduction

As cloud computing has exploded over the last two decades, so has the need for security professionals who understand how the cloud works. Enter the Certified Cloud Security Professional (CCSP) certification. The CCSP was introduced in 2015 and has quickly become the de facto standard for cloud security certifications around the globe. Today, more than 10,000 security professionals have earned the coveted CCSP designation worldwide, and that number is quickly growing!

Cloud computing, as we know it, first became widely available circa 2006 when Amazon created the first enterprise cloud service offering, Amazon Web Services (AWS). Since then, Google, Microsoft, and a host of other companies have burst on the scene with their very own cloud services. Today, cloud computing is more mainstream than ever, with most research firms estimating the public cloud market to top $1 trillion worldwide by 2028. With most estimates putting cloud spend above 60 percent of all tech spend, the need for informed cloud professionals has never been greater.

While we continue to experience this massive cloud boom, cloud security has not so quietly become front-and-center for most organizations. Companies want to ensure that their most important business and customer data remain safe when moved to the cloud, and they need skilled and qualified practitioners to make that happen. That's where you (and the CCSP) come in!

You may be familiar with the CCSP's bigger sibling: the Certified Information Systems Security Professional (CISSP). The CISSP certification has been around since 1994 and has amassed quite a following in information security circles. (As of this writing, there are more than 160,000 CISSPs worldwide.) The CCSP serves the same purpose for one of the fastest growing information security subareas — cloud security. It's all but inevitable that the CCSP will continue its ascent among the most essential industry certifications around the world.

About this Book

Information security is one of the broadest domains of Information Technology. Add to that the complexities of cloud computing, and it's easy to see why many people are scared off by the field of cloud security. A true cloud security professional is a Jack (or Jill) of all trades — they know the ins and outs of data security and protection and also understand how cloud architectures are designed, managed, and operated. The CCSP credential seeks to validate that the holder has mastered the sweet spot between the two worlds. This task may sound daunting, but don't fret! *CCSP For Dummies* breaks these topics down into bite-sized chunks to help you digest the material, pass the exam, and apply your knowledge in the real world.

While you can find tons of books and resources available to study information security, cloud security resources are a bit harder to come by. Perhaps the field is still too young, or maybe it really is too daunting for some authors and publishers to assemble. Many of the books that do exist either don't cover all of the necessary facets of cloud security or are overly complex encyclopedic volumes.

In *CCSP For Dummies*, Wiley and I have put together a book that covers all of the topics within the CCSP Common Body of Knowledge (CBK) in a straightforward, easy-to-read manner. And this second edition has been updated to address the latest and greatest topics from the CCSP Exam Outline and beyond. You'll find this book to be overflowing with useful information, but written with the battle-tested *For Dummies* approach and styling that helps countless readers learn new topics. In addition, I try to inject many of my own experiences working in cloud security to give you practical views on some otherwise abstract topics.

As wonderful as I think this book is — and I hope you feel the same way after reading it — you shouldn't consider any single resource to be the Holy Grail of cloud security. *CCSP For Dummies* creates a framework for your CCSP studies and includes the information you need to pass the CCSP exam, but will not single-handedly make you a cloud security know-it-all. Reaching the top of the cloud security mountain requires knowledge, skills, and practical experience. This book is a great start, but not the end of your cloud security journey.

Foolish Assumptions

I've been told that assumptions are dangerous to make, but here I am making them anyway! At a minimum, I assume the following:

>> You have at least five years of general IT experience, at a minimum — preferably more. In order to follow the topics in this book and pass the CCSP exam, you need to have a great deal of knowledge of the technologies that form the foundation of cloud computing. This assumption means that you're comfortable referring to basic computing terms like CPU and RAM and also have experience with things like databases, networks, and operating systems.

» You have at least a high-level understanding of information security concepts and technologies. You should be familiar with things like access control and encryption, and you should understand the concepts of confidentiality, integrity, and availability. I expect that many readers have already achieved the prestigious CISSP certification. If you're among this group, then you're not only ready for this book, but you also satisfy all of the CCSP's experience requirements (which I discuss in Chapter 1). If you don't have sufficient information security knowledge or if you need to brush up on some basic security concepts, then you're in luck — I've written Chapter 2 just for you!

» You have a minimum of one year paid work experience in one or more of the six domains of the CCSP CBK (that make up Chapters 3 through 14 of this book). This expectation is not just an assumption, but an explicit requirement of the CCSP exam. Certain educational and certification achievements (such as earning CSA's CCSK) can be substituted for this experience requirement.

» You will use what you know and what you learn in this book for good, not evil. You'll be a responsible security professional and abide by the (ISC)² Code of Ethics (which is a requirement for CCSP certification).

Icons Used in This Book

This book is full of useful information, but every once in a while, something extra useful or important pops up and deserves some extra attention. Keep an eye out for the following icons throughout this book. Each has its own specific meaning, and identifies something you should take note of.

TIP

The Tip icon marks tips (duh!) and extra tidbits of information that can help you grasp some of the more challenging concepts in the text. When I use this icon, I'm trying to point out some extra information that can help you on your exam.

REMEMBER

These icons may not help you remember your spouse's birthday, but they'll surely come in handy for the CCSP exam. I use the Remember icon to point out stuff that's especially important to know for the exam. These are the things that might trip you up on the exam if you don't commit them to your long-term memory. Consider these your CCSP lifesavers.

TECHNICAL STUFF

The Technical Stuff icon marks information of a highly technical nature that may not necessarily be needed for the CCSP exam, but gives you deeper insight, if you want it. If you're a fan of tech jargon, then keep an eye out for this icon.

WARNING

The Warning icon is the closest I can get to flashing red lights and sirens. I use this icon to tell you to watch out! It marks important information that may save you headaches — or missed points on the exam. Keep an eye out for Warning icons, as they point out those silly mistakes that are otherwise easy to avoid.

Beyond the Book

CCSP For Dummies comes with a few extra goodies to help you prepare for the CCSP exam. My hope is that the book gives you the foundation you need to pass the test, but these extra resources can help put you over the top.

In addition to the book you're reading right now, you have access to some helpful Cheat Sheets that you can use to quickly reference things like common cloud security risks and the shared responsibility model. Keep these Cheat Sheets handy to reference whenever you may not have this book at your fingertips. To access your Cheat Sheets, head over to www.dummies.com and type **CCSP For Dummies Cheat Sheet** in the Search bar.

To help you assess your knowledge, you also have access to 100 flashcards and 200 online practice questions (two sets of 100 questions). You can use the flashcards to reinforce some key CCSP terms, topics, and concepts. I reference the relevant chapter that each flashcard comes from so that you can revisit specific subjects, if necessary. I've written the practice questions to mimic the multiple-choice style of questions you'll see on the CCSP exam. Use these practice sets to verify your mastery of important topics, and identify topics or domains that you may need to brush up on.

To access your flashcards and online practice questions, simply follow these steps to register your book and activate your account:

1. Register your book or ebook at Dummies.com to get your PIN. Go to www.dummies.com/go/getaccess.

2. Select your product (in this case, it's *CCSP For Dummies*) from the dropdown list on that page.

3. Follow the prompts to validate your product, and then check your email for a confirmation message that includes your PIN and instructions for logging in.

If you do not receive this email within two hours, please check your spam folder before contacting us through our Technical Support website at http://support.wiley.com or by phone at 877-762-2974.

Now you're ready to go! You can come back to the practice material as often as you want — simply log on with the username and password you created during your initial login. No need to enter the access code a second time.

Your registration is good for one year from the day you activate your PIN.

Where to Go from Here

So, what's next? While you can certainly read this book from cover to cover, you don't have to! *CCSP For Dummies* is broken into several parts, each with chapters that stand on their own. If a particular topic interests you, visit Part 2 and explore any (or all) of the CCSP domains.

If you need a primer on information security, then you may want to head over to Chapter 2 before diving into the CCSP domains.

If you still have no idea where to go from here, you can't go wrong with Chapter 1!

1

Starting Your CCSP Journey

Chapter **1**

Familiarizing Yourself with (ISC)² and the CCSP Certification

I n this chapter, you develop an understanding of the (ISC)² organization and CCSP certification, including what you need to know before the exam, what to expect during the exam, and what to do after you pass the exam!

Appreciating (ISC)² and the CCSP Certification

The *International Information System Security Certification Consortium* — more easily referred to as (ISC)² — is a nonprofit organization that has been training and certifying cybersecurity professionals since 1989. With more than 190,000 certified members and associates worldwide, (ISC)² is widely regarded as the world's leading cybersecurity professional organization. Its flagship certification, launched in 1994, is the Certified Information System Security Professional (CISSP). Since then, the organization has launched other certifications, including three CISSP concentrations. As of today, (ISC)² offers the following ten professional certifications and concentrations:

>> Certified in Cybersecurity (CC)

>> Certified Information Systems Security Professional (CISSP)

- Information Systems Security Architecture Professional (CISSP-ISSAP)

- Information Systems Security Engineering Professional (CISSP-ISSEP)

- Information Systems Security Management Professional (CISSP-ISSMP)

>> Systems Security Certified Practitioner (SSCP)

>> Certified Cloud Security Professional (CCSP)

>> Certified Authorization Professional (CAP)

>> Certified Secure Software Lifecycle Professional (CSSLP)

>> HealthCare Information Security and Privacy Practitioner (HCISSP)

In addition to managing a broad assortment of cybersecurity certifications, (ISC)² also organizes the annual (ISC)² Security Congress conference, which provides continuing education, networking, and career advancement opportunities for thousands of security professionals every year.

In 2015, (ISC)² and the Cloud Security Alliance (CSA) introduced the Certified Cloud Security Professional (CCSP) certification to the world. The CCSP is a standalone credential, but builds on certifications like the CISSP and CSA's Certificate of Cloud Security Knowledge (CCSK). The main objective of the CCSP is to certify that the credential holder has the knowledge, skills, and experience required to design, manage, and secure data in cloud-based applications and infrastructures.

Knowing Why You Need to Get Certified

According to (ISC)², a CCSP applies information security expertise to a cloud computing environment and demonstrates competence in cloud security architecture, design, operations, and service orchestration. In preparing for the CCSP exam, you expand your knowledge of information security and cloud computing concepts, making you a more well-rounded professional, while also improving your job security. Achieving the CCSP credential is a great way to strut your stuff in front of employers who seek verified cloud security expertise — say hello to increased visibility and new career opportunities!

REMEMBER

While the CCSP isn't generally a strict requirement for most cloud security positions, it does differentiate you to potential employers. It shows that you have the technical skills and experience they need as they seek to securely build and manage their cloud environments. The CCSP is a vendor-neutral certification, meaning the knowledge and skills it certifies can be applied to various technologies and methodologies. By not being limited to a single vendor, the CCSP designation is as versatile as it is valuable and can help you start or build a long-lasting career in cloud security.

Studying the Prerequisites for the CCSP

Along with passing the CCSP exam, you must satisfy a few other requirements to achieve the CCSP designation. As a CCSP candidate, you must have at least five years of paid work experience in Information Technology, and at least three of those years must include Information Security experience. Further, you must have at least one year of experience working in one or more of the six domains of the CCSP Common Body of Knowledge (CBK).

(ISC)² emphasizes practical, real-world experience to fulfill the work experience requirements. In other words, it's not enough to have IT or Information Security listed as a line-item on your resume — you must have regularly applied relevant knowledge and skills to perform your job duties. Some examples of full-time jobs that may satisfy these requirements include, but aren't limited to

>> Cloud architect

>> Enterprise architect

>> Information systems security officer

>> Security administrator

>> Security analyst

>> Security engineer

>> Systems architect

>> Systems engineer

If you don't have acceptable full-time work experience, (ISC)² also accepts part-time work and internships under the following guidelines:

>> **Part-time:** 2,080 hours of part-time work equals one year of full-time experience.

>> **Internships:** For paid or unpaid internships, you must provide documentation on company letterhead that confirms your experience.

TIP

If you already hold CSA's CCSK certificate, (ISC)² waives the requirement for one year of experience in one or more of the six CCSP domains. Even better, if you hold the CISSP credential, then you're all set for 100 percent of the CCSP experience requirements!

TIP

If you don't already have the required work experience, you can still take the CCSP exam. When you pass, you'll earn the Associate of (ISC)² designation and be given six years to earn the required experience and become a fully certified member. You can learn more about CCSP experience requirements at www.isc2.org/Certifications/CCSP/experience-requirements.

Understanding the CCSP Domains

Six security domains are within the CCSP Common Body of Knowledge (CBK), and I cover them fully in Chapters 3 through 14. Think of these domains as the six subject areas that you must master in order to pass the exam. The CCSP domains (and their respective weightings on the exam) are

>> **Domain 1:** Cloud Concepts, Architecture, and Design (17 percent)

>> **Domain 2:** Cloud Data Security (20 percent)

>> **Domain 3:** Cloud Platform and Infrastructure Security (17 percent)

>> **Domain 4:** Cloud Application Security (17 percent)

>> **Domain 5:** Cloud Security Operations (16 percent)

>> **Domain 6:** Legal, Risk and Compliance (13 percent)

Domain 1: Cloud Concepts, Architecture, and Design

Domain 1: Cloud Concepts, Architecture, and Design counts for 17 percent of the CCSP exam and is the foundational domain that lays the groundwork for your understanding of cloud computing. You should think of this domain as your gateway to cloud mastery — everything else simply builds on the elements and concepts outlined here.

In this domain, you learn how to identify and define everyone's role in a cloud implementation, including both the cloud provider and cloud customer. Domain 1 gives you an understanding of the key technical characteristics of cloud computing and also introduces you to the various capabilities, categories, and deployment models of cloud architectures.

You must consider specific design requirements in order to develop a functional and secure cloud environment. Some of these requirements coincide with your traditional data center, so you should see some familiar content. However, certain features of cloud computing require additional consideration and new approaches. Domain 1 introduces the cloud security data lifecycle and discusses how things like cryptography, network security, and access control should be used to protect against the many unique threats that cloud environments and cloud data face.

Domain 1 also introduces various methods for cloud customers to evaluate and verify cloud providers against established security standards and certifications. Cloud customers cannot manage and control cloud environments the way they control their data centers, so there needs to be a way for them to validate the security and operations of the cloud services they use. Cloud providers can earn certifications across their entire environments and applications, or they can opt for various certifications aimed at specific components and products, such as FIPS 140-3 certification. You learn about all of these topics in Domain 1.

Domain 2: Cloud Data Security

Domain 2: Cloud Data Security is the most heavily weighted domain on the CCSP exam, at 20 percent, and covers identifying, classifying, and securing cloud data. The domain begins with coverage of the cloud data lifecycle and identifies the most important security considerations, from data creation through data destruction.

Each of the cloud service categories (IaaS, PaaS, and SaaS) leverages its own data storage types. Domain 2 defines these types, identifies the threats they face, and explores various unique considerations around securing each of them. While many of the data security technologies used in the cloud are similar to those used in traditional data centers, how they are used varies based on the specific cloud architecture and any regulatory or contractual obligations the cloud provider may have. This domain covers designing and implementing a data security strategy that fits your particular cloud architecture.

The topics of data discovery and data classification are core to any data security strategy. Domain 2 explores these concepts as they pertain to cloud computing and focuses on the cloud-specific challenges associated with each. Here, you learn how multitenancy and the large geographic footprint of most cloud providers make discovering and classifying sensitive data a big challenge and what to do about that. Among the many solutions, this domain covers Information Rights Management (IRM) technologies and how they can be used to enforce specific security and privacy requirements for data in (or outside of) the cloud. In addition to protecting data, this domain covers the concepts of data retention, deletion, and archiving.

Ensuring effective data security also requires that you ensure the auditability, traceability, and accountability of data events. Domain 2 covers the identification of data sources by cloud service category, and the logging, storing, and analyzing of relevant data events. Among the many requirements you explore, this domain emphasizes ensuring chain of custody and nonrepudiation for data events. Don't worry, Chapters 5 and 6 cover all this jargon, and more!

Domain 3: Cloud Platform and Infrastructure Security

Cloud Platform and Infrastructure Security (Domain 3) counts for 17 percent of the CCSP exam and focuses on the practical matters of securing a cloud platform and its infrastructure. You explore what makes up a cloud's virtualized (logical) environment and how that relates to the physical environment underneath it — you also dive into what it takes to secure both the logical and physical components of a cloud environment.

In Domain 1, you focus a lot of your attention on the architecture of cloud environments. It's there that you learn about the virtual infrastructure that enables the power of cloud computing, and appreciate how the underlying physical infrastructure supports all that cloudy goodness. In Domain 3, you explore the unique security concerns and requirements associated with a cloud's logical and physical environment. Mastery of these concepts requires that you understand a host of cloud-specific risks, including virtualization risks, and learn what security controls and strategies to implement as a result. In Domain 3, you learn all about what it takes to design a secure data center at the logical and physical layers.

A major component of any secure system is ensuring appropriate identity and access management. This domain hits on identification, authentication, and authorization for cloud infrastructures and covers how these topics should be managed by cloud customers who rely on a shared, third-party resources, like the cloud.

Last, but not least, Domain 3 covers the essential topics of business continuity and disaster recovery (BCDR). These concepts are hugely important for any company on any kind of architecture — cloud or legacy. While cloud environments inherently provide a great deal of redundancy over traditional data centers, organizations must understand how cloud usage fits into their overall BCDR strategy. This domain dives into what it takes to develop a comprehensive strategy, including defining your scope, generating your requirements, and appropriately assessing BCDR risks to your organization. While an effective strategy requires lots of planning, it's also important that your plan is regularly tested to ensure its feasibility and effectiveness.

Domain 4: Cloud Application Security

Domain 4: Cloud Application Security is weighted at 17 percent of the CCSP exam and covers the most critical application security concerns that are relevant to cloud environments. This domain starts with coverage of common cloud-related application security pitfalls and then introduces some of the most significant categories of cloud application vulnerabilities.

One of the primary focal points of Domain 4 is the secure software development lifecycle (SDLC) process. In this domain, you learn all about the phases of that process and how to apply it to secure application development in cloud environments. You not only explore the most common SDLC methodologies (waterfall and agile), but you also take a look at threat modeling and explore how it pertains to secure cloud development and configuration management.

A major part of software development, whether in cloud environments or not, is application testing. In Domain 4, you learn about static and dynamic application security testing (SAST and DAST) — you gain an understanding of the pros and cons of each and how they can be used together to form a comprehensive cloud application testing strategy. You learn about the differences of black box and white box testing and identify when to use each method. To wrap up your study of security testing methodologies, Domain 4 introduces the practices of vulnerability scanning and penetration testing. You learn that these are not the same things and gain an appreciation for how they complement each other as part of your comprehensive application testing strategy.

Between Domain 1 and Domain 4, you learn that cloud environments and applications can be made up of multiple components, services, and integrations from various sources. In this domain, you explore the importance of using verified secure software components. You dive into topics like supply-chain management and third-party software management and gain an understanding of using secure and approved Application Programming Interfaces (APIs) and Open Source Software (OSS). After laying this groundwork, Domain 4 covers the architecture of cloud applications and highlights specific security components that you should understand. In this domain, you revisit topics like cryptography and Identity and Access Management (IAM) and learn how they apply specifically to cloud-based application development.

Domain 5: Cloud Security Operations

Domain 5 covers the broad topic of security operations in the cloud, which includes everything from managing your data center's security to collecting and preserving digital evidence using cloud forensics techniques. This domain is worth 16 percent of the total CCSP exam.

Domain 5 begins with coverage of topics related to implementing and building a cloud infrastructure, both at the physical and logical layers. You learn about secure hardware configuration requirements (such as BIOS security) and also explore how to securely install and configure virtualization management tools. Next, the domain takes you from building your cloud infrastructure to securely operating it. This domain covers the nitty-gritty details associated with access controls for local and remote access, securing your network configurations, and using baselines as a guide, to harden the operating systems throughout your cloud environment. You learn how to securely manage stand-alone hosts, clustered hosts, as well as guest operating systems on the virtualized infrastructure.

Aside from building and operating a secure cloud infrastructure, Domain 5 has a strong focus on securely managing your physical and logical cloud infrastructure, which includes all of the technical, management, and operational activities and controls necessary to keep your cloud environment securely running. This domain covers things like patch management, performance and capacity monitoring, hardware monitoring, and backup and restore functions. You spend some time learning about additional network security controls, like honeypots and network security groups, and also learn about securing and securely using the management plane. Much of this information feeds into the domain's coverage of the Security Operations Center (SOC) and how a SOC can be used to monitor security controls across a cloud's physical and logical environment.

One of the most important aspects of Domain 5 involves coverage of operational controls and standards, like ITIL, and how to apply and implement those standards in your cloud environment. You explore common IT topics like change management, incident management, and configuration management, as they specifically pertain to cloud computing. Domain 5 wraps up with an important discussion about managing communication with customers, vendors, and other relevant parties.

Domain 6: Legal, Risk, and Compliance

Domain 6 counts for roughly 13 percent of the CCSP exam and focuses on the many legal and regulatory requirements that pertain to cloud environments. Cloud computing environments often extend across national borders and are subject to multiple different jurisdictions and regulations. You can picture one big cloud that's hovering over three different countries. Each country has its own regulations and policies, and within that country are several different states or jurisdictions that have their own laws. If that's not enough, there are also regulations specific to banking, healthcare, education, and the list goes on — but there's just that one large cloud hovering above, trying to cover everyone down below. Yikes! Maintaining compliance in each territory and industry can be overwhelming. This domain focuses on how cloud providers and customers can handle all their legal, risk, and compliance obligations.

In Domain 6, you learn that a pretty common legal challenge in cloud computing comes in the form of an e-Discovery order to produce data for a court or other government entity. In this domain, you examine the notion of e-Discovery and digital forensics in the cloud, as well as the challenges that come with it.

It's not good enough for cloud providers to do a bunch of security things and tell their customers trust them — auditing is a huge part of maintaining and demonstrating compliance to regulators and customers. This domain explores the different types of audits and how they impact cloud environments and their design. You explore the auditing process, standards that govern the process, reporting, and the stakeholders involved.

In addition to legal and regulatory requirements, Domain 6 covers the subject of risk management as it pertains to cloud computing. Cloud computing creates a paradigm shift from owning and controlling everything to the Shared Responsibility Model (don't worry, I discuss this in Chapter 3). With this change, customers need to think about how they assess, manage, and monitor risk different than they ever have. Domain 6 includes various risk frameworks and focuses on applying them in the cloud.

Preparing for the Exam

You can prepare for the CCSP exam in many ways. Self-study (like reading this book) is a very popular way to prepare, but you can include lots of other components in your study plan. Whether it's practical hands-on experience at work (which is not only helpful, but a requirement for certification) or formal classroom training, you should put together a mix of study elements that works best for your personal learning style.

TIP

When preparing for the CCSP exam, I recommend that you establish and commit to a study plan. Your study plan should include a firm timeline, study materials of choice, studying methodology, and your selected method(s) of practicing. I recommend either a 90-day or 120-day timeline, depending on your level of experience. If you've already passed the CISSP or have many years of Information Security experience, then a 90-day plan should suffice. If you're starting from a more junior level, consider giving yourself a full four months. The key is to set an aggressive timeline that is realistic based on your current knowledge and time commitments. Make sure that you consider your planned work and family commitments. I will not be held accountable for angry husbands, wives, children, or pets!

TIP

To successfully prepare for the CCSP exam, you really have to know your learning style and cater to it. Personally, I learn best by locking myself in a room and reading books in silence. Other people prefer small study groups, and some opt for classroom learning. I present some options in the following sections, but it's up to you to find the ones that work best for you.

Studying on your own

Self-study is probably the most common way for people to prepare for the CCSP and other exams like it. Many self-study resources are available for you, including books, practice exams, and a host of Internet resources. (See Appendix B for some resources that complement this book.)

Your first step should be to download the official CCSP Certification Exam Outline (www.isc2.org/CCSP-Exam-Outline). I've aligned this book with the topics in that document, and it's a good idea to review it to get an idea of the subjects that you're about to learn.

Your next step is my personal favorite: Read this book. *CCSP For Dummies* is (ISC)²-approved and covers of the content in the CCSP CBK. By starting with this book, you get a thorough review of all the topics that you can expect when you sit for the CCSP exam. It doesn't matter if you read *CCSP For Dummies* cover to cover or hop around the chapters out of order — the book is modular and meant to be read in any way you want, although upside-down might be a bit tough!

REMEMBER

The purchase of this book grants you access to online practice questions and flashcards (see the Introduction for more information). Use these resources to assess your learning after you complete the book.

After reading this book, you should then read any other study resources you can get your hands on to strengthen your understanding and retention of the exam topics. Additional resources can include other books (just make sure they're

(ISC)²-approved!), web resources (see Appendix B), or the wealth of resources that ISC2 recommends on its website (www.isc2.org/certifications/References).

WARNING

Don't rely on any single book (including this awesome one!) as your only resource to prepare for the CCSP. The exam covers a wide range of information, and you should get multiple views to ensure you fully understand each topic.

Another key to self-study is validating that you've learned and retained critical information. You should answer a whole lot of practice questions. In addition to the ones that come with this book, lots of resources are available for CCSP practice exams and questions. (Check out Appendix B to get you started.) You should know that no practice exams perfectly mirror the CCSP exam — some may be unbearably difficult, while others fail to cover half the exam topics. That's why I recommend answering as many practice questions from as many sources possible — just make sure that you get your practice questions and exams only from trusted sources.

Once you've read through all your study materials and you've tested your knowledge with practice questions, you should revisit this book one last time before taking the exam. Maybe you just focus on any notes you've taken in the margins or perhaps you do a quick reread of the entire book. Either way, I recommend revisiting this book closer to test day to remind yourself of any details you may have forgotten and clarify any topics that are still fuzzy.

Learning by doing

As Julius Caesar once said, "Experience is the best teacher." You could read all the cloud security books in the world, but nothing compares to practical hands-on learning.

You might work in a role in which you can use all of the things you learn in this book. If so, you're really lucky! Use every opportunity you get to apply the wealth of information from this book to what you do at work. If you don't have a related role, that's fine, too. Perhaps your company is migrating to the cloud? Or maybe your business already uses cloud services? Find teams and people involved in your organization's cloud endeavors and seek ways to get involved.

Getting official (ISC)² CCSP training

While many people are successful using self-study resources to prepare for the CCSP, some opt to attend a seminar or boot camp to brush up on the topics covered in the CCSP CBK. If you're in the latter group, (ISC)² offers multiple training options to fit your learning style and schedule. For the most flexibility, you can choose (ISC)²'s self-paced training option. Self-paced training includes online access to recorded instruction and course content, chapter quizzes, learning activities, and more. The course costs $920 for 180 days of access. The course also qualifies you to receive 40 Continuing Professional Education (CPE) credits. This is a great access-anywhere option that puts you in complete control of your learning journey.

Some people learn best in a traditional classroom setting, and (ISC)² has an answer for that, too. You can sign up for classroom-based training led by (ISC)² or an official (ISC)² training provider. These are offered on-site — at an (ISC)² classroom or partner facility — as five- or six-day training seminars that cover the entire CCSP CBK in less than a week.

TIP

(ISC)² also offers private on-site training for groups of ten or more. This is ideal if your organization wants to train an entire team at once as(ISC)² sends an authorized instructor to the location of your choosing. If you're looking for the best of both worlds, (ISC)² offers an option that is led by an authorized instructor, but accessed from the comfort of your own home (or wherever you might be). You can choose a university-style course that meets online with a variety of scheduling options, including weekdays, weekends, and evenings.

You can find course schedules, costs, and additional information regarding official (ISC)² training at www.isc2.org/training.

Attending other training courses

While (ISC)² and their official partners provide excellent training courses, other legitimate organizations also offer quality training options. As any IT certification grows in popularity, so do the number of companies offering training services — it never fails.

REMEMBER

Make sure that you do your research before handing over your hard-earned money to one of these companies. Search online to learn more about the company and course instructor. Ask your friends and colleagues whether they've taken the course or had any experiences with the training organization. Get as much information as possible to make sure the company is reputable and the training is useful.

Practice, practice, practice

Practice questions are the best way to confirm that you understand the topics that you'll be tested on when you take the CCSP exam. You should definitely start with the practice questions included with this book (see the Introduction for more information). After that, you can search for additional sample questions and practice exams — just make sure you're using reputable sources. When answering practice questions, make note of the types of questions you get wrong and revisit those topics in this book and your other study materials.

TIP

It's a good idea to time yourself when taking practice exams. You have four hours to answer 150 questions on the real exam, so make sure you're averaging under roughly 90 seconds per question.

Ensuring you're ready for the exam

Okay, so you read this book and answered the included practice questions. Then you read some more books and took additional practice exams. Maybe you found a CCSP study group or perhaps you decided to take a five-day bootcamp — when are you ready for the exam? You could easily study for months on end and spend lots of money on study material, but at some point, you just have to challenge the exam.

I recommend laying out a 90- or 120-day study plan and sticking to it. *CCSP For Dummies* has all the information you need to pass the CCSP exam. Read this book, take plenty of notes, and answer the practice questions until you grasp the content. Follow up by reading other books and study materials, and answering as many other practice questions as possible.

REMEMBER

The key to any effective plan is having a clear end-goal. Once you can consistently score 85 percent in each domain, I'd say you're ready for the exam!

Registering for the Exam

I recommend picking an exam date and registering for the exam at the beginning of your CCSP journey. The sooner you decide to register, the sooner you can have a firm goal to work toward!

TIP

Exam prices, taxes, and currency depend on your location. The current exam fee is $599 in the United States.

The CCSP exam is a computer-based test (CBT) and can be taken at a Pearson VUE testing center nearest you; Pearson VUE is the exclusive administrator for all (ISC)² exams around the world.

Registering for the exam is pretty easy if you follow these steps:

1. **Navigate to the Pearson VUE website by visiting** www.pearsonvue.com/isc2.

2. **Create an account for yourself with Pearson VUE.**

3. **Select the exam you're registering for.**

    Hopefully that's the CCSP, or else I'm writing the wrong book!

4. **Find the day, time, and Pearson VUE testing center that works best for you.**

5. **Pay your exam fee and register for the exam.**

TIP

(ISC)² offers reasonable and appropriate accommodations for test takers who have a legitimate need for special accommodations (such as a medical condition, for example). If you require special accommodations, contact (ISC)² before registering for your exam. Visit www.isc2.org/Register-for-Exam for more information.

WARNING

If you arrive at your test center more than 15 minutes after your scheduled exam time, you'll be considered late. If this happens, the testing center may choose to turn you away. If you're deemed late or if you miss the exam, you can kiss your exam fee goodbye!

You can reschedule or cancel your exam by contacting Pearson VUE, by phone, at least 24 hours before your scheduled exam. If you want to reschedule or cancel online, you have up to 48 hours before your scheduled exam to do so. Pearson VUE charges $50 to reschedule your exam, while it will run you $100 to cancel.

Taking the Exam

The CCSP is a computer-based testing (CBT) exam that consists of 150 multiple-choice questions. You have a maximum of four hours to complete the exam — that's about 96 seconds per question. (ISC)² uses a scaled scoring approach and requires you to achieve at least 700 out of a possible 1,000 points to pass the CCSP exam.

TECHNICAL
STUFF

On every CCSP exam, 50 of the 150 questions are known as pre-test items that are included for research purposes only. Pre-test items do not count toward your score and are used by (ISC)² to try new questions. You won't know which questions are pre-test items, so it's important that you do your best to answer each of the 150 questions accurately.

TIP

If you've never taken a CBT exam, you can watch a demo and take a tutorial on the Pearson Vue website by visiting www.pearsonvue.com/athena/athena.asp.

When you get to the Pearson Vue testing center, you must check in before sitting for the exam. The standard check-in process involves the following steps:

>> Present two forms of ID (refer to the (ISC)² website or your exam confirmation email for acceptable forms of ID.

>> Have your photo taken.

>> Provide your signature.

>> Submit to a palm scan (unless it's prohibited by law).

Before your exam begins, you are granted five minutes to read the (ISC)² Non-Disclosure Agreement (NDA). If you fail to read and accept it within the allotted time, your exam will end, and you lose your exam fees! Instead of dealing with this kind of pressure right before answer 150 tough questions, I recommend you download and read the NDA before test day. You can find a link to download the NDA in Appendix B.

TIP

Some questions on your exam may appear to have multiple right answers, but success on the CCSP requires that you select the *best* answer for each question. Use the process of elimination to get rid of two answers that are clearly wrong. You'll be left with the correct answer and what *psychometricians* (people who study the science of testing) call a distractor. If you take a deep breath and dig deep into your memory bank, you'll have a great shot at eliminating the distractor and choosing the single correct answer.

Identifying What to Do After the Exam

After four grueling hours (or less) and 150 mind-bending questions, you're all done with your CCSP exam! So, now what? Well, in most cases, you'll have your unofficial test results as soon as you finish the exam — hopefully you've passed, and you can go celebrate!

If, for whatever reason, you don't pass the exam on your first try, don't fret! It's not uncommon for folks to need a couple tries on such a tough exam — although *CCSP For Dummies* is here to help you avoid that fate! Candidates who fail their first try must wait 30 days before taking the exam again. If failure happens to you, I strongly recommend you read this book again and take lots of practice exams within that 30 days. If you fail a second time, you must wait 90 days to try again.

If you fail again, I need you to eat, drink, and sleep cloud security for that 90 days! Read and reread this book (and review your other resources) until you know all six domains inside and out.

Okay, enough about that — you're here to pass the CCSP! Once you receive formal notification that you've passed the exam, you have nine months to complete the CCSP endorsement process. Endorsement is the act of having an existing (ISC)² credential holder attest to your work experience and give (ISC)² the thumbs-up to welcome you into the family. Visit www.isc2.org/endorsement for more information.

Once you pass the exam and complete the endorsement process, you are officially a Certified Cloud Security Professional! But this isn't the end of your journey — in fact, your CCSP journey is a lifelong one. You must remain a member in good standing by doing two things:

>> **Paying your annual maintenance fee (AMF):** All (ISC)² certified members must pay an AMF of $125 every year on their certification anniversary (except those who hold only the CC certification — they pay $50 per year). (ISC)² uses members' AMFs to maintain their certifications and all the support systems and benefits that come with being a member.

>> **Completing your Continuing Professional Education (CPE):** Once you're a CCSP credential holder, you must demonstrate ongoing maintenance and enhancement of your cloud security knowledge by earning CPEs. As a CCSP, you must earn at least 90 CPE credits every three years, with a suggested minimum of 30 CPEs annually. You can earn CPE credit by completing activities that are directly related to the CCSP domains, including (but not limited to)

- Attending a conference, seminar, or presentation

- Finishing a project that's outside your normal work duties

- Writing a whitepaper or book

- Volunteering for a charitable organization

- Taking a higher education course

- Reading a book or magazine

IN THIS CHAPTER

» Recognizing the pillars of information security

» Identifying threats, vulnerabilities, and risks

» Discovering how to control access to your data

» Exploring encryption

» Planning for and responding to security incidents

Chapter **2**

Identifying Information Security Fundamentals

I n this chapter, you find out about the core security concepts crucial to passing the exam. You discover the most fundamental security topics and begin to set the stage for what you need to know to pass the exam. You need to understand a few foundational principles before embarking on your CCSP journey. This chapter serves as your information security primer.

REMEMBER

Although many CCSP candidates have already attained the CISSP or other security certifications, it's not a requirement to sit for the CCSP exam. If you already hold one of these certifications — or if you already have a strong grasp of security topics — you can probably skip this chapter and dive right into the CCSP domain chapters in Part 2.

Exploring the Pillars of Information Security

Information security is the practice of protecting information by maintaining its confidentiality, integrity, and availability. These three principles form the pillars of information security, and they're often referred to as the *CIA triad* (see Figure 2-1). Although different types of data and systems may prioritize one over the others, the three principles work together and depend on each other to successfully secure your information. After all, you can't have a triangle with two legs!

FIGURE 2-1: The CIA triad is the foundation of information security.

Confidentiality

Confidentiality entails limiting access to data to authorized users and systems. In other words, confidentiality prevents exposure of information to anyone who is not an intended party. If you receive a letter in the mail, the principle of confidentiality means that you're the intended recipient of that letter; opening and reading someone else's letter violates the principle of confidentiality. The concept of confidentiality is closely related to the security best practice of *least privilege*, which asserts that access to systems or information should only be granted on a need to know basis.

In order to enforce the principle of least privilege and maintain confidentiality, it's important that you classify (or categorize) data by its sensitivity level. You explore data classification in Chapter 5, but for this chapter, keep in mind that it plays a critical role in ensuring confidentiality. You must know what data you own and how sensitive it is before determining how to protect it and who to protect it from.

TIP

Privacy is a hot topic that focuses on the confidentiality of personal data. Personal information such as names, birthdates, addresses, and Social Security numbers are referred to as *personally identifiable information (PII)*. You can find out more about privacy in Chapter 13.

Integrity

Integrity involves maintaining the accuracy, validity, and completeness of information and systems. It ensures that data is not tampered with by anyone other than an authorized party for an authorized purpose. If your mail carrier opens your mail, destroys the letter inside, and seals it back up — well, you have a pretty mean mail carrier! In addition to not being a very nice person, your mail carrier has violated the principle of integrity: The letter did not reach the intended audience (you) in the same state that the sender sent it.

A *checksum* is a value derived from a piece of data that uniquely identifies that data and is used to detect changes that may have been introduced during storage or transmission. Checksums are generated based on cryptographic hashing algorithms and help you validate the integrity of data. You can find out more about cryptography in the "Deciphering Cryptography" section, later in this chapter, and hashing in Chapter 5.

Availability

Availability is all about ensuring that authorized users can access required systems and data when and where they need it. Availability is sometimes the forgotten little sibling of the principles mentioned in the two preceding sections, but it has a special place in the cloud given that easy access to data is often a major selling point for cloud services. If your letter gets lost in the mail, then availability is a clear issue — the message that was intended for you to read is no longer accessible for you to read.

One of the most common attacks on availability is *Distributed Denial of Service*, or *DDoS*, which is a coordinated attack by multiple compromised machines causing disruption to a system's availability. Another common and rapidly growing attack on availability is *ransomware*, which involves an attacker blocking system or data owners from accessing their own systems and data until a sum of money is paid. Aside from sophisticated cyber-attacks, something as simple as accidentally deleting a file can compromise availability.

REMEMBER

Availability is a major consideration for cloud systems.

Security controls

So, you know all about confidentiality, integrity, and availability — that's great! Now, how do you enforce those concepts in your systems? A *security control* is a specific mechanism or measure implemented to safeguard systems or assets against potential threats and vulnerabilities — said another way, security controls protect the confidentiality, integrity, and availability of your systems and data.

TIP You'll often see "security controls" referenced as just "controls."

Security controls can be categorized in a couple of ways: by their type and by their function. Types of security control include

>> *Technical controls* use technology (shocking, I know!) to protect information systems and data. Things like firewalls, data loss prevention (DLP) systems, and encryption fall under this category.

>> *Physical controls* involve the use of physical measures to protect an organization's assets. This can include things like doors, gates, surveillance cameras, and physical disposal of sensitive information (including things like shredding and degaussing).

>> *Administrative controls* include the set of policies, procedures, guidelines, and practices that govern the protection of systems and data. This can be anything from incident response plans (see later in this chapter) to security awareness training.

Functions of security controls include

>> *Preventative controls* keep negative security events from happening. This includes things like security awareness training, locked doors, and encryption.

>> *Detective controls* identify negative security events when they do happen. Examples of detective controls include log monitoring and video surveillance.

>> *Corrective controls* fix or reduce damages associated with a negative security event and may include measures to prevent the same negative event from happening again. Backups and system recovery features are the most common examples of corrective controls.

Threats, Vulnerabilities, and Risks . . . Oh My!

They aren't lions, tigers, or bears — but for many security professionals, threats, vulnerabilities, and risks are just as scary. Threats, vulnerabilities, and risks are interrelated terms describing things that may compromise the pillars of information security for a given system or an *asset* (the thing you're protecting).

The field of *risk management* deals with identifying threats and vulnerabilities and quantifying and addressing the risk associated with them. Being able to recognize threats, vulnerabilities, and risks is a critical skill for information security professionals. It's important that you're able to identify the things that may cause your systems and data harm in order to better plan, design, and implement protections against them.

Threats

A *threat* is anything capable of intentionally or accidentally compromising an asset's security. Some examples of common threats include

>> **Natural disasters:** Earthquakes, hurricanes, floods, and fires can cause physical damage to critical infrastructure, leading to loss of connectivity, power outages, or even complete destruction of systems.

>> **Malware:** Malicious software such as viruses, worms, and ransomware can infect systems, steal data, or disrupt normal business operations.

>> **Phishing attacks:** Deceptive emails, messages, or websites designed to trick individuals into revealing sensitive information like passwords, credit card numbers, or personal data.

>> **Denial of service (DOS) attacks:** Deliberate attempts to overload a network, server, or website with excessive traffic, making it unavailable to legitimate users.

Though only a few examples, the preceding short list shows how threats can come in all shapes and sizes, and how they can be natural or manmade, malicious or accidental.

Vulnerabilities

A *vulnerability* is a weakness or gap existing within a system; it's something that, if not taken care of, may be exploited in order to compromise an asset's confidentiality, integrity, or availability. Examples of vulnerabilities include

>> **Unpatched software:** Failure to install updates or patches for operating systems, applications, or firmware, leaving security vulnerabilities open to exploitation.

>> **Lack of environmental protection:** Missing or faulty fire suppression systems or other physical protections, leaving infrastructure vulnerable to natural disasters and other environmental threats.

>> **Insecure passwords:** The use of commonly used or otherwise insecure passwords, making it easier for attackers to gain unauthorized access to accounts or systems.

>> **Untrained employees:** Lack of security awareness training for employees and system users, leaving them susceptible to phishing attacks.

Threats are pretty harmless without an associated vulnerability, and vice versa. A good fire detection and suppression system gives your data center a fighting chance, just like (you hope) thorough security awareness training for your organization's employees will neutralize the threat of an employee clicking on a link in a phishing email.

Risks

Risk is the intersection of threat and vulnerability that defines the likelihood of a vulnerability being exploited (by a *threat actor*) and the impact should that exploit occur. In other words, risk is used to define the potential for damage or loss of an asset. Some examples of risks include

>> A fire wipes out your data center, making service unavailable for five days.

>> A hacker steals half of your customer's credit card numbers, causing significant reputational damage to your company.

>> An attacker gains root privilege through a phishing email and steals your agency's Top Secret defense intelligence.

REMEMBER

Risk = Threat x Vulnerability. This simple equation is the cornerstone of risk management. Find out more about risk management in Chapter 14.

Understanding Identity and Access Management (IAM)

So much of information security requires you to first have a strong understanding of who your users are and then controlling their actions based on their identity. Think about it this way: The principle of confidentiality is pretty hard to enforce if you don't first understand who does and doesn't qualify as an authorized user, right? In this section, I introduce some key concepts associated with identity and access management, or IAM.

IAM consists of four key elements: identification, authentication, authorization, and accountability.

Identification is the act of establishing who (or what) someone (or something) is. In computing, *identification* is the process by which you associate an entity (i.e., a system or user) with a unique identity or name, such as a username or email address.

Authentication takes identification a step further and validates a user's identity. During authentication, you answer the question "Are you who you say you are?" before authorizing access to a system.

Passwords are the most obvious and common forms of authentication, but *authenticators* (things used to verify identity) can vary. Authenticators generally fit into one of three *factors* (or methods):

>> **Something you know:** Passwords and PINs (Personal Identification Numbers) fall into this category.

>> **Something you have:** Security tokens and smart cards are examples of this factor.

>> **Something you are:** Examples of this factor include fingerprints, iris scans, voice analysis, and other biometric methods.

REMEMBER

Due to the imperfect nature of any one of the preceding factors, many organizations require *Two-Factor Authentication* (2FA) or *Multifactor Authentication (MFA)*. MFA has become standard practice for enforcing stronger validation of a user's identity. Because passwords can be hacked and security tokens can be stolen, the idea here is to require more than one form of authentication to reduce the risk of granting access to someone impersonating someone else.

Once you verify a user's identity, you can determine what access to grant them. *Authorization* is the process of granting access to a user based on their authenticated identity and the policies you've set for them. You can control access to systems and data in many ways, but that topic is largely outside the scope of this book.

The final major element in IAM is *accountability*, which involves assigning and holding an entity responsible for their actions within an information system. Accountability requires establishing unique user identities, enforcing strong authentication, and maintaining thorough logs to track user actions.

TIP

You can explore cloud-related IAM in Chapter 3.

Deciphering Cryptography

Cryptography is the science of encrypting and decrypting information to protect its confidentiality and/or integrity. It is easily one of the most daunting topics in the information security field, but it's incredibly foundational for so much of what you do to protect data's confidentiality and integrity. You don't have to be a Math Ph.D. to grasp the most critical concepts of encryption, and the following sections tell you what you need to know.

Encryption and decryption

Encryption is the process of using an algorithm (or *cipher*) to convert plaintext (or the original information) into ciphertext. The ciphertext is unreadable unless it goes through the reverse process, known as *decryption*, which then allows an authorized party to convert the ciphertext back to its original form using the appropriate encryption key(s). An *encryption key* is a piece of information that allows the holder to encrypt and/or decrypt data.

Types of encryption

Encryption can either be *symmetric-key* or *asymmetric-key*. The two encryption types function very differently and are generally used for different applications.

>> **Symmetric-key encryption** (sometimes referred to as *secret-key encryption*) uses the same key (called a *secret key*) for both encryption and decryption (see Figure 2-2). Using a single key means the party encrypting the information must give that key to the recipient before they can decrypt the information.

WARNING

The secret key is typically sent to the intended recipient as a message separate from the ciphertext. Symmetric-key encryption is simple, fast, and relatively cheap.

A notable drawback of symmetric-key encryption is it requires a secure channel for the initial key exchange between the encrypting party and the recipient. If your secret key is compromised, the encrypted information is as good posted on a billboard.

>> **Asymmetric-key encryption** (more commonly known as *public-key encryption*) operates by using two keys — one public and one private. The *public key,* as you might guess, is made publicly available for anyone to encrypt messages. The *private key* remains a secret of the owner and is required to decrypt messages that come from anyone else (see Figure 2-3). Although public-key encryption is typically slower than its counterpart, it removes the need to secretly distribute keys and also has some very important uses (see the next section).

Lastly, in cloud environments, there are different ways that asymmetric keys are generated and even managed. Each has their own benefits and drawbacks. This is covered in Chapter 5.

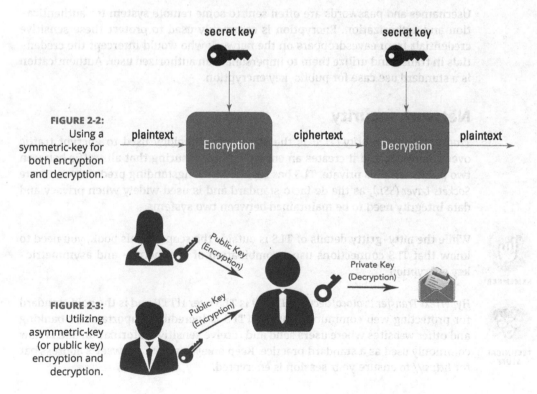

FIGURE 2-2:
Using a symmetric-key for both encryption and decryption.

FIGURE 2-3:
Utilizing asymmetric-key (or public key) encryption and decryption.

Common uses of encryption

Encryption plays an important part in protecting information systems, and its applications are wide ranging. This section discusses some of the most common uses of encryption.

Data protection

Arguably the most widely used application of encryption is to protect the confidentiality of data. Data that has been encrypted (using strong algorithms) is protected from unauthorized viewers in the event it falls into the wrong person's hand. You'll typically see encryption used for data protection for both *data-at-rest* (things like files on a hard drive or in a database) and *data-in-motion* (communication over a network, for example).

Both symmetric-key and asymmetric-key encryption are commonly used in data protection applications.

Authentication and authorization

Usernames and passwords are often sent to some remote system for authentication and authorization. Encryption is commonly used to protect these sensitive credentials from eavesdroppers on the network who would intercept the credentials in transit and utilize them to impersonate an authorized user. Authentication is a standard use case for public-key encryption.

Network security

Transport Layer Security (TLS) is the standard technology used to encrypt traffic over a network, and it creates an encrypted link ensuring that all traffic between two points remains private. TLS has replaced its longstanding predecessor, *Secure Sockets Layer (SSL)*, as the de facto standard and is used widely when privacy and data integrity need to be maintained between two systems.

REMEMBER

While the nitty-gritty details of TLS is outside the scope of this book, you need to know that TLS connections use a combination of symmetric- and asymmetric-key encryption.

TECHNICAL
STUFF

Hypertext Transfer Protocol Secure (HTTPS) is TLS over HTTP and is the gold standard for protecting web communications. HTTPS is incredibly important for banking and other websites where users send and receive sensitive information and is now commonly used as a standard practice. Keep an eye on your browser's address bar for *https://* to ensure your session is encrypted.

Digital signatures

Much like your handwritten signature is used to verify your identity, a *digital signature* is a piece of information that asserts or proves the identity of a user. Digital signatures operate on a public-key scheme and require a sender to use their private key to electronically sign a message. Recipients can then use the sender's public key to verify their identity.

In addition to helping to identify users, digital signatures support the principle of *nonrepudiation*, which is the information security concept that ensures that a party cannot deny the integrity or authenticity of a digital communication or transaction. Nonrepudiation provides assurance that the communication or transaction took place and that the parties involved cannot later deny their involvement.

Virtual private networks (VPNs)

Encryption provides a secure means for users to connect from one network to another. A virtual private network (VPN) encrypts communication between the two networks, over the Internet, to create a secure tunnel for communication. You commonly see VPNs used for people who *telework* by connecting to their organization's network from home. Similar to the network security example in the earlier section, VPNs use a mix of symmetric-key and asymmetric-key encryption.

Crypto-shredding

Standard data deletion involves overwriting data with a series of zeroes, ones, or both. This process is both slow and not completely effective at ensuring bits and pieces of data aren't left behind. A better process, known as *crypto-shredding*, involves encrypting data and then destroying the keys. With no key left behind to decrypt the data, it's effectively considered deleted.

TIP

If you guessed that symmetric-key encryption is best for crypto-shredding, you'd be correct! In addition to being simpler, faster, and cheaper, there's only one key to delete!

Grasping Physical Security

"I'm an IT gal/guy. Why should I care about physical security?" I'm glad you asked! While most information security discussions focus on using technical controls to protect the data that resides on machines, the protection of physical assets is just as important.

An uncontrolled fire wiping out your data center may not compromise your data's confidentiality or integrity, but what about availability? If it impacts one or more of the three pillars of information security, then you, as a security professional, definitely care about it. (For more on this topic, see the section "Exploring the Pillars of Information Security," earlier in this chapter.)

REMEMBER

Information security professionals are concerned with anything that impacts the confidentiality, integrity, or availability of data or systems. Don't ignore legitimate risks that are present outside of the computer hardware and software.

In addition to the environmental considerations that come with physical security, keep in mind that you can spend all your time throwing sophisticated technical protections at your systems, but it means nothing if an attacker can simply pick the lock to your data center and walk out with a server! You can find out more about secure physical design in Chapter 11.

Realizing the Importance of Business Continuity and Disaster Recovery

You can't always stop bad things from happening. The unfortunate reality is some factors will always be outside of your control — and when bad things do happen, business continuity and disaster recovery are paramount.

Business continuity (BC) refers to the policies, procedures, and tools you put in place to ensure critical business functions continue during and after a disaster or crisis. The goal of business continuity is to allow essential personnel the ability to access important systems and data until the crisis is resolved.

REMEMBER

When you think of disasters and crises, you're not only concerned with malicious cyberattacks, but also accidental disruptions, natural disasters, and major system failures.

Disaster recovery (DR) is a subset of business continuity focusing on (you guessed it!) recovering your IT systems that are lost or damaged during a disaster. In other words, DR is the part of BC focused on restoring full operation of and access to hardware, software, and data as quickly as possible after a disaster. Unlike business continuity — whose focus is on making a business operational — disaster recovery focuses on activities like recovering off-site backups, for example.

WARNING

Though business continuity and disaster recovery are closely related, they're not the same. Business continuity broadly focuses on the procedures and systems you have in place to keep a business up and running during and after a disaster. Disaster recovery more narrowly focuses on getting your systems and data back after a crisis hits. The terms are often misused, so make note of the distinction.

You need to be aware of a couple important related metrics:

» *Recovery Time Objective (RTO)* is the amount of time within which business processes must be restored in order to avoid significant consequences associated with the disaster. In other words, RTO answers the question "How much time can pass before an outage or disruption has unacceptably affected my business?"

» *Recovery Point Objective (RPO)* is the maximum amount of data loss that's tolerable to your organization. It answers the question "How much data can I lose before my business is unacceptably impacted by a disaster?" RPO plays an important role in determining frequency of backups.

Business continuity and disaster recovery are typically big selling points of cloud computing. The cloud's robust infrastructure and redundancy features contribute to increased reliability and resilience, making cloud computing a central part of many organization's business continuity and disaster recovery plans.

As a cloud security professional, there are a couple things you should keep in mind regarding business continuity and disaster recovery:

» You should ensure that the cloud infrastructure and applications being used have appropriate security measures in place to protect systems and data during both normal operations and disaster scenarios. This includes ensuring encryption, access controls, and other mechanisms remain in place during a disaster.

» You should maintain integrity and availability throughout the disaster recovery process with regular backups, testing, and validation procedures to verify that the backups remain reliable and can be restored successfully, when needed.

WARNING

Cloud providers commonly advertise their uptime and other availability metrics, but cloud infrastructures and applications are not immune from availability risks. You should conduct regular audits and compliance checks of your cloud services to ensure that their disaster recovery and business continuity plans align with industry regulations and your organization's own requirements.

Understanding Logging and Monitoring

Logging and monitoring are separate, but related, practices that your organization uses to help detect, escalate, and respond to security events.

Logging is the process of recording and storing the key actions, activities, and events that occur within an information system. Logging involves capturing important information and storing it in files (or logs) for future reference and analysis.

Examples of key log types include

>> System logs that capture events related to the operating system, such as startups and shutdowns, logins and logouts, system errors and warnings.

>> Security logs that capture things like failed login attempts, changes to access permissions, intrusion attempts, and other suspicious activities that may indicate a security incident.

>> Network logs that capture information about network traffic, such as connection information, source and destination IP addresses, and traffic volumes.

>> Database logs that capture changes made to a database, including access, modifications, and queries.

TIP

The log types that you should be aware of depends on your particular environment and use cases. The list here is only a starting point.

Logging is great and all, but logs serve little purpose if they are not actively monitored. Just like a bank might have security personnel who actively monitor the surveillance systems, monitoring, in the context of information security, involves continuously observing and analyzing your information systems. By monitoring your systems, you can detect and respond to security events in a timely manner.

Monitoring activities include vulnerability scanning, intrusion detection (through the use of intrusion detection systems, or IDS), threat intelligence analysis, and log analysis.

TECHNICAL
STUFF

The amount of log data in even a small organization can quickly become overwhelming and impossible to analyze manually. *Security Information and Event Management (SIEM)* is a category of tools used to collect, centralize, and analyze large volumes of log data from all over your environment. A SIEM tool can help automatically correlate security events and logs from various sources and enable your organization to conduct real-time threat detection and incident response.

Implementing Incident Handling

It would be great if you could just do your security magic, and nothing bad would ever happen. Unfortunately, you can't fix every vulnerability or stop every threat . . . so it's important that you're prepared to handle whatever comes your way. The field of *incident handling* deals with preparing for, addressing, and recovering from security incidents.

I want to define some important terms up front. NIST SP 800-61 defines the following:

>> An *event* is any observable occurrence in a system or network.

>> *Adverse events* are events with negative consequences.

>> A computer security *incident* is a violation or imminent threat of violation of computer security policies, acceptable use policies, or standard security practices.

TIP

While the focus in this section is specifically on computer security incidents, keep in mind that these principles apply to power failures, natural disasters, and so on.

Though every incident starts as an event (or multiple events), every event is not necessarily an incident. To take the distinction even further, not every event is even considered adverse or negative. Some examples of events include

>> A website visitor downloads a file.

>> A user enters an incorrect password.

>> An administrator is granted root access to a router.

>> A firewall rejects a connection attempt.

>> A server crashes.

Of the preceding events, only the last one is inherently adverse — and without further information, you can't call any of them incidents. The following list includes some examples of incidents:

>> A hacker encrypts all your sensitive data and demands a ransom for the keys (i.e., a ransomware attack).

>> A user inside your organization steals your customers' credit card data.

>> An administrator at your company is tricked into clicking on a link inside a phishing email, resulting in a backdoor connection for an attacker.

>> Your HR system is taken offline by a *Distributed Denial of Service (DDoS)* attack.

WARNING

Make sure you don't use the terms *event* and *incident* interchangeably — they're not the same. I have heard IT professionals refer to simple events and/or alerts as incidents, and that's a great way to sound alarms that don't need to be sounded!

Incident handling starts well before an incident even occurs and ends even after things are back to normal. The *Incident Response (IR) lifecycle* (shown in Figure 2-4) describes the steps you take before, during, and after an incident. The key components of the IR lifecycle are

>> Preparation

>> Detection

>> Containment

>> Eradication

>> Recovery

>> Post-Mortem

FIGURE 2-4: The Incident Response (IR) lifecycle.

| Preparation | Detection | Containment | Eradication | Recovery | Post-Mortem |

I cover the preceding concepts in the remaining sections.

Preparing for incidents

You can easily overlook preparation as part of the incident response process, but it's a critical step for the rapid response to and recovery from incidents. This phase of incident handling includes things like

>> **Developing an incident response plan.** Your *incident response plan* identifies procedures to follow when an incident occurs, as well as roles and responsibilities of all stakeholders.

>> **Periodically testing your incident response plan.** Determine your plan's effectiveness by conducting table-top exercises and incident simulations.

>> **Implementing preventative measures to keep the number of incidents as low as possible.** This process includes finding vulnerabilities in your

systems, conducting threat assessments, and applying a layered approach to security controls (things like network security, host-based security, and so on) to minimize risk.

>> **Setting up incident analysis equipment.** This process can include forensic workstations, backup media, and evidence-gathering accessories (cameras, notebooks and pens, and storage bags/bins to preserve crucial evidence and maintain chain of custody).

Detecting incidents

During this phase, you acknowledge that an incident has indeed occurred, and you feverishly put your IR Plan into action. This phase is all about gathering as much information as possible and analyzing it to gain insights into the origin and impact of the incident. Some examples of activities during this phase are

>> **Conducting log analysis and seeking unusual behavior.** A good Security Information and Event Management (SIEM) tool can help aggregate different log sources and provide more intelligent data for your analysis. You're looking for the smoking gun, or at least a trail of breadcrumbs, that can alert you to how the attack took place.

>> **Identifying the impact of the incident.** Which systems were impacted? What data was impacted? How many customers were impacted?

>> **Notifying the appropriate individuals.** Your IR Plan should detail who to contact for specific types of incidents. During this phase, you'll need to enact your communications plan to alert proper teams and stakeholders.

>> **Documenting the findings.** The situation will likely be frantic, so organization is critical. You want to keep detailed notes of your findings, actions taken, chain of custody, and other relevant information. This activity helps with your post-mortem reporting later on and also helps you keep track of important details that can assist in tracing the attack back to its origin. In addition, many incidents require reporting to law enforcement, regulators, or other external parties. Thorough notes and a strong chain of custody help support any investigations that may arise.

TIP

Depending on various factors (the nature of the incident, your industry, or any contractual obligations), you may be responsible for notifying customers, law enforcement, regulators, or even US–CERT (part of Department of Homeland Security). Make sure that you keep a comprehensive list of parties to notify in case of a breach.

Containing incidents

The last thing you want to deal with during an incident is an even bigger incident. Containment is extremely important to stop the bleeding and prevent further damage. It also allows you to use your incident response resources more efficiently and avoid exhausting your analysis and remediation capacity. Some common containment activities include:

>> Disabling Internet connectivity for affected systems

>> Isolating/quarantining malware-infected systems from the rest of your network

>> Reviewing and/or changing potentially compromised passwords

>> Capturing forensic images and memory dumps from impacted systems

Eradicating incidents

By the time you reach this phase, your primary mission is to remove the threat from your systems. *Eradication* involves eliminating any components of the incident that remain. Depending on the number of impacted hosts, this phase can be fairly short or last for quite some time. Here are some key activities during this phase:

>> Securely removing all traces of malware

>> Disabling or re-creating impacted user and system accounts

>> Identifying and patching all vulnerabilities (starting with the ones that led to the breach!)

>> Restoring known good backups

>> Wiping or rebuilding critically damaged systems

Recovering from incidents

The objective of the Recovery phase is to bring impacted systems back into your operational environment and fully resume business as usual. Depending on your organization's IR Plan, this phase may be closely aligned or share steps with the

Eradication phase. It can take several months to fully recover from a large-scale compromise, so you need to have both short-term and long-term recovery objectives that align with your organization's needs. Some common recovery activities include:

>> Confirming vulnerabilities have been patched and fully remediated

>> Validating systems are functioning normally

>> Restoring systems to normal operations (for example, reconnecting Internet access, restoring connection to your production network, and so on)

>> Closely monitoring systems for any remaining signs of undesirable activity

Conducting a post-mortem

After your systems are back up and running and the worst is over, you need to focus your attention on the lessons learned from the incident. The primary objective of the Post-Mortem phase is to document the lessons and implement the changes required to prevent a similar type of incident from happening in the future. All members of the Incident Response Team (and supporting personnel) should meet to discuss what worked, what didn't work, and what needs to change within the organization moving forward. Here are some questions to consider during post-mortem discovery and documentation:

>> What vulnerability (technical or otherwise) did this breach exploit?

>> What could have been done differently to prevent this incident or decrease its impact on your organization?

>> How can you respond more effectively during future incidents?

>> What policies need to be updated, and with what content?

>> How should you train your employees differently?

>> What security controls need to be modified or implemented?

>> Do you have proper funding to ensure that you are prepared to handle future breaches?

TIP

For a more in-depth review of handling security incidents, refer to NIST's Computer Security Incident Handling Guide (SP 800-61).

Utilizing Defense-in-Depth

One final security concept to explore is *defense-in-depth*, or *layered security*. These two terms describe the same idea of applying multiple, distinct layers of security technologies and strategies for greater overall protection. The thought behind this concept is that each layer has its own strengths and weaknesses, which you'd like to complement one another. A weakness in one layer can be compensated by the strengths in other layers. By applying two or more of the control mechanisms discussed in this chapter (access control, cryptography, and physical security), you can implement defense-in-depth and gain greater overall protection. (I cover additional security controls that support defense-in-depth throughout the remainder of this book.)

Of course, this approach isn't foolproof — vulnerabilities will still exist. However, a well-executed defense-in-depth approach makes it much harder for attackers to find and exploit vulnerabilities in your system, and much easier for you to detect an incident sooner rather than later. You explore the concept of defense-in-depth as it relates to the cloud throughout the rest of this book.

2

Exploring the CCSP Certification Domains

Chapter **3**

Domain 1: Cloud Concepts, Architecture, and Design, Part 1

In this chapter, you begin tackling the material at the heart of the exam by taking a deep dive into key concepts related to cloud computing, architecture, and design. Domain 1 represents 17 percent of the CCSP certification exam, and this chapter covers the first half of Domain 1.

The great news for security professionals is that many of the concepts from traditional data center models still apply in cloud environments. Having said that, a detailed understanding of cloud computing concepts is critical when creating and managing security cloud security programs. In this chapter, you learn about cloud's essential characteristics, service models (or categories), deployment models, and more.

Understanding Cloud Computing Concepts

Before you create and manage secure cloud architectures, you need to get comfortable with some cloud computing fundamentals. To help you talk the talk, this section explains the most important cloud terminology, as well as introduces you to important roles, characteristics, and technologies associated with cloud computing.

Defining cloud computing terms

According to NIST, "*Cloud computing* is a model for enabling ubiquitous, convenient, on-demand network access to a shared pool of configurable computing resources (e.g., networks, servers, storage, applications, and services) that can be rapidly provisioned and released with minimal management effort or service provider interaction. This cloud model is composed of five essential characteristics, three service models, and four deployment models."

The following list is based on ISO/IEC 17788, "Cloud Computing — Overview and Vocabulary" and defines some important terms used in the cloud computing industry. Additional terms are defined throughout the rest of the book (and in Appendix A), but these terms are the basics you need to be comfortable with to get the most from this book:

>> **Cloud application:** An application that is accessed via the Internet rather than installed and accessed locally.

>> **Cloud data portability:** The ability to easily move data from one cloud provider to another.

>> **Cloud deployment model:** The way in which cloud services are made available through specific configurations that control the sharing of cloud resources with cloud users. The cloud deployment models are public, private, community, and hybrid.

>> **Cloud resources:** Compute, storage, and networking capabilities that a cloud provider shares with a cloud user. These resources include the physical equipment located in the cloud provider's data centers as well as virtual resources like operating systems and applications.

>> **Cloud service:** Capabilities made available to a cloud user by a cloud provider through a published interface (a management console or command line, for example).

>> **Cloud service category:** A collection of cloud services that share a common set of features or qualities. Cloud service categories are labelled XaaS (where the *X* can be *Anything* as a Service).

>> **Cloud service customer data:** Any data objects under the control of the cloud service customer and that were input to the cloud service by the cloud customer or generated by the cloud service on behalf of the cloud customer.

>> **Cloud service derived data:** Any data objects under the control of the cloud service provider and that were derived by interaction of the cloud customer with the cloud service. Derived data may include access logs, utilization information, and other forms of metadata (or data about data).

>> **Cloud service provider data:** Any data objects related to the operation of the cloud service and that are fully under the control of the cloud service provider. Provider data may include cloud service operational data, information generated by the cloud service provider to provide services, and similar data not owned or related to any specific cloud customer.

The topic of data ownership in the cloud can be a contentious one, and has many legal and compliance implications. It's important that cloud providers share clear terms as to what data they own and what the customer owns, as this has an effect on who is responsible for securing what.

>> **Community cloud:** Cloud deployment model where cloud services are provided to a group of cloud service customers with similar requirements. It is common for at least one member of the community to control the cloud resources for the group.

>> **Data portability:** The ability to easily move data from one system to another, without needing to re-enter the data.

>> **Hybrid cloud:** Cloud deployment model that uses a combination of at least two different cloud deployment models (public, private, or community).

>> **Infrastructure as a service (IaaS):** Cloud service category that provides infrastructure capabilities to the cloud service customer.

>> **Measured service:** Delivery of cloud services in such a way that its usage can be monitored, accurately reported, and precisely billed.

>> **Multitenancy:** Allocation of cloud resources such that multiple tenants and their data are inaccessible from other tenants who share those resources.

>> **On-demand self-service:** A characteristic of cloud that allows a cloud service customer to provision cloud resources and capabilities with little or no interaction with the cloud service provider.

>> **Platform as a service (PaaS):** Cloud service category that provides platform capabilities to the cloud service customer.

>> **Private cloud:** Cloud deployment model where cloud services are provided to a single cloud service customer who controls their own cloud resources.

>> **Public cloud:** Cloud deployment model where cloud resources are controlled by the cloud service provider and cloud services are made available to any cloud service customer.

>> **Resource pooling:** Aggregation of a cloud service provider's resources to provide cloud service to one or more cloud service customers.

>> **Reversibility:** Capability for a cloud service customer to retrieve their cloud service customer data and for the cloud service provider to delete this data after a specified period or upon request.

>> **Software as a service (SaaS):** Cloud service category that provides software/application capabilities to the cloud service customer.

>> **Tenant:** One or more cloud service users sharing access to a set of cloud resources.

Identifying cloud computing roles and responsibilities

When you (or your customers) move data into the cloud, questions like "Who does what?" may arise. It's important that you become familiar with the common roles in cloud computing environments and understand how the various roles work together to keep cloud data secure:

>> **Cloud auditor:** A cloud service partner who is responsible for conducting an audit of the use of cloud services. An audit may be for general security hygiene, but is often for legal or compliance purposes.

>> **Cloud service broker:** A cloud service partner who negotiates relationships between cloud service providers and cloud service customers.

>> **Cloud service customer:** A person or group that is in a business relationship to provision and use cloud services from a cloud service provider.

>> **Cloud service partner:** A person or group that supports the provision, use, or other activities of the cloud service provider, the cloud service customer, or both.

>> **Cloud service provider (CSP):** An entity making cloud services available for use. I refer to cloud service provider as the CSP in this book.

>> **Cloud service user:** A person or entity (which may be a device, for example) that uses cloud services on behalf of the cloud service customer.

Recognizing key cloud computing characteristics

Five characteristics must be present for a service or offering to be considered cloud:

» On-demand self-service
» Broad network access
» Resource pooling
» Rapid elasticity

» Measured service

Looking at these five essential cloud characteristics, you can see some major themes: convenience, efficiency, and transparency, among others. While cloud has evolved to present a strong case for being secure and cutting-edge, keep in mind that the heart of cloud computing is really all about making resources easy to access, manage, and monitor.

TECHNICAL STUFF

Although the features described are the five key cloud computing characteristics, a sixth characteristic is worth mentioning: multitenancy. *Multitenancy* is a feature of most clouds that involves having multiple customers sharing physical hardware. Whereas traditional data centers rely on cages and physically separate servers and network devices to segregate customers, cloud environments rely on logical technologies (like encryption, virtualization, segmentation, and so on) to keep one customer's data virtually separated from others. While this is very standard in cloud computing, I explain an exception when I discuss the private cloud deployment model in the "Cloud deployment models" section.

If the five key characteristics are not present in a service or offering, then it is not true cloud computing. Some of these features are defined in the previous sections, but I cover them all in depth in the following sections.

On-demand self-service

By design, cloud service providers allow customers to procure and provision cloud resources by anyone who wants or needs them. On-demand self-service means that a customer can request, set up, and use cloud services in an automated fashion and without interacting with another human. On-demand self-service allows full cloud usage without approval from your manager, legal team, or finance department.

The upside to on-demand self-service is the tremendous ease of procurement. Cloud computing is designed to be easy to get started with; if you can pay for it, you can use it. Though self-service is helpful for productivity, security teams should be aware of the risks that come with it and implement policies and procedures to help govern the use of cloud services.

TECHNICAL STUFF

Shadow IT refers to the use of unsanctioned or unauthorized technology (such as cloud services) within an IT environment, which may lead to unauthorized sharing of information with unapproved third parties. Shadow IT is one of the key risks related to on-demand self-service in cloud computing and poses significant security risks to your organization's data governance and compliance efforts.

Broad network access

Cloud resources should be accessible to any authorized cloud user with an Internet connection. The principle behind this characteristic is that cloud computing should make resources and data ubiquitous and easily accessed when and where they're required.

Mature cloud offerings make accessing their resources device-agnostic, allowing cloud users the ability to connect to their cloud services from a variety of endpoint devices that include laptops, desktops, tablets, and even smartphones. From a security standpoint, this ability gives customers deploying cloud applications some additional considerations, as cloud computing extends their data to a variety of devices, that may not be within the enterprise's control. For this reason, many companies need to examine their mobile device management policies when moving to or operating in the cloud.

WARNING

Bring your own device (BYOD) has become increasingly common and means that companies are allowing employees to connect their own smartphones, tablets, and laptops to corporate systems. BYOD has the benefit of enabling broad access to cloud systems from many devices, but adds concerns regarding device management and secure access methods. Fortunately, cloud computing mitigates some risk of BYOD because it encourages users to store their data in cloud storage rather than on their devices. Additionally, cloud computing can also extend security capabilities (like device checks and monitoring) onto your BYOD devices. Even still, be mindful of your company's BYOD policies and consider how cloud systems might impact them.

Resource pooling

One of the most critical concepts in cloud computing, *resource pooling* occurs when a CSP groups (or pools) its cloud resources for shared use between multiple cloud customers. What resource pooling allows the CSP to do is scale resources up and down, on a per-customer basis, as each customer's resource needs increase or decrease. CSPs can have many thousands of servers, networking devices, and other resources available; pooling allows them to efficiently manage those resources between customers, with minimal waste.

TIP

Some organizations prefer or require maintaining segregation between their data and other organizations' data, which goes against the concept of resource pooling. Private clouds and some community clouds address this concern with data segregation or isolation needs.

Resource pooling works closely with rapid elasticity to provide cloud customers a dynamic set of compute, storage, and network resources that are allocated based on each customer's needs.

Rapid elasticity

At the core of cloud computing, rapid elasticity allows a cloud customer to quickly obtain additional cloud resources as the user's needs require. Think of a retail website during the Black Friday or Cyber Monday shopping frenzy. Rapid elasticity allows that website to seamlessly accommodate a sudden spike in traffic, without the cloud customer's intervention, by automatically scaling and provisioning (referred to as *auto-scaling* and *auto-provisioning*) resource based on load.

TIP

It's not uncommon for many businesses to have peak-hours or peak-seasons, during which their resource utilization may drastically increase. Outside of these peaks, many businesses can see their resource demands plummet for long periods of time. Rapid elasticity and resource pooling work together to give cloud customers as much compute, storage, and networking power as needed, and nothing more. This capability is important because cloud also leverages a pay-as-you-use model.

Measured service

Cloud computing makes it exceedingly easy for cloud customers to monitor, measure, control, and report on their resource usage. Measured service works in a similar manner to how you might have a measured (or metered) use for your water or electric bill. Similar to these home utilities, CSPs charge customers only for the resources that they use. As such, providing measured services that allows full transparency between a CSP and cloud customer is paramount.

TIP

Measured service allows your organization to continuously monitor resource utilization in your cloud environment and can help you detect unusual activity (such as Shadow IT or suspiciously high usage volumes resulting from certain compromises). Measured service provides detailed usage logs that assist with security audits and incident investigations.

Building block technologies

Many technologies at the heart of cloud computing architectures are very familiar if you've worked with traditional IT hardware and software. Any cloud computing environment, at the most fundamental level, consists of compute (CPU), memory (RAM), storage, networking, virtualization, and orchestration technologies. The customer will have greater or lesser responsibility over these building block technologies, depending on the cloud service category. The following sections explore some of the key building block technologies that exist in cloud environments.

Storage

Cloud storage technologies include object storage (ideal for unstructured data like documents and images) and block storage (ideal for high-performance use cases like virtual machines and databases).

Modern cloud providers offer a wide range of database storage services that support relational databases (such as MySQL, SQL Server, and PostgreSQL) and NoSQL databases (such as DynamoDB, MongoDB, and Cassandra).

Networking

Key cloud networking technologies include virtual networks, firewalls, load balancers, VPNs, and content delivery networks (CDNs). These networking technologies enable secure and efficient communication in the cloud, and they support several of the key cloud computing characteristics mentioned in the previous section.

Virtualization

Virtualization is a central concept in cloud computing involving the creation of virtual instances that simulate the behavior of physical hardware, including servers, storage devices, and networking equipment. Virtualization abstracts the underlying hardware and allows multiple virtual computing environments to run on a single physical machine.

REMEMBER

Virtual machines (VMs) are the most easily identifiable form of virtualization, but you should know that storage, networking, compute, and memory resources are all virtualized in a cloud environment.

Orchestration

Orchestration, in cloud computing, refers to the coordination and management of cloud resources and services. Orchestration involves creating and executing workflows to provision, deploy, scale, and manage cloud infrastructure and applications.

Orchestration tools help streamline the management of complex cloud environments, enabling efficient resource allocation and ensuring consistent deployment and operations.

TECHNICAL STUFF

AWS CloudFormation, Azure Automation, Puppet Bolt, and Terraform are a few popular cloud orchestration tools, but there are many others.

TIP

Cloud automation is a subset of cloud orchestration that involves programming repetitive tasks, such as spinning up and configuring virtual machines. Cloud automation helps you achieve repetitive tasks with minimal human intervention, while cloud orchestration involves coordinating and managing a collection of automated tasks.

Describing Cloud Reference Architecture

Several key components fit together to create the complete picture of a cloud architecture and implementation. These components include the activities and capabilities required to develop and manage a cloud environment, as well as the cloud service categories and cloud deployment models that describe how the service is delivered, configured, and managed.

In this section, you learn how about cloud reference architectures, including the three main cloud service categories and the Shared Responsibility Model.

Cloud computing activities

Similar to traditional computing environments, cloud computing requires a number of activities to be performed by several parties in order to build, deploy, secure, audit, and manage systems and data. This section serves as a high-level overview of the key activities performed by the cloud service provider, cloud service customer, and cloud service partner.

Cloud service provider

The following are key roles and activities performed by the cloud service provider:

>> **Cloud service operations manager:** Oversees and manages the operation and performance of cloud services provided to customers.

>> **Technical account manager:** Provides account support and high-level technical guidance to cloud customers.

Cloud service customer

The following are key roles and activities performed by the cloud service customer:

>> **Cloud architect:** Evaluates cloud technologies and services and designs the overall architecture of the cloud deployment to meet organizational requirements.

>> **Cloud service user:** Uses services provided by the CSP.

>> **Cloud service administrator:** Configures, manages, and monitors the use of cloud services.

Cloud service partner

The following are key roles and activities performed by the cloud service partner:

>> **Cloud auditor:** Performs audits of cloud environments and provides audit reports.

>> **Cloud service broker:** Provides a marketplace for approved services, manages contracting, and securely integrates cloud services with on-prem applications.

Cloud service capabilities

You should familiarize yourself with three primary cloud service capabilities:

>> **Infrastructure service capability:** The cloud customer can provision and maintain granular control over compute, storage, and network resources.

>> **Platform service capability:** The cloud customer can run code and develop applications using programming libraries that are managed and controlled by the cloud service provider.

>> **Software service capability:** The cloud customer can use applications that are fully developed and managed by the cloud service provider.

Cloud service categories

Cloud service categories generally fall into three main groups:

>> Infrastructure as a service (IaaS)

>> Platform as a service (PaaS)

>> Software as a service (SaaS)

Aside from these three, you may have seen other iterations of the XaaS paradigm. Things like DBaaS (database as a service), BaaS (blockchain as a service), and others are increasingly used in some circles. In this section, I focus on the three primary cloud service categories listed in Table 3-1.

TABLE 3-1   **Primary Cloud Service Categories**

IaaS	PaaS	SaaS
Compute, storage, and network resources	CSP provides libraries, services, and development environments	CSP provides fully functional application
Underlying infrastructure is fully managed by the CSP	Customer creates and deploys applications	CSP manages the entire infrastructure and platform
Customer can run software and services on the infrastructure	CSP patches and deploys systems	Customer leases or borrows licenses, as needed
Customer may have limited control over select networking devices	Customer maintains control over deployed applications and may be able to configure hosting environment	Customer may have limited control of application configuration settings

Infrastructure as a service (IaaS)

Infrastructure as a service, or IaaS, is in many ways what people first think of when they hear cloud computing. It's the service category where the CSP provides compute, storage, and networking resources and the customer has the greatest level of control and customization over those resources. Think of things like virtual machines and storage containers or buckets — that's IaaS.

NIST 800-145 describes IaaS as "the capability provided to the consumer is to provision processing, storage, networks, and other fundamental computing resources where the consumer is able to deploy and run arbitrary software, which can include operating systems and applications. The consumer does not manage or control the underlying cloud infrastructure but has control over operating systems, storage, and deployed applications; and possibly limited control of select networking components (e.g., host firewalls)."

IaaS key characteristics and benefits include

>> **Cost efficiency:** By using the IaaS service model, customers do not need to spend money on buying and managing hardware up front or as the need for additional resources grow. With IaaS, customers can trade Capital Expenditure (CapEx) for Operational Expenditure (OpEx). In addition, customers also benefit from the cloud provider paying for and managing physical security of the datacenters.

>> **Availability and reliability:** Infrastructure as a service provides customers with options for load balancing and redundancy across vast infrastructures that can span many regions or even countries. These vast infrastructures provide customers with assurance that their resources will be highly available and resilient against availability threats (DDoS and others).

>> **Scalability:** With IaaS service models, additional resources can be procured, provisioned, and expanded quickly and with ease to support growing demand. Whereas on-premise solutions would require a customer to purchase and set up new servers to support increased utilization, IaaS allows automatic scaling when necessary.

Platform as a service (PaaS)

Platform as a service, or PaaS, sits on top of the IaaS layer in the cloud stack and begins to shift control (and responsibility) over resources away from the cloud customer and back to the cloud provider. In PaaS offerings, the user is generally building their own application or solution using prepackaged libraries and features provided by the cloud provider. Having the infrastructure and development environment taken care of by the CSP allows the customer to focus on development rather than managing servers, virtual machines, and other granular resources. As a result of PaaS offerings, the barrier to entry for software development continues to fall. Developers, large and small, spend less time and money developing infrastructures and managing resources and more time on being innovative.

You may be familiar with terms like *up the stack* and *down the stack* from TCP/IP discussions, and they carry over to the cloud computing world. In cloud, these terms refer to the way the three cloud service categories stack on top of each other to provide full cloud functionality. IaaS sits at the bottom of the stack and moves up to PaaS, followed by SaaS at the top.

NIST 800-145 describes PaaS as "the capability provided to the consumer is to deploy onto the cloud infrastructure consumer-created or acquired applications created using programming languages, libraries, services, and tools supported by the provider. The consumer does not manage or control the underlying cloud infrastructure including network, servers, operating systems, or storage, but has control over the deployed applications and possibly configuration settings for the application-hosting environment."

Though PaaS customers inherit many of the same benefits of IaaS, some will be unique to PaaS.

PaaS key characteristics and benefits include

>> **Cost efficiency:** Similar to IaaS, the PaaS service category offers cost savings because application developers pay only for the systems and resources they use. As customers progress through the development cycle, they can scale up or down with ease and without incurring unnecessary costs.

>> **Flexibility:** Developers receive a great deal of flexibility during their application development lifecycle when they use PaaS cloud offerings. Within a given cloud environment, developers can often easily switch between operating systems and software versions to suit their needs. Many cloud providers provide open source environments and applications for developers, which prevents vendor lock-in and affords them the ease of moving between environments, platforms, and even cloud providers.

>> **Simplicity:** With the underlying infrastructure and operating systems being managed by the cloud provider, hardware and software upgrades and system patches are handled for the developer. Upgrading to the latest version of software is commonly as simple as clicking a few buttons, which minimizes downtime and lets developers focus on creating their applications rather than managing systems.

>> **Ease of access:** Being cloud-based means that development platforms and tools are easily accessed from anywhere in the world. This ease of access makes it incredibly easy for global development teams to collaborate on projects, as opposed to on-prem development platforms that may require out of band collaboration (like emailing updated files or using less reliable technologies like shared drives).

TECHNICAL STUFF

Serverless computing is a cloud computing model that allows developers to run their code without needing to provision or manage servers. A *serverless function* is a small piece of code that is executed in response to an event or trigger. In serverless computing, developers just need to write and deploy their application code and define event–driven functions. The CSP takes care of all of the infrastructure and scaling needs.

Function as a service (FaaS)

The increased adoption of serverless computing has given rise to another popular cloud service category, Function as a Service (FaaS). FaaS is similar to PaaS in that it provides a platform for developers to create, run, and manage application code while hiding infrastructure management from the developers. While PaaS requires you to manage servers and scaling, FaaS (and serverless) is more focused on code execution, and it doesn't require any server process to constantly run; application code only executes when a function is invoked.

Serverless computing has been around for some time, but FaaS was first made popular with the announcement of AWS Lambda in 2014. Since then, Microsoft Azure, Google Cloud Platform, and other CSPs, large and small, have launched serverless offerings that continue to grow in adoption.

Software as a service (SaaS)

Software as a service, or SaaS, sits at the top of the cloud stack and provides fully operational software applications to the customer. SaaS moves the majority of resource management to the cloud provider, allowing the end user to simply use the provided application to meet their needs. Examples of SaaS offerings include Google Docs, Dropbox, and DocuSign; these cloud-based applications require little to no configuration by the customer.

NIST 800-145 describes SaaS as "the capability provided to the consumer is to use the provider's applications running on a cloud infrastructure. The applications are accessible from various client devices through either a thin client interface, such as a web browser (e.g., web-based email), or a program interface. The consumer does not manage or control the underlying cloud infrastructure including network, servers, operating systems, storage, or even individual application capabilities, with the possible exception of limited user specific application configuration settings."

SaaS customers inherit many of the previously mentioned benefits from IaaS and PaaS, but SaaS does have some unique features and benefits.

SaaS key characteristics and benefits include

>> **Cost efficiency:** You're probably seeing a theme here: Cloud helps customers cut costs. Similar to IaaS and PaaS, software as a service helps customers manage costs by eliminating the need for system administrators and dedicated hardware and software. For SaaS applications, customers only need a device to access the given application and an Internet connection.

>> **Licensing:** With SaaS, customers effectively lease or borrow licenses as they use software. Leasing eliminates the need for customers to purchase full sets of licenses, which may go underutilized for long periods of time. Cloud providers, due to the scale of their environments, can take advantage of friendlier licensing fees from third-party vendors, and some of those savings are able to be realized by the end user.

>> **Standardization:** By nature, cloud applications are standardized regardless of who's accessing or where they're accessing the application from. From an application standpoint, standardization helps ensure consistent experiences from one user to another and makes sure that all users are using the latest and greatest software versions, with little to no action taken by the customer.

Cloud deployment models

Four main types of cloud deployment models exist:

>> Public

>> Private

>> Community

>> Hybrid

These deployment models describe how cloud services are hosted, who controls and operates them, and what cloud customers may access them. Table 3-2 highlights the main features of the four main types of cloud deployment.

TABLE 3-2 Overview of the Cloud Deployment Models

Public	Private	Community	Hybrid
Open to the general public	Used exclusively by a single organization	Used exclusively by a community of similar organizations (like government agencies)	Shares features of two or more cloud models
May be owned by a private company, government organization, academic institution, or a combination	May be owned by the organization, a third party, or co-owned	May be owned by a community member, a third party, or co-owned	Allows customers to have control over their most critical systems
Highly scalable resources	May exist on- or off-premises	Supports disaster recovery for customers considering private cloud	Customer maintains increased ownership and control over their resources

Public cloud deployment

According to NIST SP 800-145, "[public] cloud infrastructure is provisioned for open use by the general public. It may be owned, managed, and operated by a business, academic, or government organization, or some combination of them. It exists on the premises of the cloud provider." In English, *public cloud* is a set of computing services that can be accessed by anyone willing and able to pay for them.

With enterprise offerings from tech giants like Google, Amazon, and Microsoft — as well as Apple's consumer cloud product, iCloud — public cloud is typically what consumers think of when they think about "the cloud."

Public cloud benefits and uses include

>> **Easy to set up and manage:** In public cloud deployments, the cloud service provider owns and operates the infrastructure, which means the customer isn't responsible to manage infrastructure like data center facilities, networking hardware, and operational expenses. In addition, public cloud commonly offers streamlined access to resources through easy-to-use interfaces.

>> **Highly scalable resources:** Public clouds typically have vast infrastructures that are ready and able to handle heavy workloads.

>> **Resource efficiency and cost-effective:** Customers don't have to worry about wasted resources, as public clouds automatically scale a customer's resources up or down, based on their usage and bill them only for what they use. Unused resources from one customer can be used (and paid for) by another.

Private cloud deployment

According to NIST SP 800-145, "[private] cloud infrastructure is provisioned for exclusive use by a single organization comprising multiple consumers (e.g., business units). It may be owned, managed, and operated by the organization, a third party, or some combination of them, and it may exist on or off premises." In other words, *private cloud* offers similar services to those offered by public cloud, but private cloud can only be accessed by members of a single organization.

Private cloud is sometimes referred to as an *internal cloud* and is often used for legal, compliance, or security purposes. In certain highly regulated industries, customers often want the convenience and features that cloud provides, without their data being mixed (or comingling) with other customers' data.

Private cloud benefits and uses include

>> **Increased ownership:** With private clouds, the customer/user is the same party that owns and operates it. As such, private clouds give users a greater level of ownership and the ability to control everything about it. One common example is for customers with data location requirements — for example, a bank may have regulations that require its data remains within the European Union (EU). The standard way to satisfy this requirement has historically been to build or use a private cloud that allows that bank to only let data travel to data centers within the EU. Newer offerings from some public cloud infrastructures are now allowing these customers to meet these types of requirements without managing their own private cloud.

>> **High level of system and data control:** Similar to the point mentioned in the previous bullet, private clouds give customers increased control over all resources. Private cloud customers can control things like bandwidth, system patching, and software/application availability, whereas these things are often only controlled by the CSP in public clouds.

Community cloud deployment

According to NIST SP 800-145, "[community] cloud infrastructure is provisioned for exclusive use by a specific community of consumers from organizations that have shared concerns (e.g., mission, security requirements, policy, and compliance considerations). It may be owned, managed, and operated by one or more of the organizations in the community, a third party, or some combination of them, and it may exist on or off premises." Think of community clouds as private clouds that are extended to a limited set of related organizations.

Community clouds are common in highly regulated industries. Government customers, for example, will often seek out the moniker *GovCloud* for assurance that only government data resides within a given cloud. While the term GovCloud may entail a bit of marketing, it's a great example of the intent of the community cloud deployment model.

Community cloud benefits typically mirror those of public clouds. The added benefit comes from all members of the cloud user base sharing a common set of privacy, security, or compliance requirements. A community of users with the same (or highly similar) set of requirements can ensure that the cloud meets their requirements exactly.

Hybrid cloud deployment

According to NIST SP 800-145, "[hybrid] cloud infrastructure is a composition of two or more distinct cloud infrastructures (private, community, or public) that remain unique entities, but are bound together by standardized or proprietary technology that enables data and application portability (e.g., cloud bursting for load balancing between clouds)." Simply put, *hybrid cloud* consists of some combination of public, private, and/or community cloud features.

As you may expect, hybrid cloud models attempt to bring the best of multiple worlds together; when using a hybrid cloud deployment, customers are generally seeking public cloud features and scalability with private or community cloud control.

Hybrid cloud benefits include

» **Re-use of existing infrastructure and technology:** Many customers want the benefits and features that public clouds provide, but they may already have an expensive infrastructure that's up and running. A hybrid cloud allows customers to reap the benefits of public clouds while still utilizing their private clouds, as necessary. A hybrid cloud is sometimes a stepping stone for customers dipping their toe in the cloud waters, but there are often compliance, legal, or other business reasons for customers maintaining private cloud (or on-premises) infrastructure.

» **Control over critical or sensitive systems:** With hybrid cloud deployment models, customers are able to keep data that they are most concerned about in their private cloud, while moving less sensitive data to a public cloud. By sharing characteristics of public and private (or community) clouds, customers are able to maintain a high level of control and ownership without missing out on the benefits that public cloud provides.

» **Disaster recovery support:** One common use case for hybrid cloud is in supporting disaster recovery. Customers already running on a fully functional private cloud can benefit from the redundancy and reliability assurance that many public clouds provide. Customers can continue to use their private clouds as normal, but can configure their resources to failover to the public cloud in the event of a disaster. Because the public cloud would be used only in case of emergency, customers will usually incur little to no costs under normal circumstances (because you're billed for what you use).

TECHNICAL STUFF

The hybrid cloud deployment model shares similarities with the concept of multi-cloud. *Multi-cloud* refers to a strategy where an organization uses multiple CSPs rather than just a single cloud provider. This often includes the use of multiple public cloud providers — so while all hybrid cloud deployments are multi-cloud, not all multi-cloud deployments are hybrid.

Cloud shared considerations

Cloud computing involves organizations outsourcing the management and maintenance of their computing infrastructure to one or more third-party cloud providers. As such, moving to the cloud is not only a technology decision, but also a business decision. As with any business decision, you must consider several factors before moving forward. In this section, you explore several universal cross-cutting aspects that anyone thinking about moving their data to the cloud should consider.

Interoperability

Interoperability is the ability for two or more systems to seamlessly work together by sharing information and using that information as necessary. In cloud systems, interoperability ensures that cloud services can understand standard data formats, APIs, configurations, and identification and authorization mechanisms so that these cloud-based systems can work with the organization's existing technologies or even other clouds.

Portability and reversibility

Portability is the ease with which a party can move or reuse application or service components. Portability means that the service provider, underlying platform, operating system, API structure, format of data, or other factors do not present obstacles to seamlessly moving services from one solution to another.

Vendor lock-in occurs when any of these factors prevents a customer from moving from one cloud provider to another. Portability ensures that an organization is able to easily move between cloud providers or cloud deployment models (from public to private cloud, for example), and host some or all of those components in different environments. Highly interoperable systems provide customers flexibility as their needs change and also tend to keep cloud providers on their toes because customers are able to migrate at any time.

Availability

As discussed in Chapter 2, availability is one of the pillars of information security and one of the greatest considerations for organizations moving to the cloud. In many ways, the availability of resources and systems can make or break a cloud provider's success and their reputation. When an organization relies on a cloud provider for their infrastructure, platforms, or applications, the cloud provider's failure to deliver can mean substantial impact to the customer's business. It's not uncommon for CSPs to commit to 99.9 percent (or higher) availability. Failure to meet this commitment can result in penalties, loss of customers, and degraded brand reputation.

Resiliency

Resiliency measures the ability of a cloud provider to continue providing fully functioning services in the event of disruption. In many ways, resiliency goes hand in hand with availability. As you learn in Chapter 2, disaster recovery and business continuity planning are two key reasons users move to the cloud. Given that CSPs commonly have incredibly vast amounts of resources (servers, storage, networking equipment, bandwidth, and so on), it's easier for cloud-based systems to be highly redundant and resilient in the event of natural disaster, power failure, or other equipment outage. Potential cloud adopters should pay close attention to any resiliency commitments made in their contracts or SLAs.

Security and privacy

Security is often the top concern for potential cloud customers, and it can either be a major selling point or a barrier to adoption for any given CSP. For many organizations — especially smaller ones — moving to the cloud can significantly increase security capabilities, because large scale cloud providers are able to provide world-class security controls that some organizations either cannot afford or are not yet sophisticated enough to implement.

Many cloud providers will publicly state their baseline levels of security or share some of their most marketable security features, but they will typically fall short of listing specific security controls to avoid arming potential attackers with sensitive information that could lead them to compromising the CSP's security. In general, the most mature cloud providers are able to offer just about any security feature a customer could want, but additional security can often incur additional costs.

WARNING

Not all cloud providers are created equally, and not all are able to meet the same levels of security standards. As cloud security professionals, it's important to not only understand what security features are available, but also which ones are enabled by default. Too many cloud breaches occur because users falsely assume that an advertised security feature is enabled without their action.

If security is concern 1A, privacy is often 1B for potential users of cloud services. The very nature of cloud means that customers' data is not always 100 percent within their control. Remember that the global nature of cloud means that a customer's data may exist in multiple locations around the world. Privacy laws and regulations are increasingly influencing CSPs' behavior, but no universal or international set of laws or directives currently consistently enforce privacy standards from one CSP to another, across different geographical locations. Depending on a customer's privacy needs, it may be necessary to negotiate specific requirements as part of contracts or SLAs. (I cover SLAs later in the section "Service-level agreements.")

It might go without saying that cloud computing and high performance are intertwined. Few customers will select or stay with a cloud provider that can't deliver consistently strong performance. The largest CSPs have been in a bit of an "arms race" for years and are releasing stronger, better, and faster compute, memory, and storage capabilities at least every year.

In the upcoming section "Impact of related technologies," you can see some key emerging applications for cloud computing that rely on high performance.

Governance

Governance relates to the policies, procedures, roles, and responsibilities in place to ensure security, privacy, resiliency, and performance. Governance is required at the start of any cloud migration and continues through the entire lifetime of a cloud deployment. In other words, governance activities are ongoing from day zero until cloud services are no longer being used.

Many cloud providers make governance easier than it is with traditional data center models because they offer tools to generate reports and monitor relevant statistics and metrics. The ability to schedule and automate reporting enhances governance activities and allows customers to focus on their mission.

Service-level agreements

In cloud, a *service-level agreement (SLA)* is an agreement between a cloud service provider and cloud customer that identifies the minimum level of service that must be maintained.

SLAs can include anything from amount of uptime to minimum response time to customer service inquiries. In many ways, an SLA serves as a warranty when a customer moves to the cloud. Similar to the warranty you get when purchasing a car, a cloud SLA gives customers assurance that they are getting what they expect and provides remedies (like fee reimbursement) if those agreed upon expectations aren't met.

Here are some examples of things you should look for in a service-level agreement. Keep in mind that this list is not exhaustive:

>> **Availability:** How much uptime is the CSP committing to? The standard is 99.9 percent or more, but pay attention to the period of time over which this guarantee is made.

>> **Performance:** What are standard and maximum response times?

>> **Data ownership:** Who owns your data once it's in the cloud?

>> **Location of the data:** What geographical locations might your data be located? The location may have privacy or compliance implications.

>> **Portability of the data:** Are you able to move your data to another provider whenever you choose?

>> **Data security and privacy:** Is data encrypted at rest? In transit? Who is permitted to access your data?

>> **Disaster recovery:** What solutions and processes are in place for DR and backup?

Maintenance and versioning

The cloud service category being used will determine just how much consideration a customer must give to maintenance and versioning. With SaaS offerings, the CSP is responsible for just about all patching, maintenance, and versioning. Moving up the stack to PaaS and even more with IaaS, the customer has increasing responsibility for these actions.

Maintenance and versioning responsibilities should be agreed upon and understood early on, and they should be specifically called out in contracts and SLAs. With versioning, customers should be aware of what ability the CSP grants for rolling back to previous versions, and what responsibility they have to upgrade (or rollback) from one version to another.

Regulatory compliance

Regulatory compliance is the requirement for an organization to meet or satisfy regulations, guidelines, policies, and laws relevant to its business. A company failing to meet these requirements may face financial penalties, legal action, or even termination of business operations. As a result, regulatory compliance is a major concern for potential cloud users, and it's important to note that the nature of cloud means satisfying compliance is a shared responsibility between a CSP and its customer.

TIP

Having worked on compliance teams at two of the largest cloud providers, I can say firsthand that cloud customers often struggle to understand what is commonly called the *Shared Responsibility Model*. As a CCSP, it's paramount that you understand what your organization is responsible for securing and what your CSP or customer is responsible for. The most transparent CSPs will provide substantial documentation to support your understanding of the Shared Responsibility Model; if this documentation is not readily available, it's best to ask for sufficient details.

Many, many regulations and laws impact technology. Some key examples that impact cloud-based environments include Health Insurance Portability and Accountability Act (HIPAA), Payment Card Industry Data Security Standard (PCI DSS), System and Organization Controls (SOC), the Federal Information Security Management Act (FISMA), and the Federal Risk and Authorization Management Program (FedRAMP), among others. It's important that cloud security professionals understand how their industry influences which of these or other regulations they are required to satisfy.

TIP

In the context of regulatory compliance, you may see SOC (i.e., SOC 1, SOC 2, or SOC 3) described as either System and Organization Controls or Service Organization Controls.

Auditability

As a CCSP candidate, auditability in the cloud is an area you should pay very close attention to because of the Shared Responsibility Model. Because customers do not have full control over the cloud environment the way they would in a traditional data center model, it's important that they're able to audit their compliance with various regulatory requirements, as well as monitor important user and system activity.

The CSP is responsible for providing logging and auditing capabilities to the customer and demonstrating that they are capturing and reporting on any events the customer may want to audit. Most mature cloud service providers offer a wealth of auditing and reporting capabilities, but it is up to the customer to use them in accordance with their compliance obligations.

Impact of related technologies

One of the recently updated sections to the CCSP Common Body of Knowledge (CBK) addresses critical technologies that cloud security professionals should stay abreast of. The following list of emerging technologies are closely related to cloud and represent some of the fastest growing applications of cloud computing.

Artificial Intelligence (AI) and machine learning (ML)

Broadly speaking, *Artificial Intelligence* is the field devoted to helping machines process things in a smart manner; AI involves giving machines the ability to imitate intelligent human behavior. AI burst onto the public scene in a big way with the release of the AI-enabled chat app, ChatGPT, at the end of 2022. As of this writing in 2023, ChatGPT has over 100 million active users and generates 1.8 billion visitors per month, demonstrating the meteoric rise of mainstream AI, which has been enabled and driven by cloud computing.

Machine learning is a subset of AI that focuses on allowing machines to alter themselves as they are exposed to additional data. Much like a child learns language by being exposed to different words in different contexts over time, ML occurs when a machine learns new information without requiring it to be explicitly programmed.

Cloud providers like Amazon Web Services (AWS), Google Cloud Platform, and Microsoft Azure offer services that make it easy for organizations and users to access AI and ML capabilities without requiring advanced skills in data science. Many of these services offer pre-built machine learning models and large datasets from which those models can begin "learning" for your application.

Data science

Data science is a multidisciplinary approach to studying large and complex datasets and extracting meaningful insights using machine learning and various statistical techniques. Cloud computing plays a significant role in data science by providing scalable and flexible infrastructure and computational resources, allowing data scientists to store and process huge amounts of data using cutting-edge ML capabilities.

Blockchain

In April 2021, the price of 1 Bitcoin peaked at close to a whopping $65,000! Since then (as of this writing), the price has trended downward, but interest in cryptocurrencies and other blockchain applications continues strong. In simplest terms, a *blockchain* is a string of digital information that is chained together by cryptography. Each block of information contains a cryptographic hash of the previous block, transaction data, and a timestamp. Several industry leading cloud providers now offer platforms to help users build their blockchain-based applications without needing PhDs in cryptography.

Internet of things (IoT)

Internet of things is a fancy way of describing everyday devices that are connected to the Internet. My TVs, refrigerator, oven range, and dishwasher are all equipped with devices that connect to the Internet and that allow them to send and receive data (hopefully not to Skynet). Outside of the home, IoT has many commercial and industrial applications; you can find entire warehouses run by Internet-connected devices. Because these devices collect and generate a large amount of data, cloud systems play a pivotal role in drawing insights from IoT systems. For systems with thousands or even millions of IoT sensors, cloud computing allows data to be aggregated, processed, and analyzed more quickly and efficiently.

Edge computing

In simple terms, *edge computing* is a form of computing that involves capturing, processing, and analyzing data at its source. Edge computing reduces latency and improves performance by bringing the power of the cloud to the edge of the networks and doing all of the processing on-site instead of sending data to a central cloud data center. In a smart home, for example, edge computing can be used to process and control devices like security cameras and thermostats directly in the home instead of sending all data to a cloud server.

Confidential computing

Confidential computing is a cloud-based technology focused on protecting sensitive data by isolating it in a protected central processing unit (CPU) during processing. Confidential computing keeps sensitive data encrypted in a secure enclave that is separate from the rest of the environment, offering assurance that even the cloud provider cannot access the data in plaintext.

Containers

Containers are a growing technology that involves logically decoupling an application from its environment so that the containerized application can be developed, deployed, and run consistently in different environments (public cloud, private cloud, or even a personal laptop). Containers were made popular with the development of *Kubernetes*, an open-source platform for managing containerized workloads. With Kubernetes and other container platforms, cloud users are able to develop applications and seamlessly move and run them from one platform to another. Containers are particularly useful in hybrid cloud deployments, for example, where a customer might run the same application on-prem and in the cloud.

Quantum computing

In October 2019, Google announced that it had achieved *quantum supremacy* — basically, the ability of a quantum computer to solve a problem that a classical computer could not solve in a practical amount of time. Though quantum computing is still in its infancy, tech giants like Google, IBM, and Microsoft are pushing forward with solutions to bring the power of quantum computing to cloud applications.

TECHNICAL STUFF

The field of quantum computing revolves around using the principle of quantum mechanical superposition to process information exponentially faster than even modern supercomputers. The physics behind quantum mechanics and quantum computing is outside the scope of this book, but worth further research if you find yourself working on cloud-based quantum applications.

DevSecOps

DevSecOps is a software development practice aimed at combining security and IT operations into every stage of the software development lifecycle (SDLC). Cloud computing plays an important role in supporting and enabling DevSecOps practices in modern technology environments. The scalability, flexibility, and automation features within cloud environments support automating security processes and enabling development teams to include security throughout the entire development lifecycle.

Chapter **4**

Domain 1: Cloud Concepts, Architecture, and Design, Part 2

I n this chapter, you explore the key information security concepts that are critical to securing cloud environments as either the cloud provider or the cloud user. You also learn about some important considerations when evaluating and selecting a cloud provider for your organization. Domain 1 represents 17 percent of the CCSP certification exam, and this chapter covers the second half of Domain 1.

Identifying Security Concepts Relevant to Cloud Computing

Chapter 2 contains an information security primer that introduces many of the security concepts applicable to data centers or any security model. If you're not familiar with topics like cryptography, access control, and media sanitization, you should check out Chapter 2 before proceeding with this chapter. While those concepts and others are broadly applicable, you need to consider specific points when securing cloud environments.

Cryptography and key management

As a cloud security professional, it's up to you to evaluate the need for cryptography for your cloud-based data and systems. You should be carefully examining the type of data you're securing, the threats to that data, and any regulatory or contractual requirements related to securing the data. Based on your analysis, the proper encryption controls allow you to protect the confidentiality and integrity of your information without impacting legitimate system usage and data access.

Generally speaking, three states of digital information exist:

>> Data at rest

>> Data in transit

>> Data in use

Understanding these states and what happens to information during each phase is important when thinking about how to apply cryptography.

Data at rest

Data at rest refers to data that is stored on a system or device, and not actively being read, written to, transmitted, or processed. This data may be spreadsheets on a hard drive, documents stored on tape, or entire databases in a cloud-based backup.

If you think about data at rest, it's essentially information that can be a sitting duck for attackers, if not properly protected. Large pools of data staying in one location are generally at greater risk than data that's moving from point A to point B. Because data at rest is often exposed for long periods of time, you should pay special attention to encryption as a control against unauthorized access. Common options include encrypting sensitive files prior to storage and/or encrypting the entire storage volume or drive itself. You can even use field level encryption for granular control over your most sensitive information.

TECHNICAL STUFF

Field-level encryption is a form of encryption that lets you encrypt individual fields as opposed to entire files or databases. Field-level encryption offers more granular protection over your most sensitive information, and it's often used to provide extra protection over regulated data. Let's say you have a cloud database that stores customer information like names, addresses, phone numbers, and credit card numbers. Using field-level encryption, each field within the database (such as the credit card number) can be encrypted using its own unique key. This ensures that even if the database is compromised, the sensitive information remains protected.

REMEMBER

Not all cloud data at rest solutions are created equal. Some CSPs enable encryption by default for all data at rest, while others require various levels of configuration to enable it. As a cloud security professional, make sure you refer to the CSP's product configuration guides to understand what's already done and what is your responsibility.

Data in transit

Data in transit (or *data in motion*) refers to data that is actively being transmitted across a network or between multiple networks. Data in transit can include data moving from a user's laptop across the Internet to a cloud provider, data traveling between systems or services within a cloud environment, or any data traversing a trusted or untrusted network. Common examples of data in transit are email traffic, file downloads from the Internet, and commands sent over SSH.

WARNING

The threats posed to data in transit differ from those of data at rest, and it's important to understand how you can use cryptography to protect data without causing unintended consequences. Some pitfalls to watch out for are interoperability challenges caused by improper or incompatible encryption between systems, as well as performance impacts due to the processing requirements that encryption adds.

TIP

Always evaluate encryption compatibility across all systems and environments that your data flows and remember to consider whether the risk the encryption is mitigating is greater than the performance hit it'll have.

Pitfalls aside, sensitive cloud data in transit should be protected with encryption. Encryption helps ensure that data makes it from the user to the cloud (and back) without unauthorized access or compromised integrity. Some key protocols and technologies for encrypting data in transit include TLS (including HTTPS), IPsec, PGP, and VPNs. Several of these technologies are introduced in Chapter 2.

Data in use

Data in use is sometimes forgotten, but this third state of digital data refers to information that is actively being processed or manipulated by a system or application. Data in use can be data that is being created, modified, or even erased; any data that is neither stagnant nor being transmitted from one point to another can generally be considered data in use.

TECHNICAL STUFF

Data in use is synonymous with data that resides in a system's Random Access Memory (RAM) or cache memory.

Data in use can be very tricky to secure. For one, data in the cloud can generally be processed only in unencrypted form; indexing, searching, and analysis of encrypted data is anywhere from impractical to impossible. Even scarier, data in use often contains very sensitive data; things like encryption keys and certificates are commonly found in memory. Because of the limitations associated with encryption, cloud security professionals typically look to other security controls to manage risks to data in use. A layered security approach that leverages approaches like network segmentation and isolation, secure containers, and multifactor authentication helps protect data in use.

Key management

Just as important as it is to encrypt sensitive data, it's paramount that you have a method for generating, issuing, organizing, and managing encryption keys. A cloud security architect will generally assess an organization's use of encryption and identify their needs for key management. When using public cloud, customers often want to use their own key management system as an added layer of privacy and control over their data. In doing so, customers remove dependency on the cloud provider to manage their keys and also avoid potential vendor lock-in due to using a CSP's proprietary key management platform.

TIP

Most large-scale cloud providers offer key management services. It's important that you understand how using those services impact the security or portability of your data. Don't forget to check contractual terms, SLAs (service level agreements), and config guides associated with encryption and key management.

Customers commonly use two key management services (KMSs) with cloud environments:

>> **Remote KMS:** In remote KMS, the CSP generates, holds, and manages the encryption keys, and the customer encrypts and decrypts their data using those keys. Remote KMS is typically used when high availability or scalability is a top priority, because the CSP can ensure that encryption keys are always available. On the flip side, remote KMS also means that the CSP has access to the keys, which is a concern for many customers, particularly those with regulated data.

>> **Client-side KMS:** A client-side KMS is owned, operated, and maintained on premises by the customer. This configuration gives the customer complete control over who can generate or access cryptographic keys. Something to

keep in mind with client-side KMS is that it requires constant network connectivity between the cloud customer and CSP; disruptions in connectivity may prevent encryption and decryption functions from operating. Client-side KMS also means that the customer is responsible for managing the keys and ensuring that they remain protected. While client-side KMS offers the most control, it is also the more expensive option.

Identity and access control

Access control and its related technologies give way to *Identity and Access Management (IAM)*, which is the sum of all the technologies, processes, and personnel that are responsible for controlling access to resources. As a cloud security professional, you should pay careful attention to validating cloud users' identities and controlling their access to systems and data. I provide an introduction to IAM in Chapter 2; check that out for a primer. There are three foundational types of access that you should be aware of:

>> *User access* refers to the permissions granted to individual users within a system or environment. It determines the level of access a user has to resources and data based on their identity. User access is typically managed through user authentication (like username and password or MFA), authorization, and role-based access controls (RBACs).

>> *Service access* refers to the permissions granted to systems, applications, and services; it includes all of the credentials required for these systems, applications, and services to interact with each other and controls their access to resources within a cloud environment. Services access controls, such as secure API keys, ensure that only authorized services can communicate with or access specific resources.

>> *Privileged access* refers to elevated permissions granted to certain users or service accounts; these elevated permissions typically grant access to sensitive data and administrative tasks. As such, privileged access requires strict control, as described in the "Privileged access management" section just ahead.

In addition to what you've learned this far, IAM can be broken down into the following components:

>> Account provisioning and deprovisioning

>> Directory services

>> Privileged access management

Account provisioning and deprovisioning

Access management begins and ends with account provisioning and deprovisioning, and both are critical pillars of IAM. Account provisioning deals with creating user accounts and enabling access to cloud resources, whereas deprovisioning is the opposite and entails removing users and their access.

Account provisioning should be designed to create an efficient account creation process that is consistent and easily monitored and audited. The goal is to have a standardized process by which new users are created and/or new access is granted for existing users.

Account deprovisioning is perhaps even more important, from a security perspective. Account deprovisioning is the process of removing access and disabling an account when a user no longer requires access to cloud resources. The easy use case is when someone leaves a company, but keep in mind that account deprovisioning also comes into play when users change roles or job functions; a user's required access to resources would likely change if they moved from the IT department to a role in Finance, for example. Deprovisioning is all about enforcing the principle of least privilege and minimizing the risk associated with unnecessary access.

Directory services

Directory services are another key pillar of IAM and security, both in traditional IT settings and in the cloud. A *directory service* is a relational hierarchy of cloud identities that manages the storage and processing of information and acts as the single point through which cloud users can locate and access cloud resources. In the on-prem world, Active Directory is a key example of a directory service, and it offers authentication, policy enforcement, and other services for an enterprise organization.

While many traditional directory services providers were slow to migrate to the cloud, several third-party directory services offerings have become popular in cloud environments. Most major CSPs now offer cloud-native directory services, many of which can integrate with a customer's existing on-prem directory services (like Active Directory). Within cloud environments, directory services play a huge role in establishing and maintaining a trusted source for organizational identities and access policies.

TECHNICAL STUFF

Cloud directory services use protocols like Lightweight Directory Access Protocol (LDAP) and Security Assertion Markup Language (SAML) to link user identities to cloud applications.

Privileged access management

Users with the highest privileges (root, admin, and so on) present the most risk to that system, both because of insider risk and due to the impact should those accounts be compromised by a malicious actor outside the company. Privileged access management includes the technologies and processes involved in managing the entire lifecycle of these sensitive accounts: from provisioning to deprovisioning, and everything in between.

While monitoring all accounts for suspicious activity is best practice, this monitoring is extremely important for privileged users accounts. Cloud security professionals should track and monitor successful and failed authentications and include information like date, time, user identifier, and location (or IP) of access. Effective privileged access management should seek to implement ad-hoc privileged access (for example, elevated privileges only when needed) rather than long-term privileged access and provide continuous visibility of privileged access to cloud resources.

Data and media sanitization

Conversations about cloud computing are often focused on migrating to the cloud, but many cloud customers also want to understand how they can remove their data from the cloud whenever that time should come. A standard practice of cloud providers is to physically destroy media once it's no longer needed, but because CSPs store data from multiple customers on the same servers and drives, prudent customers want the ability to fully remove their data from the cloud at any time they chose. The standard method of data deletion is to overwrite content with a series of random 0s and 1s, sometimes multiple times. I introduce a more effective method, crypto-shredding (or cryptographic erasure) in Chapter 2. For even more information on data and media sanitization, check out NIST Special Publication 800-88, Guidelines for Media Sanitization.

Network security

Networking and network security play huge roles in cloud computing. The very nature of cloud requires that data move from one point to another over the Internet, among other networks. Cloud computing typically entails multiple cloud users connecting to a cloud provider's externally exposed networking devices. Keeping this point in mind, you can understand the criticality of ensuring that both a CSP's internal networks are secure and that the connection from users to the CSP remain secure.

Whereas traditional data centers can rely on a clean segmentation point between public and private networks (such as the physical boundary where network traffic comes into the data center), cloud environments rely on multiple internal private networks to separate customers from one another. This added architectural complexity means that as a CCSP, you should have a solid understanding of how networks work and how to secure them.

There are two key technologies you should consider when it comes to network security in the cloud:

>> **Virtual Private Cloud (VPC):** A *virtual private cloud (VPC)* is a logically isolated network within a shared cloud environment — it's like your own private cloud within a public cloud. With a VPC, you can define your own private IP address range, create subnets, and control inbound and outbound network traffic through your private network. VPCs are the key technology behind network segmentation and isolation in the cloud.

>> **Network security groups:** A *network security group* is a cloud-based virtual firewall that allows you to control network traffic within a VPC or subnet using allow and deny rules. Network security groups allow you to enforce network security policies and restrict access to resources.

There are two key practices you should consider when it comes to network security in the cloud:

>> *Traffic inspection* is the continuous monitoring and analysis of network traffic, with the goal of enforcing security policies and detecting anomalies and potential threats. Traffic inspection includes technologies and practices like data loss prevention, intrusion detection and prevention, malware detection, TLS inspection, and more. By implementing traffic inspection, you can gain visibility into your network activity and proactively detect and mitigate security risks.

>> *Geofencing* is a technique that involves establishing virtual boundaries based on location. Geofencing uses geographic information, often based on IP addresses, to limit access to resources and data to approved locations and regions only. For example, geofencing can be used to limit access to confidential French Government information to people attempting to access from French soil, or within the European Union, if appropriate.

Another key network security concept that continues to gain popularity is zero trust networking. It's a topic so important, I think it deserves its own section — and that's what comes next.

Zero trust networking

Zero trust networking is a security model that is built on the philosophy of "never trust, always verify," and requires continuous assessment and authorization to maintain access. Whereas traditional network security models focus on establishing a secure network perimeter and treating anything inside of that network as trusted, a zero trust networking approach assumes that the network is already breached. Network segmentation is used to limit lateral movement within a zero trust network; this segmentation divides the network into smaller "microperimeters," restricting communication between them and minimizing the "blast radius" of a compromise.

The broader topic of zero trust architecture (ZTA) is covered in Chapter 7, in the section titled "Designing a Secure Data Center."

Virtualization security

As mentioned in Chapter 3, virtualization is the act of creating virtual (in other words, not actual) resources like servers, desktops, operating systems, and so on. In cloud computing, virtualization is one of the key enabling technologies for multitenancy and scalability; it separates compute environments from the physical hardware so that multiple operating systems and applications can run on a single machine.

A *hypervisor* is a computing layer that allows multiple operating systems to run simultaneously on the same piece of hardware, with each operating system seeing the machine's resources as its own dedicated resources. In other words, hypervisors virtually divide a computer's resources among several virtual machines (VMs) and manages the sharing of those resources between each VM.

The two types of hypervisors are Type 1 and Type 2. Type 1 hypervisors (also called bare metal hypervisors) run directly on the hardware, whereas Type 2 hypervisors are software-based and run on an operating system.

From a security perspective, Type 2 hypervisors have a greater attack surface because of the vulnerabilities associated with operating systems and the applications that reside on the OS with the hypervisor. OS and application vulnerabilities can be exploited and used to attack Type 2 hypervisors and their virtual machines. Type 1 hypervisors, however, generally have embedded operating systems that are tightly controlled by the vendor. This control lends itself to creating hardened operating systems that only have functionality necessary to operate the hypervisors. For many years, cloud security professionals assumed that Type 1 hypervisors were immune from attack.

Despite being less commonly exploited, Type 1 hypervisors are not exempt from security risks.

Containers (introduced in Chapter 3, in the section called "Impact of related technologies") share many of the same security concerns as virtual servers. While you're not necessarily focused on the hypervisor with container security, you should keep in mind the same principles discussed in the earlier section on hypervisor security. Access to containers must be tightly controlled, and container images must be validated to ensure that they have not been improperly tampered with. As you do with virtual servers, you must have a process in place to routinely update and patch all your containers.

Common threats

In June 2022, the Cloud Security Alliance (CSA) published "Top Threats to Cloud Computing: Pandemic Eleven." The report examines the risks inherent in cloud computing environments and identifies the top threats that organizations face when using cloud services, particularly in the post–COVID era.

TIP

CSA's annual threat report is a great resource for information regarding the cloud threat landscape. You can find a link to download the report in Appendix B. I highly recommend you check it out!

CSA's 2022 "Pandemic Eleven" threats are

>> Insufficient identity, credential, access, and key management

>> Insecure interfaces and APIs

>> Misconfiguration and inadequate change control

>> Lack of cloud security architecture and strategy

>> Insecure software development

>> Unsecured third-party resources

>> System vulnerabilities

>> Accidental cloud data disclosure

>> Misconfiguration and exploitation of serverless and container workloads

>> Organized crime/hackers/APT

>> Cloud storage data exfiltration

Insufficient identity, credential, access, and key management

Identity and Access Management (IAM) and key management are hugely important topics in any type of environment; this set of tools and processes allows users to control and monitor who can access data and systems. In the cloud, these topics get even more critical because of the shared responsibilities between CSPs and customers. I discuss IAM and key management throughout the course of this book, but for now, remember that these issues present a great deal of risk to cloud customers who don't prepare effectively.

Consider the following when you're looking to mitigate threats associated with IAM and key management:

>> Use strong passwords and multifactor authentication to protect access to sensitive data.

>> Understand your cloud provider's IAM services and examine the tradeoffs between on-prem and cloud-native IAM solutions. Along these lines, you should understand your CSP's ability to support federated identity and what that means for your organization.

>> Practice least privilege and allow only the minimal amount of access for cloud users.

>> Remove unused credentials to minimize exposure through unnecessary accounts.

>> Develop a robust key management plan that includes key rotation (automatic, where feasible).

While the cloud provider has responsibility to enable cloud customers to meet their security objectives (like IAM and key management), it is ultimately the cloud customer's responsibility to implement and monitor these controls. Neglecting to do so is often the reason for data breaches and other cloud security incidents.

Insecure interfaces and APIs

Application Programming Interfaces (APIs) are used to expose a cloud provider's capabilities to the cloud customer. APIs, along with user interfaces, allow customers to take advantage of the products, services, and features that a CSP operates. Because of their rising popularity, securing these interfaces should be one of your top priorities. Strong API security requires that you check for misconfigurations, weak authentication, excessive permissions, unpatched systems, and insufficient logging and monitoring, just to name a few. Failure to properly secure APIs can lead to data exfiltration, service interruptions, or unauthorized data modification.

As they often have public IP addresses, APIs are typically the most exposed part of a cloud environment, and if they are not protected, pose a great deal of risk to the data stored in the cloud. It's important that CSPs design these APIs with security in mind, and it's critical that cloud users appropriately govern their use of APIs.

TIP

Because of the growing use and the high volume of traffic that relies on APIs, your organization should use automation to continuously monitor API traffic, whenever possible.

Misconfiguration and inadequate change control

A leading cause of data breaches is the misconfiguration of systems and services that leaves data vulnerable to attack. Default credentials and settings, excessive permissions, and lack of basic security hygiene are some key examples of misconfiguration.

A famous example of misconfiguration occurred in 2017 when a misconfigured AWS S3 storage bucket led to the exposure of more than 100 million American's private information that was owned by Experian. More recently, in late 2021, the now Meta-owned apps Facebook, Instagram, WhatsApp, and Oculus all went offline for seven hours due to misconfigured changes that interrupted communications between Facebook's data centers. The outage also prevented anyone from using the "Log in with Facebook" feature on various third-party sites. Aside from millions of people not being able to post selfies, the Facebook outage highlighted the importance of proper change control and the value of business continuity planning.

Inadequate change control often contributes to misconfiguration in cloud environments. Whereas traditional IT environments often rely on lengthy processes and several stages of review to implement changes, cloud environments are far more dynamic and tend to automate basic and common tasks.

WARNING

Cloud customers who don't understand the differences between legacy change control and cloud-based change control are prone to miss critical things and fail to effectively configure settings in a timely fashion. While CSPs are often expected to provide support in the form of configuration guides, best practices, and so on, proper configuration of settings and adequate change control are ultimately the responsibility of the cloud customer.

Lack of cloud security architecture and strategy

Customers moving their IT infrastructure or sensitive data to the cloud should have an established cloud security architecture as well as a well-defined strategy for managing the security of their cloud environment and data. It's important that customers understand the differences between cloud and traditional IT so that they are prepared to adequately address the unique threats that cloud computing poses. Unfortunately, many companies embark on their cloud journeys without skilled cloud security professionals (like you!) to help with these unique challenges. It is paramount that customers consider how they will migrate, what security controls and configurations fit their business needs, and what processes they will follow to consistently manage the security of their data in the cloud.

Your cloud security architecture and strategy should include consideration of the cloud deployment model(s) and cloud service model(s) that you're using, and you should also determine how you're protecting user and system identities, securely managing multi-cloud usage, building for business continuity and disaster recovery, and managing third-party risk. You should develop your strategy before designing your cloud architecture and update your strategy as needed.

Insecure software development

Software development is a tough job, and the complexity of cloud environments can make it even tougher. As a CCSP, part of your job is making it easy for your software developers to create secure code.

If properly architected, your cloud strategy can allow your development teams to shift some of the burden of software security to your CSP. Remember that your CSP manages the security of the underlying infrastructure and platforms, in addition to offering your developers services for things like encryption, key management, IAM, and secure continuous integration/continuous deployment (CI/CD). You should ensure that your developers understand the security tools that come with the cloud and be mindful that your security team is enabling developers to use those tools.

REMEMBER

Reducing the risk associated with insecure software development requires teaching your developers secure coding practices and deploying application security testing methodologies (like SAST and DAST, introduced in Chapter 10).

TIP

It's too easy for security teams to become routine bearers of bad news, burdening developers with metrics describing their security posture, but doing little to help them improve those metrics. Keep in mind that scalability in the cloud also applies to vulnerabilities. So what might otherwise be a single vulnerability can easily be duplicated across 10,000 containers in a cloud environment. So, it's important that you, as a cloud security professional, help your development teams effectively prioritize their remediation activities in a risk-based manner.

Unsecure third-party resources

As a CISO, third-party risk comes in closer to the top of my list, but CSA places it comfortably in the middle of the Pandemic Eleven. When you think of cloud computing, it starts and ends with third-party resources — the IaaS provider you're using, the open source code you're adopting, and the SaaS products and APIs your leveraging — they all present third-party risk. These risks are also considered supply chain risks, because they're all components used in delivering your products or services.

TIP

While "third party" gets all the love, the risk doesn't stop there. Your third parties have third parties, and those fourth parties likely have their own third parties (your fifth parties). You'll often see and you may want to use "Nth party" to describe the vendors and suppliers at every stop along your supply chain.

A product or service is only as secure as its weakest link, and you can't always prevent vulnerabilities in code or products that you didn't create. Security teams around the world were reminded of this in late 2021, when the critical severity Log4Shell vulnerability wreaked havoc in applications using the popular Log4j logging framework. Log4Shell is considered the largest vulnerability to date, due to the popularity of the Log4j framework. By many estimates, upwards of 90 percent of all cloud environments were susceptible to the exploit.

System vulnerabilities

A *system vulnerability* is a security flaw in a cloud service platform, which can be exploited to compromise the confidentiality, integrity, or availability of systems or data. You can reduce the risk associated with system vulnerabilities through routine vulnerability scanning, patching, and other security hygiene practices.

The CSA Pandemic Eleven calls out four main categories of system vulnerabilities:

>> **Zero day vulnerabilities:** Simply put, a *zero day vulnerability* is a security flaw that is so new that vulnerability scanners won't detect it and the software developer has yet to create a patch to fix it. Hackers love zero days because there is very little a victim can do to stop them until a patch is released. Log4Shell, mentioned in the previous section, is a notable example of a zero day vulnerability.

>> **Missing security patches:** Unless a vulnerability is a zero day, there is a patch available for you to fix the flaw. Patches for your various pieces of software are released daily, and they can be hard to keep up with. You should establish a risk-based approach to deploying security patches, keeping in mind that your overall system risk increases as your number of missing patches increases.

>> **Configuration-based vulnerabilities:** This type of vulnerability occurs when you deploy a system using default or misconfigured settings. Baselining, as

discussed in the "Security hygiene" section later, is a primary protection against this type of system vulnerability.

>> **Weak or default credentials:** Lacking strong authentication credentials can present significant risk to your systems and data. Remember to use complex passwords (and MFA, where possible) and store your passwords and other credentials securely.

Accidental cloud data disclosure

As I mention multiple times in this book, the cloud makes accessing information from anywhere easy, and that's great. However, this ubiquitous data access comes with risks if you lack the right data security and governance. As cloud providers continue to offer more features and configurations, the opportunity for misconfigurations continues to increase. Having publicly exposed databases with weak or nonexistent authentication makes you an easy target for hackers who scan the Internet for exposed databases.

You should reduce access exposure by ensuring that externally facing databases implement strong IAM policies and you should implement monitoring that offers visibility over your cloud environment and helps you identify any accidental external exposures.

Misconfiguration and exploitation of serverless and container workloads

Serverless computing, introduced in Chapter 3, allows you to run function code in short-living containers, by default. The short time-to-live (TTL) of these functions reduces the risk of exploit because hackers have only a short time to compromise the function each time it "spins up" and an even shorter time to maintain access and do harm. If you choose to increase the TTL of your serverless containers, you're likely increasing the risk of those containers by allowing them to persist for longer periods.

Serverless and container technologies offer many business benefits (speed and cost, to name a couple). Here are a few additional tips to keep in mind, if your organization uses these technologies:

>> Invest in cloud security training for your developers and ensure that you're placing increased focus on application security as you migrate to a serverless architecture.

>> Create and use reusable secure cloud architecture baselines to reduce the frequency and risk of misconfigurations.

>> Be mindful of how long your containers persist to reduce the likelihood and impact of a compromise.

>> Program your application code to wipe temporary storage so that it isn't used to host or execute malware.

>> Use a Cloud Security Posture Management (CSPM) tool to implement automated security assessment and compliance checking of your cloud environment.

WARNING

Serverless and cloud-native containerized workloads require a higher degree of cloud and application security maturity than simpler cloud deployments, like basic virtual machines.

Organized crime/hackers/APT

An *advanced persistent threat* (APT) is a sophisticated attack in which a skilled hacker or team of hackers establish a long-term presence in an environment. APTs often include nation-states or organized crime gangs with significant resources. Because of these resources, APTs are often able to break into networks and remain undetected for many months, moving laterally and accessing large amounts of data in the process. A recent example of an APT incident occurred in early 2022 when the international extortion-focused hacker group, Lapsus$, broke into chipmaker NVIDIA's network, stole and began leaking sensitive information — from hashed login credentials to trade secrets.

Understanding the tactics, techniques, and procedures (TTP) used by APT groups can help you identify the early signs of an attack. The threat intelligence community studies APT groups and produces reports that can educate you on the TTPs used by APT groups that might target your organization.

TIP

The National Council of ISACs is a partnership composed of 26 organizations designated by their sectors as their Information Sharing and Analysis Centers (ISACs). These sector-based ISACs provide a forum for sharing cyber and physical threats and mitigation strategies among member organizations. Example member ISACs include FS-ISAC for Financial Services organizations, Auto-ISAC for automotive manufacturers and suppliers, and RH-ISAC for the retail and hospitality sector.

Cloud storage data exfiltration

This final security issue in the Pandemic Eleven broadly covers the unauthorized release, theft, or use of your cloud data by an individual outside your organization's operating environment. Many examples of data exfiltration include sensitive information like personally identifiable information (PII), personal health information (PHI), and cardholder data. The root cause can be anything from malware to phishing attacks.

Security hygiene

Much like brushing your teeth, there are certain security things that seem basic, but are paramount to well-being. *Security hygiene* refers to the set of best practices and measures that you should take as a starting point to maintaining good security posture; it includes things like using strong passwords, implementing proper access controls, and conducting regular backups of important information.

When it comes to security hygiene, there are two practices that are as basic and essential as brushing your teeth: baselining and patching.

Baselining

Baselining is the process of establishing a known and accepted standard of normal behavior for your system, network, or application. You can create baselines either manually or in an automated fashion by monitoring and collecting data about various aspects of your environment (things like user behavior, configuration settings, performance metrics, and so on).

By establishing a baseline, you can effectively detect deviations from the norm that might indicate a security issue. Baselines play an important role in intrusion detection, anomaly detection, and overall security monitoring. Having a baseline that defines what "good" looks like helps you more easily identify something that's not so good.

Patching

Patching is perhaps the most basic of security hygiene needs. People in cybersecurity spend a lot of time talking about vulnerabilities, and I discuss system vulnerabilities earlier in this chapter. Patching refers to the process of applying updates, fixes, or (you guessed it!) patches to your software to fix known vulnerabilities. Software vendors typically release patches when they identify a security weakness, but patches can also include performance enhancements, compatibility improvements, and other tweaks. I cover patch management more in Chapter 11.

Comprehending Design Principles of Secure Cloud Computing

You can rely on many of the same principles from traditional IT models when designing secure cloud computing environments, but the cloud does present additional considerations. Cloud computing comes with its own set of benefits and challenges in managing the data lifecycle, disaster recovery, and business continuity planning.

In addition, you must consider unique factors when conducting business impact analysis to determine whether moving to the cloud makes sense for your organization.

Cloud secure data lifecycle

I often use the phrase "security follows the data" when describing data security. What I mean by this phrase is that keeping data secure requires an understanding of where the data is, both physically and in its lifecycle. Figure 4-1 shows the cloud secure data lifecycle, and its steps are described in the following list.

1. **Create.**

   Data is either generated from scratch or existing data is modified/updated.

2. **Store.**

   Data is saved into a storage system or repository.

3. **Use.**

   Data is processed by a user or application.

4. **Share.**

   Data is made accessible by other users or systems.

5. **Archive.**

   Data is transferred from readily accessible storage to a more long-term, static storage state.

6. **Destroy.**

   Data is deleted and removed from storage, making it permanently inaccessible and unusable.

Understanding the differences between each of these phases is an important prerequisite to defining data security processes and identifying appropriate security mechanisms. Specific data security controls are dependent on any regulatory, contractual, and business requirements that your organization must satisfy. Cloud data security is covered in detail in Chapters 5 and 6.

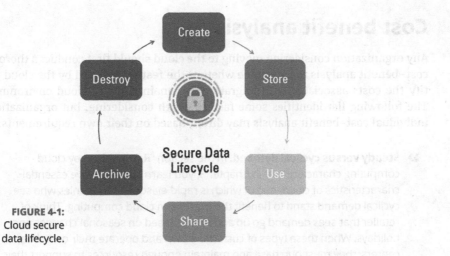

FIGURE 4-1:
Cloud secure
data lifecycle.

Cloud based business continuity (BC) and disaster recovery (DR) planning

You can visit Chapter 2 if you need an introduction to BCP and DR. This section gives you some tips, as a CCSP candidate concerned with business continuity planning and disaster recovery in cloud environments. Some important points to consider are

>> Understand how the shared responsibility model applies to BCP/DR.

>> Understand any supply chain risks that exist (for example, vendor or third-party factors that may impact your ability to conduct BCP/DR activities).

>> Consider the need to keep backups offsite or with another CSP.

>> Ensure that SLAs cover all aspects of BCP/DR that concern your organization, including RPOs, RTOs, points of contact, roles and responsibilities, and so on.

REMEMBER

Service Level Agreements (SLAs) are tremendously important to consider when planning for business continuity and disaster recovery. SLAs should clearly describe requirements for redundancy and failover, as well as address mitigating single points of failure in the cloud environment. In addition, you should look for clear language on your ability to move to another cloud provider should your DR and BC requirements not be met. While having all of this documented and agreed upon is a must, it's also important that you periodically review and test that these agreements continue to hold true.

Cost benefit analysis

Any organization considering moving to the cloud should first conduct a thorough cost-benefit analysis to determine whether the features offered by the cloud justify the costs associated with migrating and maintaining a cloud environment. The following list identifies some factors worth considering, but organizations' individual cost-benefit analysis may differ, based on their own requirements:

>> **Steady versus cyclical demand:** In the section "Recognizing key cloud computing characteristics" in Chapter 3, you learn about the five essential characteristics of cloud, one of which is rapid elasticity. Companies who see cyclical demand stand to benefit the most from cloud computing. Think of a retailer that sees demand go up and down, based on seasonal changes and holidays. When these types of customers own and operate their own data centers, they must purchase and maintain enough resources to support their highest capacity periods (Black Friday, for example). During other times of the year, these customers are still paying to operate facilities that are likely only a fraction in use. Some organizations, however, don't experience cyclical spikes, and so the equation for them is a little different. Every potential cloud customer must evaluate their own demand trends and determine whether cloud computing offers a financially attractive option for running their workloads.

>> **CapEx versus OpEx:** One of the biggest changes for companies moving to the cloud is a drastic shift from capital expenditures to operational expenditures. Rather than paying to keep data centers up and running, companies in the cloud carry OpEx costs associated with cloud oversight, management, and auditing. Organizations must evaluate whether their current org structure, business model, and staffing can support this shift. For example, some companies may realize that their current staff is not sufficiently equipped to take on new roles, and the costs of hiring new personnel may be prohibitive to moving to the cloud.

>> **Ownership and control:** Organizations who own and operate their own hardware maintain full ownership and control over their systems and data; they get to change what they want, when they want. When moving to the cloud, some of this control is traded for convenience and flexibility. While organizations can negotiate favorable contractual terms and SLAs, they will never maintain the same direct control they have with on-prem solutions. While many customers are willing to make this tradeoff, each organization will have to assess their own priorities and determine whether relinquishing some level of control is acceptable.

>> **Organizational focus:** One of the key benefits of cloud is the fact that organizations can shift their focus from operating systems to overseeing their operation; a difference that can be significant and allow organizations to focus more on their core business rather than managing IT operations. While this benefit is clear, some organizations may not be completely ready to transition their existing operations staff into other roles. Business leaders must evaluate how ready they are for such an organization shift and whether the pros outweigh potential pitfalls.

TIP

Another financial concept related to cost benefit analysis is return on investment (ROI), which is a financial metric used to compare the gains or benefits derived from the investment to the costs of the investment. Your business will often use ROI to justify an expense, so it's important for you to consider ROI when designing your secure cloud.

Functional security requirements

There are some key functional requirements to consider when designing your secure cloud. To start, cloud portability and interoperability refer to the ability to easily move applications and data between different cloud platforms.

>> **Portability** is the ability to switch between different CSPs or move data between your on-prem systems to the cloud without much hassle. This lets you take advantage of cloud features from multiple providers without much hassle. Portability helps you avoid *vendor lock-in,* which is when a customer gets stuck using specific CSPs products or services because it's too difficult to switch to another CSP.

>> **Interoperability** is the ability to use multiple different cloud systems together seamlessly. Interoperability requires setting common rules and security measures so that your different cloud services can talk to each other effectively. Interoperability ensures that security measures like user authentication and encryption are consistent and effective across all of your cloud environments.

Security considerations for different cloud categories

Each cloud category (IaaS, PaaS, and SaaS) will share some similar security concerns, but some considerations will be unique to each category due to the varying levels of responsibility shared between the CSP and customer.

IaaS security concerns

Due to the nature of IaaS architectures and services, virtualization and hypervisors play a key role as attack vectors, though other security considerations do exist.

Some key IaaS security considerations include:

>> **Colocation and multitenancy:** With on-premise solutions, organizations can be certain that their data is physically separate from anyone else's data. In cloud environments, an organization must assume that they share resources with dozens, hundreds, or even thousands of other organizations. While it is up to the CSP to logically (or virtually) segregate one tenant's data from another, it is the responsibility of each customer to protect the data they deploy in accordance with any regulatory or contractual requirements they may have.

>> **Virtual machine (VM) attacks:** Active VMs are susceptible to the same security vulnerabilities as physical servers — and whether active or offline, a compromised VM poses a threat to other VMs that share the same server. This risk is because VMs that reside on the same physical machine share memory, storage, hypervisor access, and other hardware and software resources. The CSP is responsible for preventing, detecting, and responding to malicious activity between VMs.

>> **Hypervisor attacks:** Compromising the hypervisor can be considered a gold mine for attackers. An exploited hypervisor can yield access to the physical server, all tenant virtual machines, and any hosted applications.

>> **Network security:** Cloud environments rely on virtual networks that contain virtual switch software that control the movement of traffic within the cloud. These switches, if not properly configured and secured, can be vulnerable to layer 2 attacks, such as ARP poisoning. Because customers do not have the level of control over the network as they would with on-prem solutions, it is up to the CSP to tightly control network activity and be transparent with the customer (within reason) about how their data is protected.

>> **Denial of service (DoS) attacks:** DoS attacks are a threat in both cloud environments and traditional data center environments. The nature of cloud and the sheer size of many CSPs may make it more challenging to take down a cloud service, but it's certainly not impossible. If one cloud customer is experiencing a DoS attack, it can potentially impact other customers on the same hypervisor. Even though hypervisors have mechanisms to prevent a single host from consuming 100 percent of a system's resources, if a single host consumes enough resources, it can leave insufficient compute, memory, and networking for other hosts.

PaaS security concerns

PaaS services being platform-based, rather than infrastructure-based, present a different set of security considerations.

Some key PaaS security considerations include:

>> **Resource isolation:** PaaS tenants generally have extremely little to no system-level access of the underlying environment. This assures resource isolation and prevents a single customer from impacting multiple customers with infrastructure- or platform-level configurations. If a customer can change underlying configurations within the environment, it can negatively impact other customers that share resources, as well as make it very hard for the CSP to effectively manage and secure the environment.

>> **User permissions:** It's important that each tenant in the PaaS environment is able to manage their user permissions independently. That is, each instance of the PaaS offering should allow the respective cloud customer to configure their own user-level permissions.

>> **User access management:** Cloud security professionals must evaluate their organization's business needs and determine what access model works for them in the cloud. It's crucial that you find the balance between allowing quick user provisioning with proper and secure authentication and authorization. Cloud environments offer a great deal of power to automate these tasks, thanks to elasticity and autoscaling.

>> **Malware, backdoors, and other nasty threats:** *Auto-scaling* functionality (introduced in Chapter 3) means that any time there's a backdoor or other piece of malware in a cloud environment, it can grow and scale automatically without intervention from a cloud security professional (yikes!). In addition, these threats can start with one PaaS customer and rapidly expand to other customers, if not detected and eradicated. It's up to the CSP to continuously monitor for new vulnerabilities and exploits, and it's the customer's job to use secure coding best-practices.

SaaS security concerns

SaaS presents very different security concerns from its infrastructure and platform peers. While most of these concerns will fall on the CSP, it's important that you are familiar with some key SaaS security considerations:

>> **Data comingling:** The characteristic of multitenancy means that multiple customers share the same cloud infrastructure. In SaaS deployments, many customers are likely to store their data in applications with shared servers,

storage, or even potentially shared databases. This comingling of data means that any cross-site scripting (XSS), SQL injections, or other vulnerabilities can expose not one but potentially all customers in the shared SaaS environment. It's up to the CSP to ensure that customer data is segregated as much as possible, through use of encryption and other technologies. In addition, the CSP is responsible for conducting vulnerability scans and penetration testing to identify and fix weaknesses before they are exploited.

>> **Data access policies:** When evaluating a SaaS solution, you should carefully consider your organization's existing data access policies and evaluate how well they align with the cloud provider's capabilities. Again, multitenancy means that several customers are sharing the same resources — so the level of data access configuration and customization is potentially limited. As a cloud security professional, you want to be sure that your company's data is not only protected from other cloud customers, but you also want to ensure that you're able to control access between different users in your own company (separate access for developers and HR, for example).

>> **Web application security:** SaaS applications, by nature, are connected to the Internet and are meant to be available at all times. This interconnection means that they are constantly vulnerable to attacks and compromise. Because cloud applications hang their hat on high availability, any exploit that takes down a web app can have a great impact on a cloud customer. Imagine if an organization's cloud-based payroll systems suddenly went down on pay day!

>> **Unsanctioned SaaS:** *Unsanctioned SaaS* is modern-day shadow IT, and it refers to employees using SaaS applications without proper approval or oversight by your IT department. Unsanctioned SaaS is a major concern because it introduces security and compliance risks when the applications don't meet your organization's security standards. Additionally, data in unsanctioned SaaS is harder to control and evades your monitoring, meaning data exfiltrated through a SaaS application may go unnoticed.

Evaluating Cloud Service Providers

With so many cloud service providers on the market, it's important that you understand how to consistently evaluate them, regardless of service category, deployment model, or architectural differences. In this section, you explore some of the most common frameworks used to certify the security of CSPs and their systems. Chapters 13 and 14 provide a further look, with a deep dive on compliance and related topics.

Verifying against certification criteria

A critical component of every security program is the ability to audit and verify compliance against certification criteria that may include guidelines, standards, and/or regulations. As cloud computing continues to mature, the list of regulators and standards bodies looking to certify cloud security grows right along with it. As of today, there is still no universally agreed-upon set of cloud security standards, so as a CCSP candidate, you should be familiar with several of them.

The following list is not intended to be exhaustive, but does represent the primary set of regulations, standards, and guidelines that impact cloud computing:

>> ISO/IEC 27001

>> ISO/IEC 27002

>> ISO/IEC 27017

>> SOC 1, SOC 2, and SOC 3

>> PCI DSS

>> HIPAA

>> NIST SP 800-53 and FedRAMP

ISO/IEC 27001

ISO/IEC 27001 (often referred to as just ISO 27001) is an information security standard published by the International Organization for Standardization (ISO) and the International Electrotechnical Commission (IEC). ISO 27001 is the most popular standard within the ISO/IEC 27000 family of standards and is focused on the creation and maintenance of an *Information Security Management System* (ISMS), which ISO defines as "a systematic approach to managing sensitive company information so that it remains secure." Said a different way, an ISMS is a set of people, processes, and technologies that manages the overall security of a company's systems and data, and this standard describes the overall components of an ISMS. Organizations that complete an audit demonstrating that they meet ISO 27001 requirements may be certified by an ISO accredited body.

The most recent version of ISO 27001 was published in 2022 (after a long gap since the 2013 update). ISO 27001:2022 contains 93 controls across four domains: Organizational, People, Physical, and Technological.

Although ISO 27001 is a globally recognized standard, it is not cloud specific. As such, it cannot be relied on for exhaustive and holistic examination of cloud-specific security risks and controls. Despite this fact, its overall importance and global popularity means that it will likely be relied upon by CSPs and customers as a general security benchmark.

ISO/IEC 27002

ISO 27002 is titled "Security Techniques — Code of practice for information security controls." This standard, last revised in 2022, builds on ISO 27001 by providing guidelines for organizations to select, implement, and manage security controls based on their own security risk profile. In other words, ISO 27002 becomes more prescriptive than its counterpart by providing best practice recommendations to those responsible for implementing or maintaining an ISMS.

REMEMBER

The security controls in ISO/IEC 27001 and 27002 are the same. The only difference is that ISO 27002 explains the controls in greater detail.

ISO/IEC 27017 and ISO/IEC 27018

ISO 27017 and ISO 27018 are more recent security standards from ISO, and both are cloud-specific.

>> ISO 27017:2015 (published eight years ago, as of this writing — wow!) builds on ISO 27002 and provides guidelines for security controls related to the provision and use of cloud services. The standard offers security controls and implementation guidance for both CSPs and cloud service customers.

>> ISO 27018:2019 is focused on the protection of personally identifiable information (PII) in the cloud and again builds on the existing set of controls in the previously discussed standards, but adds privacy-related controls to the mix.

SOC 1, SOC 2, and SOC 3

If you've worked in traditional data center environments for a long time, you might recall that the Statement on Auditing Standards Number 70 (or SAS 70) was for many years the go-to standard for auditing and certifying the security of data center and other service providers — even though it was initially intended for financial and accounting auditing. In 2011, SAS 70 was replaced by the more comprehensive Service Organization Controls (SOC) reporting framework, which gives organizations the flexibility to be audited based on the needs of the particular organization.

WARNING

Do not confuse SOC with SOX (Sarbanes–Oxley). SOX compliance helps protect investors from fraudulent financial reporting by corporations, and it is completely separate from SOC compliance. The acronyms are very similar, and I've seen the two mixed up more than a few times.

The three commonly used types of SOC audits and reports are aptly named SOC 1, SOC 2, and SOC 3. All three reports align with the standards outlined in Statement on Standards for Attestation Engagements (SSAE) 18, which replaced SSAE 16 in 2017; the SSAE is managed by the American Institute of Certified Public Accountants (AICPA). Here are some additional details:

» SOC 1 is a control report that focuses strictly on an organization's financial statements and a service organization's controls that can impact a customer's financial statements. A service organization that performs payroll or credit card processing would require a SOC 1 report.

» SOC 2 reports evaluate an organization based on AICPA's five "Trust Services Principles: Security, Availability, Processing Integrity, Confidentiality, and Privacy." These reports are of extreme interest to cloud security professionals, both at cloud providers and as consumers of cloud services.

» SOC 3 takes the same information contained in a SOC 2 report and abstracts all the sensitive details. In essence, a SOC 3 report will indicate whether an organization has demonstrated each of the five Trust Services principles, but will not disclose specifics. SOC 3 reports are intended to be publicly available, whereas SOC 2 reports are tightly controlled, due to the sensitivity of their contents.

Payment Card Industry Data Security Standard (PCI DSS)

The Payment Card Industry Data Security Standard (PCI DSS) is a proprietary security standard established by Visa, MasterCard, American Express, Discover, and JCB International in 2004. PCI DSS governs all organizations that accept, store, or transmit cardholder data and/or sensitive authentication data. The Standard has six goals that generally align with security best practices:

» Build and maintain a secure network and systems

» Protect cardholder data

» Maintain a vulnerability management program

» Implement strong access control measures

» Regularly monitor and test networks

» Maintain an information security policy

The six goals are broken down into 12 requirements, which are broken down further into more than 200 security controls that specify security requirements that organizations must meet to fulfill their PCI DSS compliance obligations. The 12 PCI DSS requirements are:

>> **Requirement 1:** Install and maintain a firewall configuration to protect cardholder data.

>> **Requirement 2:** Do not use vendor-supplied defaults for system passwords and other security parameters.

>> **Requirement 3:** Protect stored cardholder data.

>> **Requirement 4:** Encrypt transmission of cardholder data across open, public networks.

>> **Requirement 5:** Protect all systems against malware and regularly update anti-virus software or programs.

>> **Requirement 6:** Develop and maintain secure systems and applications.

>> **Requirement 7:** Restrict access to cardholder data by business need to know.

>> **Requirement 8:** Identify and authenticate access to system components.

>> **Requirement 9:** Restrict physical access to cardholder data.

>> **Requirement 10:** Track and monitor all access to network resources and cardholder data.

>> **Requirement 11:** Regularly test security systems and processes.

>> **Requirement 12:** Maintain a policy that addresses information security for all personnel.

Due to the technical and detail-oriented approach taken by PCI-DSS, many organizations outside of the payment card industry trust PCI-DSS as a security standard around which they can build their security standards. Many CSPs must either meet or support their customers in meeting PCI-DSS. As such, these audits are quite common in the cloud space, and understanding PCI-DSS is a valuable skill for cloud security professionals.

NIST SP 800-53 and FedRAMP

NIST releases and manages a variety of special publications related to computer security, cloud computing, and other technologies. NIST SP 800-53 — Security and Privacy Controls for Federal Information Systems and Organizations — is NIST's "bible" of information security controls. Though it's targeted toward non-defense related federal agencies in the U.S. government, it is widely considered one of the most comprehensive baselines of security controls and is used across many industries around the globe.

NIST 800-53 outlines hundreds of security controls across the following 20 control families:

» AC: Access Control

» AT: Awareness and Training

» AU: Audit and Accountability

» CA: Security Assessment and Authorization

» CM: Configuration Management

» CP: Contingency Planning

» IA: Identification and Authentication

» IR: Incident Response

» MA: Maintenance

» MP: Media Protection

» PE: Physical and Environmental Protection

» PL: Planning

» PS: Personnel Security

» PT: PII Processing and Transparency

» RA: Risk Assessment

» SA: System and Services Acquisition

» SC: System and Communications Protection

» SI: System and Information Integrity

» SR: Supply Chain Risk Management

» PM: Program Management

The latest revision of 800-53, Rev. 5, was released in 2020 and included what was, at the time, forward-leaning information on cloud security, in addition to changes that reflect the evolving threat landscape (like new control families related to supply chain risk management and the protection of PII).

The Federal Risk and Authorization Management Program, or FedRAMP, is a U.S. government-wide program that was established in 2011 to create a standardized approach to security assessment, authorization, and continuous monitoring of cloud service providers. FedRAMP effectively enforces NIST guidelines (including 800-53 and others) for any CSP that provides products or services to the U.S. government. Known for being a rigorous assessment process, the FedRAMP model has been a major influence for public sector cloud security programs around the world.

Meeting system/subsystem product certifications

While ISO 270XX, SOC, FedRAMP, and others are squarely focused on assessing and certifying the security of an organization and its services, being able to certify the security of individual products is essential in order to build secure systems at scale. Many frameworks have been established for this purpose over the years, but two leading international standards are Common Criteria and FIPS (140-2 and 140-3), discussed in the following sections.

Common Criteria

Common Criteria (CC), formally known as Common Criteria for Information Technology Security Evaluation (yeah, let's just stick to CC), establishes processes for products to be evaluated by independent laboratories to determine their level of security. CC is another ISO/IEC standard (ISO/IEC 15408) and is internationally recognized as the gold standard for identifying secure IT products.

The Common Criteria consists of two components:

» **Protection profiles:** These profiles establish a set of security standards unique to a specific type of product, such as operating systems, firewalls, antivirus, and so on.

» **Evaluation Assurance Levels (EALs):** An EAL is a numeric score that is assigned to a product to describe how thoroughly it was tested during the CC process. EALs range from 1 through 7, with the higher levels providing more assurance of the product's security claims. The seven EAL ratings are

- **EAL 1:** Functionally tested

- **EAL 2:** Structurally tested

- **EAL 3:** Methodically tested and checked

- **EAL 4:** Methodically designed, tested, and reviewed

- **EAL 5:** Semi-formally designed and tested

- **EAL 6:** Semi-formally verified design and tested

- **EAL 7:** Formally verified design and tested

For more information on Common Criteria, including details about the evaluation process, visit www.commoncriteriaportal.org.

FIPS 140-2 and FIPS 140-3

Federal Information Processing Standard (FIPS) Pub 140-3 (or FIPS 140-3) is another standard released by NIST of the U.S. government; this one is related to the assessment and validation of cryptographic modules. A *cryptographic module* is simply any hardware, software, and/or firmware combination that performs encryption, decryption, or other cryptographic functions.

After years of teasing the cryptographic community, FIPS 140-3 was published in March 2019, and it officially superseded its long-standing predecessor, FIPS 140-2, in April 2022. The new publication sets forth some very broad guidance, but most notably aligns the new standard with those set forth in ISO/IEC 19790:2012 (Security Requirements for Cryptographic Modules) and ISO/IEC 24759:2017 (Test Requirements for Cryptographic Modules). This is a big strategic move on the part of NIST, aligning U.S. government standards with those of an international standards body like ISO.

Similar to Common Criteria, FIPS 140-2 and 140-3 assessment is completed by one of several independent third-party labs, who rates each product's security levels 1 and 4. The FIPS levels are

>> **Level 1:** The lowest level of security. The basic requirement is that at least one approved algorithm is in use by the cryptographic module. The only physical security requirement is that production-grade components be used. FIPS Level 1 allows implementations of cryptographic modules that execute software and firmware on general purpose, unevaluated operating systems; higher security levels require that entire operating environments be evaluated by Common Criteria standards.

>> **Level 2:** Security Level 2 adds additional physical security considerations to those in Level 1 by requiring cryptographic modules to show evidence of tampering (tamper-evident tape or pick-resistant locks, for example). The goal with this level is to provide visible assurance of a device's integrity.

>> **Level 3:** This FIPS Security Level adds even further physical security assurance by requiring that modules take steps to detect tampering and respond by protecting the module and any data within. An example of this level would be detecting that the hardware has been breached and erasing all plaintext data within the module to prevent unauthorized access.

>> **Level 4:** This is the highest level of security, which requires rigid testing and scrutiny. Devices certified at this level require that cryptographic modules are fully surrounded by protections that are able to detect any and all

unauthorized access attempts. A successful penetration of the physical barrier requires immediate erasure of any sensitive plaintext data within the module. Additionally, Level 4 devices require that cryptographic modules are protected against environmental attacks. For example, an attacker can attempt to cause a device's security mechanisms to fail by manipulating electrical or temperature conditions of the device. This attack would be detected and responded to by a Level 4 device.

TIP

Although FIPS 140-3 was released prior to the current CCSP exam, the Certification Exam Outline includes both FIPS 140-2 and FIPS 140-3. I cover both here, for that reason. The FIPS 140-3 Publication goes into some of these topics, so it's worth a look if cryptography is important to you. You can find a link to the publication, along with other helpful resources, in Appendix B.

Chapter **5**

Domain 2: Cloud Data Security, Part 1

In this chapter, you examine the cloud data lifecycle and find out how to identify, examine, and secure data stored in the cloud. Domain 2: Cloud Data Security covers a wide range of technical and operational topics and is the most heavily weighted domain on the CCSP exam, representing 20 percent of the CCSP certification exam. This chapter covers the first half of Domain 2.

Describing Cloud Data Concepts

One of my favorite sayings, "Security follows the data," reminds you that data is the most vital component of any system, including cloud environments. Understanding cloud data concepts is critical if you want to secure cloud-based systems. As a CCSP candidate, you need to understand how data security changes throughout the various phases of the data's lifecycle.

Cloud data lifecycle phases

I introduce the cloud secure data lifecycle in Chapter 4 and explore it further in the following sections. Although the cloud data lifecycle is typically drawn as a linear cycle, data can move between the phases in any order — or skip phases altogether (for example, not all data is archived or even destroyed).

Create

The Create phase covers any circumstance where data is "new." This new data can be freshly generated content, imported data that is new to the cloud environment, or data that has been modified/updated and has a new shape or state. The Create phase presents the greatest opportunity to classify data according to its sensitivity, ensuring that the right security controls are implemented from the beginning. Decisions made during this phase typically impact the data throughout the entire lifecycle.

Aside from data classification, it's also important at this stage to consider tagging data with any important attributes, as well as assigning proper access restrictions to the data. Again, what you do during the Create phase usually travels with the data through each of the other phases. So, extra thought should be given to how the created data needs to be managed throughout its lifecycle.

Store

The Store phase often happens in tandem with (or immediately after) the Create phase. During this phase, the created or modified data is saved to some sort of digital repository within the application or system. Storage can be in the form of saved files on a filesystem, rows and columns saved to a database, or objects saved in a cloud storage system.

During the Store phase, the classification level assigned during creation is used to assign and implement appropriate security controls. Controls like encryption (at rest), Access Control Lists (ACLs), logging, and monitoring are important during this phase. In addition, this phase is when you should consider how to appropriately back up your data to maintain redundancy and availability.

Use

The Use phase includes any viewing, processing, or consumption of data that was previously in the Store phase. For the purposes of this model, the Use phase is considered read-only and does not include any modification. (Modifications are covered in the Create phase.)

One important consideration during this phase is that data must be unencrypted while in use. For this reason, the Use phase presents some of the greatest threats to data, if not properly secured. File access monitors, logging and monitoring, and technologies like Information Rights Management (IRM) are important to detect and prevent unauthorized access during the Use phase.

TECHNICAL STUFF

Information Rights Management (IRM) is a data security technology that protects data (typically files, but also emails, web pages, and other information) from unauthorized access by limiting who can view, copy, forward, delete, or otherwise modify information. With IRM, you can remotely manage users and the level of permissions they have to access and manipulate information, regardless of where that information is located. I provide further details on IRM in the section "Designing and Implementing Information Rights Management (IRM)" in Chapter 6.

Share

During the Share phase, data is made available for use by others, such as employees, customers, and partners. As it's shared, data often traverses a variety of public and private networks and locations and is subjected to various unique threats along the way. Proper encryption (in transit) is important during this phase, as well as IRM and Data Loss Prevention (DLP) technologies that help ensure sensitive data stays out of the wrong hands.

Archive

The Archive phase involves data transitioning from active use to long-term "cold" storage. Archiving can entail moving data from a primary storage tier to a slower, less redundant tier that is less expensive or can include moving data off the cloud to a separate medium altogether (backup tape, for example).

Most data is eventually archived after it's no longer needed on a regular basis. Once archived, the data must be secured and also remain available for retrieval, when necessary. Legal and regulatory requirements must be carefully considered during the Archive phase, as these requirements may influence how long specific data is required to be stored.

Destroy

The final phase of the data lifecycle is the Destroy phase. Destroying data involves completely removing it from the cloud by means of logical erasure or physical destruction (like disk pulverizing or degaussing). In cloud environments, customers generally have to rely on logical destruction methods like crypto-shredding or data overwriting, but many CSPs have processes for physical destruction, per contractual agreements and regulatory requirements.

Data dispersion

Data dispersion is the process of replicating data throughout a distributed storage infrastructure that can span several regions, cities, or even countries around the world. Data dispersion is an integral feature of cloud architecture and contributes to data security and redundancy by ensuring that a copy of the data persists even if an entire data center location is destroyed. This concept isn't unique to cloud, as on-premise models create backup tapes and store them at remote storage locations — creating a similar level of redundancy. That approach, however, is both more expensive and time consuming and also much less scalable than cloud-based data dispersion. In cloud environments, the CSP inherits the responsibility to disperse data and allows customers to determine how much dispersion (or replication) is important for their data needs. For less critical data, customers can select fewer replicas of their data at a lower cost, but data that is highly critical can be dispersed across more locations, allowing cloud customers to customize their BCP/DR experience.

TIP

A more specific implementation of data dispersion is called *data sharding*, which involves fragmenting data before dispersing it across locations, for added security benefits. This form of data dispersion is offered by some cloud providers, and it enhances data security by ensuring that a single file is divided into multiple parts and then spread out across multiple locations — meaning a compromise of any location would yield only a portion of the file. Keep data sharding in mind, in case it shows up on the exam or in the real world.

Data flows

A *data flow diagram (DFD)* is a graphical representations of the flow of data through an information system. You can use DFDs to visualize how data moves through an organization, which can help you identify security risks and other potential problems.

DFDs are made up of four basic symbols: processes, data stores, external entities, and data flows.

>> *Processes* represent a manipulation of data; any time a system takes input, analyzes or changes it, and gives you output — that's a process.

>> *Data stores* are repositories of data (like cloud storage).

>> *External entities* represent entities that interact with the system, such as users, devices, or other systems. External entities are typically either the sources or destinations of data.

>> *Data flows* represent the flow of data (surprise!) between processes, data stores, and external entities.

DFDs can be used to model any type of information system, including cloud systems. In cloud computing, DFDs can be used to visualize the flow of data between different cloud services, identify security risks in the cloud environment, and plan for disaster recovery and business continuity. For example, a DFD could be used to model the flow of data between a user's device, a cloud storage service, and a cloud computing application. A mature DFD might show you how data is encrypted when it is stored in the cloud, how it's protected in transit between the user and the cloud, and other security controls.

DFDs are valuable tools for understanding and securing cloud environments. You can use them visualize where your data goes, how it gets there, and how it's secured throughout the entire the data lifecycle.

Designing and Implementing Cloud Data Storage Architectures

The cloud service categories — IaaS, PaaS, and SaaS — all provide access to data storage, but each model uses its own storage types. Each of the service categories and storage types comes with its own specific threats and security considerations. As you design and implement your cloud data storage architecture, you must consider what service category you're building or implementing and the unique characteristics of data security associated with that service model.

Storage types

IaaS uses volume and object storage, PaaS uses structured and unstructured data, while SaaS can use a wide assortment of storage types. I describe each of these storage types in the following sections.

IaaS

The infrastructure as a service model provides cloud customers with a self-service means to access and manage compute, storage, and networking resources. Storage is allocated to customers on an as-needed basis, and customers are charged only for what they consume.

The IaaS service model uses two categories of storage:

>> **Volume:** A *volume* is a virtual hard drive that can be attached to a Virtual Machine (VM) and utilized similar to a physical hard drive. The VM operating system views the volume the same way any OS would view a physical hard drive in a traditional server model. The virtual drive can be formatted with a

filesystem like FAT32 or NTFS and managed by the customer. Examples of volume storage include AWS Elastic Block Store (EBS), VMware Virtual Machine File System (VMFS), and Google Persistent Disk.

TIP

You may also see volume storage referred to as *block storage*. The two terms can be used interchangeably.

>> **Object:** An *object* is file storage that can be accessed directly through an API or web interface, without being attached to an operating system. Data kept in object storage includes the object data and metadata and can store any kind of information, including photos, videos, documents, and more. Many CSPs have interfaces that present object storage in a similar fashion to standard file tree structures (like a Windows directory), but the files are actually just virtual objects in an independent storage structure that rely on key values to reference and retrieve them. Amazon S3 (Simple Storage Service) and Azure Blob Storage are popular examples of object storage.

TECHNICAL STUFF

Some other terms you should be familiar with are ephemeral and raw-disk storage. *Ephemeral storage* is temporary storage that accompanies more permanent storage. Ephemeral storage is useful for temporary data, such as buffers, caches, and session information. *Raw-disk storage* is storage that allows data to be accessed directly at the byte level, rather than through a filesystem. You may not be tested on this information, but you're likely to come across the terms at some point.

PaaS

Platform as a service storage design differs from IaaS storage design because the cloud provider is responsible for the entire platform (as opposed to IaaS, where the CSP is only responsible for providing the volume allocation) and the customer only manages the application.

The PaaS service model utilizes two categories of storage (see Figure 5-1).

>> **Structured:** *Structured data* is information that is highly organized, categorized, and normalized. This type of data can be placed into a relational database or other storage system that includes rulesets and structure (go figure!) for searching and running operations on the data.

TIP

Structured Query Language (SQL) is one of the most popular database programming languages used to search and manipulate structured data(bases). Remembering that SQL is a database language is an easy way to associate structured data with databases.

>> **Unstructured:** *Unstructured data* is information that cannot be easily organized and formatted for use in a rigid data structure, like a database. Audio files, videos, word documents, web pages, and other forms of text and multimedia fit into this data type.

FIGURE 5-1:
Structured versus
unstructured
data.

Structured Data   **Unstructured Data**

SaaS

For software as a service, the cloud provider is responsible for managing not only the entire infrastructure and platform, but also the application itself. For this reason, the cloud user has minimal control over what types of data go into the system; their only data storage responsibility is to put permissible data into the application.

While they're not quite true data types, the SaaS service model commonly utilizes two types (or methods) of data storage:

>> **Information storage and management:** This type of data storage involves the customer entering data into the application via the web interface, and the application storing and managing that data in a back-end database. Data may also be generated by the application, on behalf of the customer, and similarly stored and managed. This application-generated data is internally stored on volume or object storage, but is hidden from the customer.

>> **Content and file storage:** With this type of data storage, the customer uploads data through the web application, but instead of being stored in an integral database, the content and files are stored in other storage mechanisms that users can access.

Threats to storage types

The ultimate threat to any storage type is a compromise that impacts the confidentiality, integrity, or availability of the data being stored. While specific attack vectors vary based on the storage type, the following list identifies some common threats to any type of data storage:

>> **Unauthorized access or use:** This type of threat involves the viewing, modification, or use of data stored in any storage type by either an external

unauthorized party or a malicious insider who may have credentials to the environment but who uses them in an unauthorized manner. The attack vectors from external threat actors can be anything from using malware to gain escalated privileges to using phishing techniques to steal credentials from users who have credentials to access data. To protect against insider threats related to unauthorized access and usage, CSPs should have mechanisms and processes in place to require multiple parties to approve access to customer data, where possible. Mechanisms should also be in place to detect access to customer data and processes to validate that the access was legitimate. Cloud customers should consider using Hardware Security Modules (HSMs) wherever possible, to help control access to their data by managing their own encryption keys.

» **Data leakage and exposure:** The nature of cloud computing requires data to be replicated and distributed across multiple locations, often around the world. This fact increases threats associated with data leakage, if cloud providers don't pay careful attention to how replicated data is protected. Customers want to know that their data is secured consistently across locations, not only for peace of mind against leakage, but also for regulatory compliance purposes.

» **Denial of Service:** DoS and DDoS attacks are a huge threat to the availability of data stored within cloud storage. Cloud networks that are not resilient may face challenges handling sudden spikes in bandwidth, which can result in authorized users not being able to access data when they need it.

» **Corruption or loss of data:** Corruption or loss of data can affect the integrity and/or availability of data and may impact specific data in storage or the entire storage array. These threats can occur by intentional or accidental means, including technical failures, natural disasters, human error, or malicious compromises (for example, a hack). Redundancy within cloud environments helps prevent complete loss of data, but cloud customers should carefully read CSPs' data terms that include availability and durability SLOs and SLAs.

TIP

Durability (or *reliability*) is the concept of using data redundancy to ensure that data is not lost, compromised, or corrupted. The term has been used for years in traditional IT circles and is just as important in cloud security. Durability differs from availability in that availability focuses on uptime through hardware redundancy. It's very possible (but not desirable) to have a system that stays up 100 percent of the time, but all of the data in it is corrupted. The goal of a secure cloud environment is, of course, to have as close to 100 percent availability (uptime) and durability (reliability). Despite this lofty goal, CSPs' actual commitment for each tends to be 99 percent followed by some number of 9s (like 99.999999 percent).

Designing and Applying Data Security Technologies and Strategies

After you have an understanding of data storage and some of the common threats to cloud data, the next step is to consider how to implement data security technologies and design data security strategies that fit your business and security needs.

The following technologies are commonly applied as part of a comprehensive data security strategy in the cloud:

>> Encryption and key management

>> Tokenization

>> Hashing

>> Data loss prevention (DLP)

>> Data obfuscation

WARNING

This section dives deep into several important data security technologies, but simply knowing about the technologies is not enough to build an effective security architecture. The technologies you use and the data to which you apply them should be based on an assessment of the sensitivity of your cloud data and a thorough understanding of your legal, regulatory, and contractual requirements. Do not get caught in the trap of simply throwing tools and technologies at your cloud environment without a thoughtful strategy behind you!

Encryption and key management

As one of the foundational security technologies in existence, you learn about encryption throughout much of this book. As it pertains to cloud data security, encryption and key management are critical topics that must be fully understood in order to pass the CCSP exam. With resource pooling (and multitenancy) being a key characteristic of cloud computing, it's important to remember that physical separation and protections are not commonly available in cloud environments. As such, strategic use of encryption is crucial to ensuring secure data storage and use in the cloud. See Chapter 4 for treatment of encryption in each data state (at rest, in transit, and in use).

REMEMBER

When designing or implementing encryption technologies, remember that an encryption architecture has three basic components:

» The data being secured

» The encryption engine that performs all encryption operations

» The encryption keys used to secure the data

While it would seem like encrypting everything would be the best way to ensure data security, it's important to consider that encryption has a performance impact on systems; system resources are used in order to process encryption algorithms every time data is encrypted or decrypted, which can add up if encryption is used excessively. As a CCSP, it is up to you to implement encryption so that data is as secure as possible while minimizing the impact to system performance.

REMEMBER

Encryption is just one form of *data obfuscation*, which is the process of disguising data to protect its confidentiality. Other common data obfuscation techniques include tokenization, masking, and de-identification — I discuss all of these in the following sections.

Countless other challenges and considerations exist when implementing encryption technologies, both on-prem and in cloud environments. Some key cloud encryption challenges include the following:

» Almost all data processing requires that data is in an unencrypted state. If a cloud customer is using a CSP for data analysis or processing, then encryption can be challenging to implement.

» Encryption keys are cached in memory when in use and often stay there for some time. This consideration is a major point of in multitenant environments because memory is a shared resource between tenants. CSPs must implement protections against tenants' keys being accessed by tenants who share the same resources.

» Cloud data is often highly replicated (for availability purposes), which can make encryption and key managing challenging. Most CSPs have mechanisms in place to ensure that any copies of encrypted data remain encrypted.

» Throughout the entire data lifecycle, data can change states, locations, and format, which can require different applications of encryption along the way. Managing these changes may be a challenge, but understanding the cloud secure data lifecycle can help design complete end-to-end encryption solutions.

» Encryption is a confidentiality control at heart. It does not address threats to integrity of data on its own. Other technologies discussed throughout this chapter should be implemented to address integrity concerns.

WARNING

Many people wrongly consider encryption to be both a confidentiality and an integrity security control. In reality, encryption does not protect data integrity. Hashing and checksums can be used to provide integrity assurance. Remember these differences on the exam.

>> The effectiveness of an encryption solution is dependent on how securely the encryption keys are stored and managed. As soon as an encryption key gets into the wrong hands, all data protected with that key is compromised. Keys that are managed by the CSP may potentially be accessed by malicious insiders, while customer-managed encryption keys are often mishandled or mismanaged.

As the last point indicates, key management is a huge factor in ensuring that encryption implementations effectively secure cloud data. Because of its importance and the challenges associated with key management in the cloud, this task is typically one of the most complicated ones associated with securing cloud data.

When developing your organization's encryption and key management strategy, it's important that you consider the following:

>> **Key generation:** Encryption keys should be generated within a trusted, secure cryptographic module. FIPS 140-3 validated modules have been tested and certified to meet certain requirements that demonstrate tamper resistance and integrity of encryption keys. (See Chapter 4 for more on FIPS 140-3, and its predecessor, FIPS 140-2.)

>> **Key distribution:** It's important that encryption keys are distributed securely to prevent theft or compromise during transit. One best practice is to encrypt keys with a separate encryption key while distributing to other parties (in PKI applications, for example). The worst thing that could happen is sending out a bunch of "secret" keys that get stolen by malicious eavesdroppers!

>> **Key storage:** Encryption keys must be protected at rest (both in volatile and persistent memory) and should never be stored in plaintext. Keys may be stored and managed internally on a virtual machine or other integrated application, externally and separate from the data itself, or managed by a trusted third party that provides key escrow services for secure key management. A *Hardware Security Module* (HSM) is a physical device that safeguards encryption keys. Many cloud providers provide HSM services, as well as software-based HSM capabilities.

TIP

When evaluating CSP HSM capabilities, FIPS 140-2 (and FIPS 140-3) is again a useful reference — particularly, but not only, for customers in highly regulated industries, like government. I cover FIPS 140-2 and FIPS 140-3 in Chapter 4.

>> **Key rotation:** Key rotation involves generating new encryption keys and retiring old ones at predetermined intervals (90 days is a common interval). An effective key rotation strategy is heavily automated, and it is essential for safeguarding your cloud assets and ensuring compliance with standards like HIPAA, PCI, and GDPR.

>> **Key destruction or deletion:** At the end of the encryption key's lifecycle, there will be a time that the key is no longer needed. *Key destruction* is the removal of an encryption key from its operational location. *Key deletion* takes it a step further and also removes any information that could be used to reconstruct that key. To prevent a Denial of Service due to unavailable keys, deletion should only occur after an archival period that includes substantial analysis to ensure that the key is in fact no longer needed.

TIP

Cloud environments rely heavily on encryption throughout the entire data lifecycle. While encryption itself is used for confidentiality, the widespread use of encryption means that availability of the encryption keys themselves is a major concern. Pay close attention to availability as you're designing your key management systems and processes.

Tokenization

Tokenization is the process of substituting a sensitive piece of data with a non-sensitive replacement, called a *token*. The token is merely a reference back to the sensitive data, but has no meaning or sensitivity on its own. The token maintains the look and feel of the original data and is mapped back to the original data by the tokenization engine or application. Tokenization allows code to continue to run seamlessly, even with randomized tokens in place of sensitive data.

Tokenization is often used to protect cardholder data and other sensitive financial information, while encryption is more likely to be used to protect passwords, protected health information, and other sensitive personal information.

TIP

Tokenization can be outsourced to external, cloud-based tokenization services (referred to as *tokenization-as-a-service*). When using these services, it's prudent to understand how the provider secures your data, both at rest and in transit between you and their systems.

Hashing

Hashing, as depicted in Figure 5-2, is the process of taking an arbitrary piece of data and generating a unique string or number of fixed-length from it. Hashing can be applied to any type of data — documents, images, database files, virtual machines, and more.

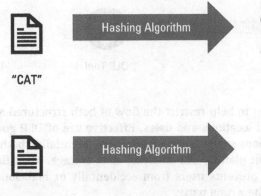

"CAT"

Hashing Algorithm

F4947AC08424777B8734CA200
0A823833E3E119BD92A87A665
D3E7F320E04665251B886C33E
AE81762D654A997003B5A570B

Unique Hashed Output for "CAT"

"CAR"

Hashing Algorithm

1140007C6EABD001DEA267199
55373B16B9A000D000D00C12E
A111D333E44EA66DA7001E11C
CBABFFF10EE77E87878755AAA

Unique Hashed Output for "CAR"

FIGURE 5-2:
Hashing.

Hashing provides a mechanism to assure the integrity of data. Hashes are similar to human fingerprints, which can be used to uniquely identify a single person to whom that fingerprint belongs. As seen in Figure 5-2, even the slightest change to a large text file will noticeably change the output of the hashing algorithm. Hashing is incredibly useful when you want to be sure that what you're looking at now is the same as what you created before. In cloud environments, hashing helps verify that virtual machine instances haven't been modified (maliciously or accidentally) without your knowledge. Simply hash your VM image before running it and compare it to the hash of the known-good VM image; the hash outputs should be identical.

WARNING

The term hashing is sometimes used interchangeably with encryption, but they are very different! Encryption is a two-way function, meaning what can be encrypted can be decrypted. Conversely, hashing is a one-way function. You can only generate a hash of an object; you cannot retrieve an object from its hash. Encryption, again, is used to provide confidentiality, while hashing provides integrity checking. Be careful not to confuse these two terms!

Several hashing algorithms are available, but the SHA (Secure Hash Algorithm) family of algorithms are among the most popular. Specific algorithms are outside the scope of this book, but you can research SHA-1, SHA-2, and SHA-3 for additional context.

Data loss prevention (DLP)

Data loss prevention (DLP), also known as data leakage prevention, is the set of technologies and practices used to identify and classify sensitive data, while ensuring that sensitive data is not lost or accessed by unauthorized parties. See Figure 5-3 for a visualization of DLP.

FIGURE 5-3:
Data loss
prevention (DLP).

Sensitive Data   Outbound Traffic   DLP Tool   Unauthorized Party

DLP can be applied to help restrict the flow of both structured and unstructured data to authorized locations and users. Effective use of DLP goes a long way to helping organizations safeguard their data's confidentiality, both on-prem and in the cloud. To put it plainly, DLP analyzes data storage, identifies sensitive data components, and prevents users from accidentally or maliciously sending that sensitive data to the wrong party.

When designing a DLP strategy, organizations must consider how the technology fits in with their existing technologies, processes, and architecture. DLP controls need to be thoroughly understood and applied in a manner that aligns with the organization's overall enterprise architecture in order to ensure that only the right type of data is blocked from being transmitted.

Hybrid cloud users, or users that utilize a combination of cloud-based and on-prem services, should pay extremely close attention to their enterprise security architecture while developing a DLP strategy. Because data traverses both cloud and non-cloud environments, a poor DLP implementation can result in segmented data security policies that are hard to manage and ineffective.

REMEMBER

DLP that is incorrectly implemented can lead to false-positives (for example, blocking legitimate traffic) or false-negatives (allowing sensitive data to be sent to unauthorized parties).

DLP implementations consist of three core components or stages:

>> **Discovery and classification:** The first stage of DLP is discovery and classification. *Discovery* is the process of finding all instances of data, and *classification* is the act of categorizing that data based on its sensitivity and other characteristics. Examples of classifications may include "credit card data," "Social Security numbers," "health records," and so on. Comprehensive discovery and proper classification is crucial to success during the remaining DLP stages.

>> **Monitoring:** Once data has been fully discovered and classified, it can be monitored. Monitoring is an essential component of the DLP implementation and involves watching data as it moves throughout the cloud data lifecycle. The monitoring stage is where the DLP implementation is looking to identify data that is being misused or handled outside of established usage policies. Effective DLP monitoring should happen on storage devices, networking

devices, servers, workstations, and other endpoints — and it should evaluate traffic across all potential export routes (email, Internet browsers, and so on).

>> **Enforcement:** The final DLP stage, enforcement, is where action is taken on policy violations identified during the monitoring stage. These actions are configured based on the classification of data and the potential impact of its loss. Violations of less sensitive data is traditionally logged and/or alerted on, while more sensitive data can actually be blocked from unauthorized exposure or loss. A common use-case here is financial services companies that detect credit card numbers being emailed to unauthorized domains and are able to stop the email in its tracks, before it ever leaves the corporate network.

Always remember "Security follows the data" — and DLP technology is no different. When creating a DLP implementation strategy, it's important that you consider techniques for monitoring activity in every data state. DLP data states are

>> **DLP at rest:** For data at rest, the DLP implementation is stored wherever the data is stored, such as a workstation, file server, or some other form of storage system. Although this DLP implementation is often the simplest, it may need to work in conjunction with other DLP implementations to be most effective.

>> **DLP in transit:** *Network-based DLP* is data loss prevention that involves monitoring outbound traffic near the network perimeter. This DLP implementation monitors traffic over Hypertext Transfer Protocol (HTTP), Hypertext Transfer Protocol Secure (HTTPS), File Transfer Protocol (FTP), and Simple Mail Transfer Protocol (SMTP), and other protocols.

WARNING

If the network traffic being monitored is encrypted, you need to integrate encryption and key management technologies into your DLP solution. Standard DLP implementations cannot effectively monitor encrypted traffic, such as HTTPS.

>> **DLP in use:** *Host-based,* or *endpoint-based, DLP* is data loss prevention that involves installation of a DLP application on a workstation or other endpoint device. This DLP implementation allows monitoring of all data in use on the client device and provides insights that network-based DLP are not able to provide.

TIP

Because of the massive scale of many cloud environments, host-based DLP can be a major challenge. There are simply too many hosts and endpoints to monitor without a sophisticated strategy that involves automated deployment. Despite this challenge, host-based DLP is not impossible in the cloud, and CSPs continue to make monitoring easier as new cloud-native DLP features become available.

After you understand DLP and how it can be used to protect cloud data, there are a few considerations that cloud security professionals commonly face when implementing cloud-based DLP:

>> *Cloud data is highly distributed and replicated across locations.* Data can move between servers, from one data center to another, to and from backup storage, or between a customer and the cloud provider. This movement, along with the data replication that ensures availability, present challenges that need to be worked through in a DLP strategy.

>> *DLP technologies can impact performance.* Host-based DLP scan all data access activities on an endpoint, and network-based DLP scan all outbound network traffic across a network boundary. This constant monitoring and scanning can impact system and network performance and must be considered while developing and testing your DLP strategy.

>> *Cloud-based DLP can get expensive.* The pay-for-what-you-use model is often a great savings to cloud customers, but when it comes to DLP, the constant resource utilization associated with monitoring traffic can quickly add up. It's important to model and plan for resource consumption costs on top of the costs of the DLP solution itself.

Data de-identification

Confidentiality is incredibly important, especially in the cloud. While mechanisms like encryption and DLP go a long way to providing data confidentiality, they're not always feasible. *Data de-identification* (or *anonymization*) is the process of removing information that can be used to identify a specific individual from a dataset. This technique is commonly used as a privacy measure to protect Personally Identifiable Information (PII) or other sensitive information from being exposed when an entire dataset is shared. Figure 5-4 depicts the purest form of data de-identification; in this example, student names have been removed in order to protect the confidentiality of their grades.

Gradebook

	Exam 1	Exam 2	Exam 3
Alice	85	100	83
Bob	79	82	82
Chris	73	79	90
Donna	77	74	84

Original Data

	Exam 1	Exam 2	Exam 3
Student 1	85	100	83
Student 2	79	82	82
Student 3	73	79	90
Student 4	77	74	84

De-identified Data

FIGURE 5-4:
Data de-identification.

Several techniques are available to de-identify sensitive information; masking (or obfuscation) and tokenization are two of the most commonly used methods and are discussed in the following sections.

Masking

Masking is the process of partially or completely replacing sensitive data with random characters or other non-sensitive data. Masking, or *obfuscation*, can happen in a number of ways, but Figure 5-5 is a visual depiction of the most popular type of data masking, which is commonly used to protect credit card numbers and other sensitive financial information.

1111 2222 3333 4567   XXXX XXXX XXXX 4567

FIGURE 5-5:
Data masking.   Original Card Number   Masked Card Number

As a cloud security professional, you can use several techniques when masking or obfuscating data. Here are a few to remember:

>> **Substitution:** *Substitution* mimics the look of real data, but replaces (or appends) it with some unrelated value. Substitution can either be random or algorithmic, with the latter allowing two-way substitution — meaning if you have the algorithm, then you can retrieve the original data from the masked dataset.

>> **Scrambling:** *Scrambling* mimics the look of real data, but simply jumbles the characters into a random order. For example, a customer's whose account number is #5551234 may be shown as #1552435 in a development environment. (For what it's worth, my scrambled phone number is 0926381135.)

>> **Deletion or nulling:** This technique is just what it sounds like. When using this masking technique, data appears blank or empty to anyone who isn't authorized to view it.

Aside from being used to comply with regulatory regulations (like HIPAA or PCI DSS), data masking is often used when organizations need to use production data in a test or development environment. By masking the data, development environments can use real data without exposing sensitive data elements to unauthorized viewers or less secure environments.

The two primary methods or strategies to conduct data masking are

>> **Static data masking:** *Static masking* is the process of duplicating the original data with sensitive components masked in the new copy. Static masking is the better option when you need to use "real" data in a development or test environment.

>> **Dynamic data masking:** *Dynamic masking* is the process of masking sensitive data as it is used in real-time, rather than creating a separate masked copy of the data. This method is sometimes referred to as on-the-fly masking, and requires a masking layer in between the storage component and the application. This type of masking is great when you need to use production environments in a confidential or private manner. One great use-case is customer service representatives who need to see only the last four digits of your SSN. The source database may have the entire SSN saved, but the first five digits are masked from the representative.

Implementing Data Discovery

Before you can protect your sensitive data, you must first locate it. *Data discovery* is the process of finding and identifying sensitive information in your environment. It is a crucial step toward data security because you can't possibly secure something if you don't know that it exists or where it resides. In addition, data discovery is an important consideration for regulatory compliance. Companies must know where they are storing PII, PHI (Protected Health Information), or other regulated data — data discovery provides these insights.

TIP

Another (very specific) definition of data discovery focuses on analyzing data and visually representing it to identify patterns and gain insights on how that data is used. While this form of business intelligence is not quite as important for the CCSP exam, it's worth keeping in mind.

While traditional discovery focuses on the contents of files and data stores, a more holistic approach examines the past and potential future flow of data. Understanding where data has been and where it might go provides helpful insights when classifying data and identifying opportunities for misuse or compromise.

The rise of cloud computing means that organizations' data is more dynamic than ever and being stored across countless applications in multiple locations. Users can access organizational data from anywhere at any time, so being able to discover and classify sensitive data is an important challenge.

The three primary approaches for data discovery are

>> **Metadata:** *Metadata* is data about data, which can include filenames, file headers, or other information that provides valuable insight about the data and its contents. Good metadata can be analyzed to glean insights about the data, and those insights can be used to locate and classify sensitive data.

>> **Labels:** Labeling similar data is another method of identifying sensitive data. Ideally an organization should have some automated process of labeling sensitive data, but this process is often manual. It's also ideal to create data labels when the data is first created, but the process can take place at any time during the data lifecycle.

>> **Content:** The final approach for data discovery is to analyze the actual content of your data, which requires conducting various forms of analysis to determine what all files contain. This form of data identification is typically the most thorough form, but it's also the most resource intensive and expensive.

Structured data

Structured data is highly organized and comes in known formats, making it ideal for discovery and analysis. Relational databases, for example, are organized into tables and columns and come with metadata that describe the database and its structure. Because they are so strictly organized, it's easier to search for and find data that needs to be classified.

Unstructured data

Unstructured data can include email, text, image files, or other binary data that is generally much harder to discover and search. Users can create and store unstructured data with few limitations around the format or location. Metadata and labels can assist in this discovery, but successful data discovery is highly reliant on including descriptive metadata and having strong processes for labeling.

Semi-structured data

Semi-structured data is data that has some structure, but not as much as structured data. It is often used to store data that is not easily categorized and uses tags to create fields and records without requiring the full structure of a relational database.

An example of semi-structured data is an XML document that contains a list of products, with each product having a name, price, and description. The XML document is semi-structured because it has some structure (the product elements), but it is not as structured as a relational database table.

Data location

Data location is the physical or logical place where data is stored. It can be stored on a variety of devices, including computers, servers, and cloud storage. The location of data can affect its accessibility, security, and compliance — data that is stored on a local computer may be more accessible to users, but it may also be less secure; data that is stored in the cloud may be more secure, but it may also be less accessible to users.

You should carefully choose your data location, based on the specific needs of your organization and the data itself. In addition to considering accessibility and security, you should also consider the compliance requirements of your data. For example, GDPR and other regulations have requirements that impact where you can and cannot store your data. I discuss GDPR and other privacy regulations in Chapter 13.

TIP

Some large public cloud providers offer "GovClouds" or other community clouds that limit where data is stored, in order to cater to organizations with strict data location requirements.

Chapter 6

Domain 2: Cloud Data Security, Part 2

I n this chapter, you learn about data classification, mapping, and labeling, and the key data security concepts that apply to various stages of the data lifecycle — data retention, deletion, auditing, and more. Domain 2: Cloud Data Security is the most heavily weighted domain on the CCSP exam, representing 20 percent of the certification. This chapter covers the second half of Domain 2.

Planning and Implementing Data Classification

Data classification is the process of categorizing and organizing data based on level of sensitivity or other characteristics. Classification is a complementary step to data discovery and is a critical component for risk management, data security, and compliance. Proper data classification is required in order to determine what policies and controls are required to protect specific data types and categories of information.

Many attributes can be analyzed as part of data classification activities. Some examples include the type of data, data location, data owner, and legal or regulatory requirements. All of these attributes (and others) can help divide data into buckets that share a common set of risks and consequently share a common set of security controls required to secure each bucket of data. The ultimate demonstration of data classification maturity is having processes and tools in place to discover and appropriately classify data and apply the right set of policies and security controls to that data, through automated means.

Data classification is not only a security best practice, but is also a pillar of many regulatory compliance guidelines and industry certifications, such as ISO 27001 and PCI-DSS. NIST's Guide for Mapping Types of Information Systems to Security Categories (NIST 800-60) was last updated in 2008, but has aged well and is a good resource that provides a step-by-step methodology to classifying data based on risk.

As important as data classification is in traditional data centers, it is even more important in cloud environments. Due to multitenancy and shared resources in the cloud, it's critical that data is properly classified at creation or modification. This classification allows the data to be stored in the right place, encrypted with the right mechanisms, and controlled in accordance with the risks associated with that particular data.

Data classification policies

Data classification policies are an important part of your organization's information security program; these policies help ensure that sensitive data is properly protected.

Data classification policies typically define different levels of sensitivity for data (such as confidential, internal, and public). They also specify the controls that should be applied to each level of data, such as encryption, access restrictions, and auditing.

A robust data classification policy can help your organization prioritize where you apply the most stringent security controls, which can help you reduce the risk of data breaches and other security incidents that impact your most important information. These policies can also help improve your compliance with industry regulations, like the General Data Protection Regulation (GDPR).

Data mapping

The use of *metadata* (data about data) to map data to security controls is an approach that can be both effective and efficient at discovering, analyzing, and categorizing sensitive data. Examples of useful metadata include filenames, file headers, and column headings within a spreadsheet.

One important consideration when relying on this type of information for classification is that your analysis is only as good as the metadata itself. A filename like PII-0123.txt alerts you to personally identifiable information that needs to be protected in a certain manner, whereas the filename 0123.txt is not very helpful on its own. It's up to you to determine what information to place in filenames, headers, and other metadata so that it's helpful without potentially leaking information to the bad guys.

An effective mapping strategy allows cloud customers to understand where their most sensitive data resides in the cloud, thus enabling them to establish effective security policies and implement the appropriate security controls for the different types of data across different applications and storage media.

Data labeling

Labels, similar to metadata, can be used to identify and classify groups of data that have a lot in common. Unlike metadata, however, labels are not a formal part of the data — rather, they are external tags that you can create to provide additional structure and support your analysis.

Much like metadata, the value of labels is only as good as the processes developed and followed to create those labels. You can rely on every file having a filename, but labels can be created inconsistently, which minimizes their value in data classification. In order to reap the most benefit from labels, make sure that your users understand which data elements should be labeled and ensure that a consistent approach is followed for developing and applying those labels to data elements in your environment.

TECHNICAL STUFF

Mature organizations can reach a point where metadata-driven processes automatically generate labels, yielding higher levels of access control and security. While I'll always advocate for automation, it's important for you to conduct periodic audits to ensure that your label-generating system functions correctly and without circumvention.

Sensitive data

If you're not using metadata or labels to categorize your data, then you're likely analyzing the content of the data itself. While I dive deep into regulatory compliance in Chapters 13 and 14, this section provides an overview of three main categories of highly regulated sensitive data.

>> Protected Health Information (PHI)

>> Personally Identifiable Information (PII)

>> Cardholder data

Personally Identifiable Information (PII)

You've likely heard of PII, as it is the most commonly used classification of data for security and privacy purposes. *Personally identifiable information* (PII) is any data that could potentially be used to identify a particular individual from other individuals. Your full name, Social Security number, passport number, and email address are all great examples of data elements that are unique to you and only you — that's PII.

PII can either be sensitive or non-sensitive. Information like your SSN and passport number are not publicly available and considered very sensitive. Non-sensitive PII includes data that can be used to identify an individual, but are publicly available — information like your name as displayed on Facebook or your business phone number as listed on your website can be used to identify you, but are publicly available and not likely to cause personal harm.

PII is further divided into direct and indirect identifiers:

>> *Direct identifiers* can be used on their own to identify an individual. Again, SSN is a perfect example because there is a 1:1 assignment of Social Security number to human being. Driver's license numbers and bank account numbers are other examples of direct identifiers.

>> *Indirect identifiers* can help narrow down a set of individuals, but cannot be used to identify a single individual on its own. Examples of indirect identifiers include birthdates, race, gender, and the like. As part of your data classification process, it's important to appropriately categorize PII and apply appropriate restrictions and protections based on the type of PII.

WARNING

Do not overlook the potential sensitivity of indirect identifiers simply because they cannot independently identify an individual. You must not neglect the notion of aggregate risk — that is, multiple pieces of information can be combined to create something more sensitive than any of its individual components. Think about this: The first name Arthur, though not super common, isn't enough to single me out as an individual. However, adding just one other indirect identifier (say, Hometown: Washington, DC) drastically narrows down the pool of individuals you could be talking about. Throw in a birthdate field and occupation, and I'm willing to bet you've just narrowed it down to yours truly.

Protected health information (PHI)

Protected health information (PHI) is information related to the past, present, or future health status of an individual that was created, used, or obtained in the course of providing healthcare services, including payment for such services. PHI can include things like diagnosis and treatment information, test results, and prescription information, as well as other PII such as gender, birthdate, and so on.

In the United States, the handling and protection of PHI is governed by the Health Insurance Portability and Accountability Act, or HIPAA (pronounced hip-uh). HIPAA controls who can access PHI, and under what circumstances they can do so. HIPAA also regulates things like data retention, archiving, and other physical and technical safeguards — and so it is a huge driver of security and privacy requirements for CSPs who serve customers with PHI data. I discuss HIPAA further in Chapter 13.

Cardholder data

Cardholder data may sound self-explanatory — and it's probably exactly what you think it is. *Cardholder data* is a specific subset of PII that is related to holders of credit or debit cards. This data includes information such as the primary account number (PAN), security codes, expiration dates, and any other information that can be used to identify a particular individual cardholder. PCI-DSS is the global standard that regulates the protection and handling of cardholder data.

Designing and Implementing Information Rights Management (IRM)

Information Rights Management (IRM) is a data security technology that protects data (typically files, but also emails, web pages, and other information) from unauthorized access by limiting who can view, copy, forward, delete, or otherwise modify information.

Information Rights Management works by combining data encryption technologies with granular identity and authorization management. IRM is an important security technology in cloud environments because it allows you to control and manage access to data even as it moves across various locations.

You may be familiar with the related term, DRM. *Digital rights management* is focused on protecting intellectual property through its distribution lifecycle. DRM became huge in the early 2000s, as applications like Napster and LimeWire contributed to the pirating of copyrighted material (music, movies, and the like). DRM technologies allow movie studios to prevent a pirated movie from playing on a computer that isn't associated with a legitimate purchase of that movie. IRM plays a similar role to that of DRM, but with a broader focus on the security and privacy of any organization's sensitive data.

Objectives

Information Rights Management is a powerful technology that takes standard encryption and access control capabilities to another level. While many of the objectives of IRM are consistent across different environments, some concepts are particularly important for you, as a CCSP candidate, to understand.

IRM manages access to information through access control lists (ACLs) that dictate who can access data and what permissions they have for that data. Whereas traditional access control mechanisms commonly allow you to grant read, write, or execute permissions, IRM affords you more granular control over access permissions. For any given data object, you can control who is able to save/download, copy, edit, print and more. Cloud environments, by design, help organizations make their information accessible by whoever needs it wherever they need it — and that's great! The granular control provided by IRM is incredibly valuable to make sure that the increased availability doesn't compromise the confidentiality or integrity of an organization's most important data.

One of the most appreciated concepts of IRM for cloud security professionals is the fact that IRM protects data regardless of the location of that data. Many standard security mechanisms rely on data being in a predictable location and either preventing the data from leaving that location or preventing unauthorized users from accessing the data in that location. With IRM technologies, ACLs are embedded directly into each protected file and travel with the file wherever it goes (inside the cloud environment and even once downloaded); IRM is the perfect example of security following the data! For cloud environments that span many regions or even countries, IRM can provide an added layer of confidentiality, no matter where the data may be located.

Information Rights Management can support data classification and can help protect data throughout the entire data lifecycle. (Refer to Chapter 5 for the stages of the cloud data lifecycle.) IRM protections can be applied to data immediately upon creation (or modification). The IRM controls can be based on any data or user attributes that are available at the time the data is created, so, you can apply access controls based on who created the data, where the data is created, and what the data is named or labeled. Having this level of control from the onset can enable an organization to maintain granular data protections throughout the entire life-cycle. These types of IRM and ACL controls can be templatized and used to create configuration baselines to enforce organizational data protection policies.

WARNING

Despite its many benefits, you need to be mindful of some potential pitfalls when using IRM in a cloud deployment. Many IRM implementations require that users install and use an IRM agent that manages identification and authentication per-missions locally, which can be a challenge for cloud environments that reach external users outside of the organization's direct control. In addition, IRM may present compatibility challenges with certain applications, operating systems, and mobile platforms. Your data security architecture should consider these fac-tors, as well as assess how IRM can integrate and work with other data security technologies in your environment, like DLP.

Appropriate tools

After you understand what Information Rights Management is and you know the key benefits and considerations when implementing IRM, you're ready to learn the key capabilities associated with IRM tools and solutions. Details about specific tools are outside the scope of this book, but this section dives into the types of features you should look for when incorporating IRM into your security architecture:

>> **Continuous protection:** A key feature of any IRM tool is ensuring that any data being managed by the IRM implementation is protected at all times, regardless of its location or data lifecycle phase. Continuous protection means that information is protected at rest and in transit, in the cloud and on-premises.

>> **Automatic expiration:** IRM tools allow an organization to set policies that automatically revoke access to data after a predetermined lifetime. As opposed to traditional systems that have no control over data once it leaves systems under you control, this feature allows an organization to ensure that data that should be accessed only for a certain period of time expires once that time is reached. This message will self-destruct in five seconds.

>> **Dynamic control:** IRM technologies allow organizations to manage access permissions even once data has been distributed. Dynamic control means that data owners have the same granular level of control over IRM'd data (that's the technical term) even once it's been downloaded, shared, or moved to remote storage.

>> **Auditability:** IRM technologies provide a continuous audit trail of access to data under its control. Organizations using IRM tools are able to monitor which users have access to data and track when they use that access. Auditability is a big help to ensuring that data access is in line with organizational policies as well as legal and regulatory requirements.

>> **Integration and support:** IRM tools maintain compatibility with most office suites and email filtering technologies, allowing granular control over not just documents and files, but also emails that move through the organization. IRM systems are generally designed and built to integrate with an organization's existing infrastructure and commonly support a wide range of data formats.

Planning and Implementing Data Retention, Deletion, and Archiving Policies

Effective data protection strategies should address risks at every stage of the data lifecycle. The topics of data retention, data deletion, and data archiving involve policies and procedures at the store, destroy, and archive stages, respectively. These concepts are essential in cloud computing, particularly in regard to maintaining compliance with legal, regulatory, and contractual obligations.

Data retention policies

A *data retention policy* is an organization's established set of rules around holding on to information. The purpose of the policy is to create guidelines for retaining data in accordance with regulations and business needs, as well as ensuring that important information is available for future use. One important consideration for data retention involves incident response. Malicious activity can potentially go unnoticed for weeks, months, or (hopefully not) years! Your data retention policy should consider your detection capabilities and retain data long enough to ensure it's available for future forensics activities.

Data retention requirements are very often based on regulatory or other compliance requirements that establish minimum data retention terms. Organizations may opt to retain data for longer periods, but it's important to understand all data retention obligations to be sure that the minimum threshold is met. Ultimately, the length of time you retain data will depend on a number of factors, including the classification of the data; it may be necessary to store one classification of data for a longer period than others.

TIP

An effective data retention policy should not only consider retention periods, but should address all factors that contribute to data being available when needed in the future. Other major considerations involve the formats, storage methods, and security mechanisms used for data retention. A holistic approach to data retention helps ensure that important information exists where it can be easily retrieved whenever it's needed.

Data deletion procedures and mechanisms

A critical and sometimes overlooked component of data protection is the secure removal of that data from systems when it is no longer needed. Lack of effective data deletion procedures can lead to data leakage and breaches or legal and regulatory compliance issues. Your organization may have data deletion requirements from regulators, customers, and partners, but a holistic review of business and technical requirements is prudent in developing your data deletion procedures and mechanisms.

Secure data deletion ensures that no files or pointers to files are left behind after deletion. The key is to remove the deleted data from the system and prevent it from ever being reconstructed after deletion. Reconstructing deleted data is already a challenge due to the distributed nature of cloud storage systems, but the following disposal options provide an added layer of assurance:

>> **Data overwriting:** Overwriting involves writing random data over the actual data one or more times. Multiple passes of overwriting provide more assurance of the actual data's destruction.

>> **Data encryption:** Simply using encryption to make the data unreadable (without the encryption key) is a basic way of "deleting" data. Taking this step further and intentionally deleting the key is *crypto-shredding,* a concept introduced in Chapter 2. Crypto-shredding is the most effective method of data deletion, and it's one of the only methods available to cloud customers because they don't maintain physical access or control over data centers and servers.

WARNING

While crypto-shredding is a cloud customer's best bet for effective data deletion, customers must consider whether or not the CSP or another third party manages their encryption keys. If so, proper attention must be given to ensuring those external keys are also fully deleted.

>> **Degaussing:** *Degaussing* is a data erasure method that involves using strong magnets to destroy data on magnetic media, like hard drives. This method is generally effective, but is not available to cloud customers because degaussing requires physical access that only the infrastructure owner has.

>> **Physical destruction:** When all else fails, physical destruction gets the job done! As it sounds, this method involves damaging the media by pulverizing, burning, or other physical means. Physical destruction is another method that is not available to cloud customers (due to physical limitations), but is a common practice used by CSPs when decommissioning hardware.

Data archiving procedures and mechanisms

Data archiving is the process of removing information from production systems and transferring it to other, longer term storage systems. In doing so, cloud customers cut costs by sending less important data to cheaper storage options and can use their production resources for more important data. Data that you no longer need for day-to-day use but that is required to be maintained as a part of an organization's data retention policy is typically archived until it's either needed or deleted.

Cloud-based data archiving policies and procedures should consider the following topics:

>> **Format:** When data is archived, it should not just be stored and forgotten. With archived data commonly being kept for many years, it's important that you pay careful attention to the format of the data being archived as well as the storage type being used. As technologies evolve over the years, organizations need to ensure that archived data can be retrieved when needed. Using reliable data formats and storage media is paramount. In addition, organizations need to consider their archived data formats as organizational changes are made over time. Without keeping this point in mind, companies run the risk of getting rid of applications, application versions, or components that may be required to support data that has previously been archived.

>> **Business continuity and disaster recovery:** Data archiving processes should align with an organization's backup and restore procedures and should include procedures for supporting business continuity and disaster recovery activities.

>> **Monitoring and testing:** Monitoring data throughout all stages of its lifecycle is important. As part of the cloud data lifecycle, archived data should be logged to make sure that it can be properly protected and monitored until restored or deleted.

>> **Protecting:** Data that is archived in long-term storage should be analyzed and classified to understand its data protection needs. Encryption is a very common mechanism used to protect archived data, and organizations must

carefully manage encryption keys for archived data. If archived data is needed after several years but the keys have been lost over time, then the entire archive is potentially useless.

>> **Restoring:** Archived data generally falls into two categories: data that will never be needed and data that will need to be retrieved and used at some point. Data that will never be needed can be disposed of in accordance with an organization's data retention and data deletion policies. For everything else, steps should be taken to plan for the eventual restoration of archived data, and these steps should be periodically tested to ensure that they remain effective as technical and organizational changes occur.

Legal hold

Legal hold is the process of preserving any data that is, will, or may be relevant during a legal investigation. A legal hold is initiated when an organization receives an official judicial or law enforcement notice that outlines what data must be preserved and how it must be preserved and secured. In general, legal holds last until all civil or criminal proceedings are final.

TIP

A related topic is that of *e-discovery*, or *electronic discovery*, which refers to the process of electronic data being collected, secured, and analyzed as part of civil or criminal legal cases. E-discovery often impacts those that work in forensics, but it's a term that every CCSP candidate should be familiar with.

An organization that receives a legal hold notice must be prepared to archive or store and protect relevant data in accordance with the requirements set forth in the notice. Cloud customers, as data owners, should consider potential legal hold roles and responsibilities when negotiating cloud contracts and SLAs with cloud service providers.

Designing and Implementing Auditability, Traceability, and Accountability of Data Events

After you understand the various stages through which data moves in cloud environments and the key methods for protecting data throughout the entire lifecycle, you're ready to find out how to identify, track, and analyze data events to ensure ongoing security in your environment.

The *Open Web Application Security Project* (OWASP) is an online community that is dedicated to providing organizations around the world with free, practical resources to support application security. OWASP provides a wealth of tools, articles, and documentation in the field of web application security — among this long list of helpful resources is a great set of definitions and guidelines around logging. The rest of this section leverages the OWASP Logging Cheat Sheet, which you can find at www.owasp.org/index.php/Logging_Cheat_Sheet. You can also refer to Appendix B for additional recommended OWASP resources.

Defining event sources and requirements of identity attribution

The Shared Responsibility Model (see Chapter 3) indicates that the responsibilities of the CSPs and cloud customers change from one cloud service category to the next. The event sources at an organization's disposal vary depending on the service category being used. The following sections outline some of the key event sources available for IaaS, PaaS, and SaaS cloud customers.

SaaS event sources

In SaaS cloud environments, the cloud service provider is responsible for the entire infrastructure as well as the application itself. This split in responsibilities is great for customers who are mostly hands off and just want a functioning application, but remember it means that these cloud customers have minimal log data at their disposal.

To understand what level of auditability, traceability, and accountability you have as a SaaS customer, you should pay close attention to terms in your SLAs and cloud contracts.

REMEMBER

Make sure that you have a very strong grasp of the Shared Responsibility Model when reviewing SLAs and contracts with cloud service providers. Reliable CSPs are transparent about what they are responsible for and what you, the cloud customer, is responsible for. When it comes to event logging, you need to understand "where the buck stops" for the CSP so that you know what's left for you to handle. Understanding the Shared Responsibility Model is essential for maintaining data security, as well as ensuring compliance with any legal or regulatory requirements your organization is accountable for.

Some event sources that are important for SaaS customers include

>> Admin logs

>> User account logs and other access logs

- » Application logs
- » Webserver logs
- » Database logs
- » Billing logs

PaaS event sources

Organizations utilizing a PaaS cloud environment inherit additional responsibilities over those required of SaaS customers, which comes with added access to and control over logging and monitoring capabilities. In PaaS environments, the CSP exposes some infrastructure-level event sources and diagnostic information.

Software applications produce tons of information events that can be used to generate log data. As an organization develops its application within a PaaS environment, it is up to application developers to expose the desired level of application event data for logging and monitoring. As a future CCSP, you must work with your organization's application development teams to understand their capabilities and limitations around providing event information. Together, cloud security professionals and application developers should design and implement capabilities for logging that allow thorough event monitoring without unnecessary burden on the software development lifecycle.

The following list from the OWASP Logging Cheat Sheet is a fantastic starting point for event sources that PaaS customers should track:

- » Input validation failures (protocol violations, unacceptable encodings, invalid parameter names and values, and so on)

- » Output validation failures (database record set mismatch, invalid data encoding, and so on)

- » Authentication successes and failures

- » Authorization (access control) failures

- » Session management failures (for example, cookie session identification value modification)

- » Application errors and system events (syntax and runtime errors, connectivity problems, performance issues, third-party service error messages, filesystem errors, file upload virus detection, configuration changes, and so on)

- » Application and related systems start-ups and shutdowns and logging initialization (starting, stopping, or pausing)

>> Use of higher risk functionality (for example, network connections, adding or deleting users, changes to privileges, assigning users to tokens, adding or deleting tokens, use of systems administrative privileges, access by application administrators, all actions by users with administrative privileges, access to payment cardholder data, use of data encrypting keys, key changes, creating and deleting system-level objects, data import and export including screen-based reports, and submitting user-generated content)

>> Legal and other opt-ins (for example, permissions for mobile phone capabilities, terms of use, terms and conditions, personal data usage consent, and permissions to receive marketing communications)

In addition to the preceding OWASP recommendations, PaaS customers may also want to track and monitor the following specific events:

>> Source code modifications

>> Configuration changes

>> Data modifications (prioritize highly sensitive data, such as PHI)

REMEMBER

PaaS cloud environments provide a combination of infrastructure-level event sources (provided by the CSP) and application-level event sources that are customized by the organization's app developers.

IaaS event sources

Organizations using the infrastructure as a service cloud model have the greatest access to logs and event sources of any cloud service category. In an IaaS cloud environment, the cloud customer has control and access over their entire environment, which means almost all infrastructure-level events and logs are available, as well as platform- and application-level logs.

To prevent any surprises, cloud customers should be sure that access to relevant logs is clearly documented in their SLAs and contracts with the cloud service provider.

IaaS customers should monitor all recommended events for SaaS and PaaS, where applicable. Some additional IaaS event sources include but are not limited to

>> Network logs

>> Hypervisor logs

>> DNS server logs

>> Management console logs

>> Virtual machine manager logs

>> API access logs

>> Billing records

Identity attribution

Ensuring that you have the right sources of event data is critical, but making sure that those event sources contain the right data is just as important! Event logs should contain as much relevant information as possible to allow cloud security professionals to effectively audit and conduct forensic activities, when necessary. The basic questions that need answering in any investigation are who, what, where, and when. The OWASP Logging Cheat Sheet provides useful guidelines for which event attributes to capture for each of these questions.

Who (this can be a human or a machine user):

>> Source address (for example, user's device/machine identifier and user's IP address)

>> User identity, if authenticated or otherwise known (such as a username, user ID, or similar)

What:

>> Type of event

>> Severity of the event (for example, error, warning, info, debug, and so on)

>> Security relevant event flag (if the logs contain nonsecurity event data, too)

>> Description of what happened

Where:

>> Application identifier (name and version, for example)

>> Application address (cluster/host name, workstation identity, or local device identifier, for example)

>> Service (name and protocol, for example)

>> Geolocation (which can often be derived from the IP address, but may be spoofed by more sophisticated attackers)

>> Window/form/page (may be the entry point URL or dialog box where the event was initiated)

>> Code location (script or module name, for example)

When:

>> Log date and time (international format is suggested)

>> Event date and time (note that the event timestamp may be different to the time of logging)

>> Interaction identifier

TECHNICAL STUFF

Per OWASP, an *interaction identifier* is a mechanism used to link all relevant events for a single user interaction. A single user event may trigger multiple subsequent events over a range of time. Rather than requiring manual correlation, some applications can determine when these separate events are all related to the same interaction from a single user.

OWASP makes further recommendations for additional event attributes to consider logging. Check out the cheat sheet, if you'd like to see more. In any event (pardon the pun), the specific attributes your organization logs and monitors should be based on the sensitivity of your data, your technical capabilities, and any relevant legal, regulatory, or contractual commitments.

While it's clearly very important to have thorough and detailed logging capabilities, some data should never be saved in logs. OWASP recommends excluding, sanitizing, or de-identifying the following data from your logs:

>> Application source code

>> Session identification values

>> Access tokens

>> Sensitive personal data (PHI, cardholder data, or government identifiers, for example)

>> Authentication passwords

>> Database connection strings

>> Encryption keys and other master secrets

>> Data of a higher security classification than the logging system is allowed to store

>> Commercially sensitive information

>> Information it is illegal to collect in the relevant jurisdictions

>> Information a user has opted out of collection or not consented to

Logging, storing, and analyzing data events

Once you know where to look for important event data and you understand what type of event attributes to include (and which ones not to include) in your log entries, you can explore the actual collection, verification, storage, and analysis of all of that valuable information.

REMEMBER

Aside from the obvious security benefits of logging, storing, and analyzing data events, maintaining robust logs in your cloud environment may be a compliance requirement. The Federal Information Security Management Act (FISMA), the Gramm-Leach-Bliley Act (GLBA), the Health Insurance Portability and Accountability Act (HIPAA), (discussed in the "Protected Health Information (PHI)" section of this chapter), and PCI-DSS are examples of regulations and standards that establish guidelines for log retention and management.

According to NIST, a *log management infrastructure* includes "the hardware, software, networks, and media used to generate, transmit, store, analyze, and dispose of log data." Log management infrastructures are generally composed of three tiers: log generation, log analysis and storage, and log monitoring. I discuss these three tiers in the following sections.

Collection

You're familiar with event sources that generate important log data. OWASP provides the following guidance for collecting event and log data:

>> Perform input validation on event data from other trust zones to ensure it is in the correct format (and consider alerting and not logging if an input validation failure occurs)

>> Perform sanitization on all event data to prevent log injection attacks

TECHNICAL STUFF

A *log injection attack* occurs when an attacker creates false log entries or injects malicious content into logs through unvalidated input. You may not be tested on this specific attack, but it's good to understand potential threats to your log data.

>> Encode data correctly for the output (logged) format

>> If writing to databases, read, understand, and apply the SQL injection cheat sheet (see https://cheatsheetseries.owasp.org/cheatsheets/SQL_Injection_Prevention_Cheat_Sheet.html)

>> Ensure that failures in the logging processes/systems do not prevent the application from otherwise running or allow information leakage

>> Synchronize time across all servers and devices, where possible

As these recommendations suggest, a great deal of attention should be given to configuring event log sources, both in terms of input and output validation. Secure log generation and collection is an important step, but logging technologies and processes must still be verified.

Verification

As with most security mechanisms, logging architectures must be periodically tested to verify that they function as intended. OWASP provides the following verification guidelines:

» Ensure the logging is working correctly and as specified.

» Check that events are being classified consistently and the field names, types, and lengths are correctly defined to an agreed standard.

» Ensure logging is implemented and enabled during application security, fuzz, penetration, and performance testing.

» Test that the mechanisms are not susceptible to injection attacks.

» Ensure that there are no unwanted side-effects when logging occurs.

» Check the effect on the logging mechanisms when external network connectivity is lost.

» Ensure that logging cannot be used to deplete system resources — for example, by filling up disk space or exceeding database transaction log space, leading to denial of service.

> Aside from preventing a DoS, keep in mind that cloud is pay-as-you-go model. It's in your best interest to validate that your cloud logs are not using unnecessary resources and driving up your bill.

TIP

» Test the effect on the application of logging failures, such as simulated database connectivity loss, lack of filesystem space, missing write permissions to the filesystem, and runtime errors in the logging module itself.

» Verify access controls on the event log data.

» If log data is utilized in any action against users (like blocking access or account lockout), ensure that it cannot be used to cause denial of service of other users.

The type and amount of verification your organization needs to perform depends on the cloud service category you're using. For IaaS deployments, the cloud customer is responsible for the vast majority of log management — including testing and verification. The burden of verification is much lower on SaaS customers, who rely on the CSP to log and monitor the majority of events. For any service category, cloud customers should review SLAs and contracts to understand how logs are managed or discuss the Shared Responsibility Model with their cloud service provider.

Storage and analysis

Cloud environments produce a whole lot of data and tons of events. Remembering that cloud providers charge customers for what they use, prudent cloud customers need to carefully consider their business, legal, and regulatory requirements when deciding which logs to store and which to purge.

Regardless of how conservative you may be with logging, it's imperative that you have a process and technology to find valuable insights among the noise. Without having a system in place to search and analyze your logs, you'd be left with a massive collection of data that can't be used for its intended security or compliance purposes.

A *Security and Information Event Management* (*SIEM*) is a software product or service that collects, aggregates, and indexes logs from multiple sources and makes those logs easily searched and analyzed.

Whereas traditional SIEM tools allowed customers to correlate events across multiple logs, modern cloud-based SIEM solutions are providing increasing functionality to support unified data and automated threat detection and response. Cloud-based SIEM tools can either be installed in a cloud environment or run as SaaS solutions that ingest log data from the customer's environment and applications.

TIP

The term SIEM is sometimes used interchangeably with the related terms SIM and SEM. *Security Information Management* (SIM) refers to products and services that provide long-term storage, analysis, and reporting of log information. *Security Event Management* (SEM) refers to real-time monitoring and correlation of events. SIEM provides the best of both worlds!

SIEM solutions are commonly used (on-prem and in the cloud) for a variety of functions, depending on an organization's specific needs. Some common SIEM capabilities include:

>> **Aggregation:** One of the most foundational functions of SIEM tools is gathering data from many sources and aggregating them into a single indexed, searchable collection of data. Logs can be aggregated from a wide variety of sources, including servers, databases, applications, network devices, and cloud resources. The primary benefit of log aggregation is that it gives you the ability to search and analyze multisource data from a single point, which

saves security analysts a great deal of time associated with logging into disparate systems and potentially forgetting to check one or more sources. Data aggregation is virtually a necessity for customers managing thousands of systems and services in a cloud environment.

>> **Correlation:** Another core functionality provided by SIEM solutions is the ability to identify and connect common attributes among separate data sources in order to provide useful information. Stated another way, SIEM tools enable event correlation that connects the dots between separate events to identify patterns.

>> **Alerting:** Once log data is aggregated and event information is correlated, SIEM tools are able to alert you of potential security incidents. Alert monitoring typically occurs around the clock and can be configured to trigger in real-time based on specific users, actions, error codes, or other parameters.

TIP

If I don't sound like a broken record yet, just wait. The cloud pay-as-you-go model means that around-the-clock monitoring and alerting may generate a costly amount of data. You must architect your logging and monitoring solutions with resource utilization in mind.

>> **Dashboards:** A *dashboard* is a single graphical view of multiple alerts and data points. When you're dealing with an insane amount of log data and potentially high volumes of alerts, SIEM dashboards can help bring order to the madness and place the most important information front and center. Most SIEM tools offer out-of-box dashboard templates with the ability to create customized dashboards to suit your needs.

>> **Forensic analysis:** SIEM solutions allow long-term storage of correlated log data and provide the ability to search historical logs that cover your entire infrastructure; this means that you can conduct forensic analysis in your environment by investigating particular users, endpoints, time periods, or other criteria.

Chain of custody and nonrepudiation

Chain of custody refers to the process of maintaining and documenting the chronological sequence of possession and control of physical or electronic evidence, from creation until its final use (often presentation in court). An electronic chain of custody consists of a comprehensive history of data's possession changes, location changes, manipulations, accesses, and so on. Chain of custody is very important for legal and law enforcement actions — and, because a verifiable chain of custody can help confirm data's integrity, it's incredibly valuable in conducting forensic analysis and incident response.

An organization that owns and operates their own data center usually finds maintaining a verifiable chain of custody easy; the organization typically has a high degree of control over their hardware, software, and personnel and can implement procedures to ensure that critical data is tracked from beginning to end. Maintaining chain of custody isn't so simple in cloud environments, due to the way data can move from one place to another — oftentimes without the customer's knowledge or direct consent. The best way for cloud customers to mitigate chain of custody concerns is by ensuring that your SLAs and contracts include requirements for your cloud provider to preserve important data and maintain chain of custody, when necessary.

Nonrepudiation is the ability to ensure that the origin or author of data cannot be disputed. Nonrepudiation is typically achieved through hashing or digital signatures that provide confidence over data's authenticity. Nonrepudiation works closely with chain of custody to provide assurance over the integrity and validity of important data. In addition to providing assurance of data's origin, nonrepudiation also provides assurance of actions (for example, confirming that a particular user logged in to a system or made a change to a file).

Chapter **7**

Domain 3: Cloud Platform and Infrastructure Security, Part 1

In this chapter, you explore all the practical matters of cloud platform and infrastructure security. You discover what makes up a cloud's physical environment and how that relates to the virtual cloud environment. You also find out how cloud providers build and secure data centers and how you secure the systems you build within them. Domain 3 represents 17 percent of the CCSP certification exam, and this chapter covers the first half of Domain 3.

Comprehending Cloud Infrastructure and Platform Components

Cloud infrastructures and platforms are made up of many parts, each playing its own important role. You can find many cloud infrastructure components in traditional data centers, but their application in cloud environments may be a little different. Aside from the infrastructure concepts that you're likely familiar with from traditional data center models, cloud infrastructure also introduces some unique components, which I describe throughout the rest of this section.

As you see in Figure 7-1, a cloud infrastructure is composed of

>> Physical environment

>> Networking resources

>> Compute resources

>> Virtualization capabilities

>> Storage resources

>> Management plane

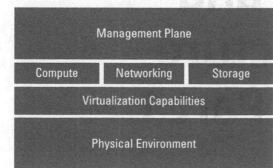

FIGURE 7-1:
Overview of cloud infrastructure components.

I break down each of these key components in the following sections.

TIP

The terms cloud infrastructure and cloud architecture are easy to use interchangeably, but they mean slightly different things. *Cloud infrastructure* includes all the tools and components needed to build a cloud, while *cloud architecture* is the blueprint that describes how those components work together to build the cloud. In other words, you can think of cloud infrastructure as your ingredient list and cloud architecture as your recipe.

Physical environment

While some less informed people may think that information in the cloud is stored in some fluffy virtual world, you and I know that the cloud has a physical environment. Cloud computing runs on actual hardware located in actual buildings. A single one of these buildings (or *data centers*) can house up to hundreds of thousands of servers, switches, and other hardware components. A single cloud environment is usually made up of several of these data centers located across multiple geographic locations.

NIST provides some helpful points to consider when securing physical environments. In NIST 800-53, the Physical and Environmental Protection control family provides guidance on the following areas that are particularly relevant to cloud infrastructures:

>> **Physical access authorization and control:** Define and enforce controls for least privilege access to physical resources.

>> **Access control for transmission medium:** Define security safeguards for power and network cables to prevent damage, disruption, tampering, and theft.

>> **Physical access monitoring:** Develop capabilities to investigate and respond to physical security incidents. Monitoring can include things like physical access logs and security cameras that monitor data center ingress and egress points.

>> **Emergency power:** This one is a biggie! Cloud computing is all about availability, and the last thing a CSP or cloud customer needs is a power outage that makes critical data unavailable.

>> **Fire and water damage protection:** These guidelines are self-explanatory.

>> **Asset monitoring and tracking:** Cloud providers must keep track of every server (and other hardware components) and ensure that they remain in authorized locations.

Although the underlying technologies in cloud computing are very similar to those in a traditional data center, the massive scale of cloud environments creates a unique and complex set of considerations for the physical environment. In addition to the preceding NIST-derived list, the following items are critical considerations for a cloud's physical environment:

>> **Data center location:** Cloud Service Providers go through very detailed assessments when determining where to build their data centers. It's essential that CSPs pay special attention to the availability of resources, as well as threats (natural and manmade) associated with the potential locations.

>> **Sufficient and redundant power and cooling:** With hundreds of thousands of servers providing services to potentially thousands of customers, cloud providers must ensure that they have enough electricity to power and enough cooling to safely run all that hardware. And if your primary power or cooling systems fail, you need to ensure that a reliable backup is in place.

>> **Sufficient and redundant network bandwidth:** Similar to power and cooling, a CSP must ensure that they can support the data needs of all their customers with significant network bandwidth. Sufficient and redundant network bandwidth ensures that the cloud is always on and that customers can reliably access their cloud resources from anywhere in the world.

Having significant and redundant power, cooling, and bandwidth can get quite expensive, and providing suitable security for large physical environments is another huge expense. Because large public clouds serve many organizations, cloud customers can realize the benefits of economies of scale that they just couldn't get by running their own data centers. I dive deeper into physical and environmental data center design in the upcoming section titled "Designing a Secure Data Center."

Network and communications

Networking is the cornerstone of cloud computing because networks and communications provide the only way for cloud customers to access their cloud-based systems and applications (and their data!). Managing the physical network is completely the responsibility of the CSP, but every CCSP candidate should understand some key functionality in cloud networks, including the following concepts:

>> **Routing:** The process of directing network traffic between endpoints on the cloud network or between the cloud network and an external network.

>> **Filtering:** The process of selectively allowing or denying traffic or access to cloud resources.

>> **Rate limiting:** The process of controlling the amount of traffic into or out of the cloud network.

>> **Address allocation:** The process of assigning one or multiple IP addresses to a cloud resource, which can be done either statically or dynamically.

>> **Bandwidth allocation:** The process of sharing network resources fairly between multiple users that share the cloud network. (I'm sure you can imagine how important this is for multitenant environments!)

Software-Defined Networking (SDN) is an approach to network management that enables a network to be centrally controlled (or programmed), providing consistent and holistic management across various applications and technologies. SDN architectures allow dynamic and efficient network configuration that improves network performance and gives cloud providers a centralized software-based view of their entire network infrastructure. As you can imagine, SDN technology is hugely important in cloud computing because it allows large CSPs to programmatically configure, manage, and secure network resources that would be a nightmare to manage through traditional network management techniques.

SDN sounds pretty cool, but you may be wondering exactly how it works. Figure 7-2 depicts a basic Software-Defined Networking architecture. As you see, SDN technology abstracts network control from network forwarding capabilities (like routing), thus creating two layers (control plus infrastructure) out of what is traditionally a combined function. The control plane contains the actual SDN control logic. This layer receives service requests from the application layer and is responsible for providing configuration and forwarding direction to network forwarding equipment in the infrastructure layer. The control plane is where the SDN magic happens; it's here that SDNs logically optimize network traffic, thus allowing cloud providers to allocate network resources in an agile and highly scalable manner. This separation between the control and data planes also provides cloud administrators with a single interface to manage thousands of network devices, without needing to individually log in and manually manage those devices.

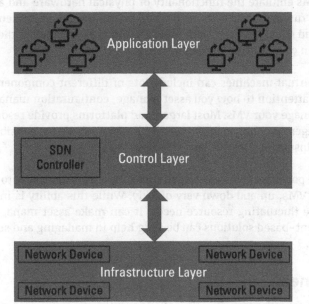

FIGURE 7-2: Software-Defined Networking (SDN) architecture.

Software-Defined Networking is a pivotal technology in cloud computing and forms the basis of many public cloud networks. With the amount of central control provided by SDN implementations, securing your Software-Defined Network is of the utmost importance. By virtualizing your entire network infrastructure, you increase your attack footprint and give attackers a central target (the SDN controller) that could be used to compromise your entire network. Pay special attention to securing SDN controllers through robust access policies, system hardening, and encrypted communications.

Compute

As the term cloud computing suggests, compute power is a big deal for cloud consumers! *Compute resources* take data, process it, and show you the output of that processing. Just like in traditional data center models, cloud-based computing comes down to compute (CPU) and processing (RAM) capabilities.

What's unique in cloud environments, however, is that these compute resources must be managed and allocated among multiple customers. Before tackling that challenge, you should be familiar with some common types of cloud compute assets, specifically virtual machines (VMs) and containers.

VMs

VMs are the most common compute mechanism in cloud computing environments. VMs emulate the functionality of physical hardware and allow cloud customers to run operating systems (OS) in a virtualized environment. In addition to the OS (and the OS kernel), your organization may include middleware or custom application code in your VM deployments.

Because virtual machines can include lots of different components, you need to pay close attention to how you asset manage, configuration manage, and vulnerability manage your VMs. Most large cloud platforms provide resources to support VM management, but it is ultimately the customer's responsibility to manage their VM instances and the data processed within them.

TIP

One of the powerful features of cloud environments is the ability to scale resources, including VMs, up and down very quickly. While this ability is incredibly helpful to manage fluctuating resource needs, it can make asset management a nightmare. Agent-based solutions can be a big help in managing and securing your VM inventory.

Containers

Containers take the virtualization of VMs to the next step and package only the necessary code, configurations, and resources needed to run a particular application. Unlike VMs, containers don't run an entire OS — instead, they use the kernel of the VM or OS that they're hosted on. In short: VMs provide virtual environments that allow organizations to run their applications, while containers isolate an application from its environment and allow the application to be run in multiple different environments. Containers are an increasingly popular technology, especially for multicloud or hybrid deployments.

REMEMBER

You may hear the term container and think of storage because . . . well, because containers in the real world are used to store things. Remember, however, that this compute technology is actually used to run applications and process information.

Because containers allow you to scale up and down resources even more rapidly than VMs, asset management and configuration management are even bigger security concern for containers. Most container technologies come with support for managing your container deployment lifecycle, but it's up to you to ensure that you aren't spinning up containers that haven't been properly patched or managed.

Reservations, limits, and shares

The use of reservations, limits, and shares allows you to allocate a single host's compute resources.

A *reservation* guarantees that a cloud customer has access to a minimum amount of cloud compute resources, either CPU or RAM. Much like a restaurant reservation ensures that you have a seat when you need it, compute reservations are used to make sure that your VMs have the right amount of computing and processing power when they need it. Reservations are an important feature in cloud environments because they can help protect customers against Denial of Service due to other resource-intensive tenants.

A *limit* acts just the opposite of a reservation and sets a maximum amount of cloud compute resources that can be used. In cloud environments, limits can be set either for a VM or for a customer's compute utilization as a whole. Limits can help customers ensure that they don't use more resources than they've budgeted for, and they can also help ensure that a single cloud tenant doesn't use a tremendous amount of resources at the harm of other tenants. Limits may be configured as fixed (for example, "use no more than 16GB of RAM"), but I've most often seen dynamic limits used in practice. Dynamic limits allow customers to temporarily use additional resources depending on given circumstances or requirements being met.

WARNING

Limits are particularly useful in development environments, where cost may supersede any other consideration. Use limits in production environments very carefully to avoid potential Denial of Service.

The concept of a *share* is used to mediate resource allocation contentions. *Resource contention* is just a fancy way of saying that there are too many requests and not enough resources available to supply all those requests. When resource contention occurs, share values are used to allocate resources to all tenants assigned a share value. Tenants with a higher share value receive a larger portion of available resources during this period.

TIP

You should understand what resource contention is for your exam and know that shares are one way to negotiate and remediate it. However, you should also know that this occurrence is fairly uncommon in most large, mature cloud providers. Two of the key cloud computing characteristics, rapid elasticity and resource pooling (see Chapter 3), are focused on ensuring that large amounts of customers can share cloud resources with minimal disruption. CSPs with routine resource contention are very likely not built at a scale large enough for their customer base.

Virtualization

Chapter 3 introduces the concept of virtualization. *Virtualization* is the process of creating software instances of actual hardware. VMs, for example, are software instances of actual computers. Software-Defined Networks, discussed earlier in this chapter, are virtualized networks. Nowadays, you can pretty much find any traditional hardware available as a virtualized solution.

Virtualization is the secret sauce behind cloud computing, as it allows a single piece of hardware to be shared by multiple customers. Concepts like multitenancy and resource pooling would not exist as they do today — and you wouldn't be reading this book — if it weren't for the advent of virtualization!

Virtualization offers many clear benefits. Following is a list of some of the most noteworthy:

>> **Increases scalability:** Virtualized environments are designed to grow as your demand grows. Instead of buying new hardware, you simply spin up additional virtual instances.

>> **Allows faster resource provisioning:** It's much quicker and easier to spin up virtualized hardware from a console than it is to physically boot-up multiple pieces of hardware.

>> **Reduces downtime:** Restoring or redeploying physical hardware takes a lot of time, especially at scale. Failover for virtualized resources can happen much more quickly, which means your systems remain up and running longer.

» **Avoids vendor lock-in:** Virtualization abstracts software from hardware, meaning your virtualized resources are more portable than their physical counterparts. Unhappy with your vendor? Pack up your VMs and move to another one!

» **Saves time (and money):** Virtualized resources can be easily centrally managed, reducing the need for personnel and equipment to maintain your infrastructure. In addition, less hardware usually means less money.

The preceding list reiterates why virtualization is such a critical technology and reminds you of the deep connection between virtualization and cloud computing.

The most common implementation of virtualization is the hypervisor (see Chapter 4). A hypervisor is a computing layer that allows multiple guest operating systems to run on a single physical host device. Figure 7-3 shows an overview of hypervisor architecture.

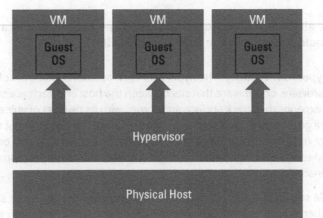

FIGURE 7-3: Hypervisor overview.

The hypervisor abstracts software from hardware and allows each of the guest OSes to share the host's hardware resources, while giving the guests the impression that they're all alone on that host. The two categories of hypervisors are Type 1 and Type 2. A Type 1 hypervisor is also known as a bare metal hypervisor, as it runs directly on the hardware (see Chapter 4). Type 2 hypervisors, however, run on the host's operating system. Figure 7-4 shows a comparison of the two.

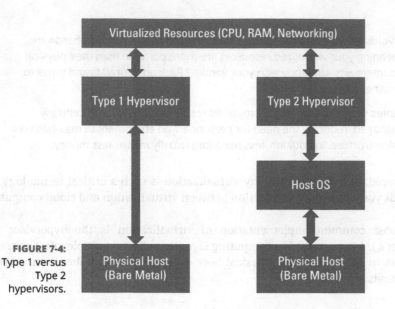

FIGURE 7-4:
Type 1 versus
Type 2
hypervisors.

Virtualized Resources (CPU, RAM, Networking)

Type 1 Hypervisor

Type 2 Hypervisor

Host OS

Physical Host
(Bare Metal)

Physical Host
(Bare Metal)

Despite all the advantages of virtualization and hypervisors, as a CCSP candidate, you should remember some challenges as well:

>> **Hypervisor security:** The hypervisor is an additional piece of software, hardware, or firmware that sits between the host and each guest. As a result, it expands the attack surface and comes with its own set of vulnerabilities that the good guys must discover and patch before the bad guys get to them. If not fixed, hypervisor flaws can lead to external attacks on VMs or even VM-to-VM attacks, where one cloud tenant can access or compromise another tenant's data.

>> **VM security:** Virtual machines are nothing more than files that sit on a disk or other storage mechanism. Imagine your entire home computer wrapped up into a single icon that sits on your desktop — that's pretty much what a virtual machine comes down to. If not sufficiently protected, a VM image is suscepti-ble to compromise while dormant or offline. Use controls like Access Control Lists (ACLs), encryption, and hashing to protect the confidentiality and integrity of your VM files.

>> **Network security:** Network traffic within virtualized environments cannot be monitored and protected by physical security controls, such as network-based intrusion detection systems. You must select appropriate tools to monitor inter- and intra-VM network traffic.

**TECHNICAL
STUFF**

The concept of *virtual machine introspection* (VMI) allows a hypervisor to monitor its guest operating systems during runtime. Not all hypervisors are capable of VMI, but it's a technique that can prove invaluable for securing VMs during operation.

> » **Resource utilization:** If not properly configured, a single VM can exhaust a host's resources, leaving other VMs out of luck. Resource utilization is where the concept of limits (discussed in the "Reservations, limits, and shares" section of this chapter) comes in handy. It's essential that you manage VMs as if they share a pool of resources — because they do!

Storage

At the most fundamental technical level, cloud storage isn't much different from traditional data center storage. Storage typically begins with Hard Disk Drives (HDD) or Solid State Drives (SSD), depending on the performance needed by a particular customer or workload. The drives are grouped and arranged into RAID (Redundant Array of Inexpensive Disks) or SAN (Storage Area Network) configurations and then virtualized for multitenant access. On their own, these storage units have no filesystem. Instead, a filesystem is created and applied by the guest OS whenever a tenant deploys a virtual machine.

In Chapter 5, you learn that IaaS cloud generally uses two categories of storage. *Volume storage* is similar to traditional block storage and is used when cloud storage is allocated to a VM and used as if it were a regular hard drive attached to that machine. *Object storage* is file storage that isn't attached to any particular VM or application and is kept on a separate system that is accessed through APIs or web interfaces.

TIP

Make sure that you understand the differences between volume and object storage for your exam and for practical reasons. You should be able to identify the type of storage for a given cloud service, and you should know the key properties of each.

Volume storage

For volume storage, the hypervisor takes a chunk of the physical storage infrastructure and virtually assigns it to a VM. A *logical unit number* (LUN) is a unique identifier that's used to label each individual chunk. A LUN can represent a single disk, a partition of a disk, or an array of disks, depending on how much storage space a cloud tenant provisions. In any case, LUNs are virtually mounted to the virtual machine for use as virtualized storage.

Volume storage is great when you need a fixed chunk of storage for with a filesystem, but keep in mind that volume storage can be used only with that filesystem and at runtime.

Object storage

Object storage is a bit newer of a concept than volume storage, and it gives developers additional options for storing and retrieving unstructured data. Instead of files being broken down into blocks, LUNs, or volumes, object storage deals with whole files that are accessed via network call. Object storage is ideal for images, documents, web pages, and any other data without a specific schema or structure.

Another key benefit of object storage is that cloud providers can charge for the exact amount of data you use (in other words: the total size of your objects is what you pay for), whereas with volume storage you're likely to have volumes with more space allocated than you're using at any given time. (Think of volume storage as having a 256GB hard drive with only 200GB being used.)

Management plane

The *management plane,* in cloud computing, is the interface and set of functions that supports and enables control of a cloud environment and the hosts within it. The management plane is typically restricted to highly privileged CSP administrators, with a limited subset of capabilities externalized to customer cloud admins.

Management planes not only allow you to start, stop, and pause your virtual hosts and services, but also allow you to provision the desired resources (CPU, memory, and storage, for example) for your environment. The management plane is the cloud administrator's primary, centralized interface to connect with the cloud infrastructure and configure their environment.

Most modern cloud providers expose the management plane to customers through a set of APIs, CLIs, or proprietary web interfaces. (AWS refers to theirs as a management console, Google's is named Cloud Console, while Microsoft's is called the Azure Management Portal.) Regardless of what each company's marketing departments might've come up with, management planes provide the interface and tools customers need to manage their cloud infrastructure, platforms, and applications.

As you can probably tell, the management plane is a very powerful tool — and with great power comes great responsibility! Because it provides a consolidated view and single-point access into your cloud environment, the management plane must be tightly locked down, with access granted to the fewest amount of people with absolute need for such permissions. In addition, all management plane access should be closely monitored, logged, and regularly audited for misuse.

Despite the increased risk associated with consolidated access, management planes offer security benefits by providing a holistic view of all your cloud resources. You're able to examine all your cloud assets and know exactly what you're running and how it's configured at any given time. This level of transparency is hard to achieve in traditional data centers, which often require the use of multiple tools, interfaces, and processes to identify and manage your IT assets.

Designing a Secure Data Center

Cloud customers are moving their data to the cloud at a rapid rate. Many of these customers are thrilled by the opportunity to offload mundane infrastructure management and security responsibilities to companies who make their money doing just that. Other customers, however, are migrating to the cloud because of regulations and guidelines like the Cloud Smart Strategy in the United States (see the aptly-named sidebar). These organizations and others are often making the move to cloud with a great deal of anxiety — and understandably so. It's easy to appreciate the reluctance an organization might have losing control and oversight of their own data centers; these companies have often done things a certain way for a very long time and have a high level of confidence in the way they secure their infrastructures. Giving that up to a CSP who says "Trust us, we've got this" is not always easy. Transparent CSPs share some (but not all) of the details behind how they secure their environments.

Whether you're a cloud customer or a cloud provider, it's essential that you understand the principles behind secure data center design. You should bear in mind that effective data center security involves a layered approach (or defense-in-depth, as I discuss in Chapter 2). This layered approach requires logical, physical, and environmental security controls that every CCSP candidate should understand.

UNITED STATES CLOUD SMART STRATEGY

The United States Cloud Smart Strategy, released in October 2018, builds upon the U.S. Government's earlier Cloud First Policy by providing a flexible framework for federal agencies to migrate to the cloud. The Cloud Smart Strategy recognizes that not all IT solutions are best suited for the cloud and encourages agencies to make technology decisions that align with their mission needs. "Cloud Smart" emphasizes the importance of security, procurement optimization, workforce skills development, and leveraging emerging technologies such as artificial intelligence and edge computing. This policy acknowledges the evolving technology landscape and aims to strike a balance between cloud adoption and other IT strategies.

Logical design

A data center's network and software design is fundamentally important to keeping customer data secure. For example, CSPs often design with tenant partitioning in mind — keeping data and resources of different tenants separate from each other. While logical data center security controls are discussed in-depth later in this chapter and in Chapter 8, this section is a good time to introduce the topic of zero trust.

NIST 800-207, zero trust architecture, defines zero trust as "a collection of concepts and ideas designed to minimize uncertainty in enforcing accurate, least privilege per-request access decisions in information systems and services in the face of a network viewed as compromised." That's quite a mouthful.

In short, though, *zero trust architecture* (ZTA) is a security model that's built on the idea that no entity inside or outside of an organization's security perimeter should be trusted. Instead of considering parties within the security perimeter as trusted, ZTA requires that identities and authorizations are always verified. This requirement prevents the common security risk associated with compromised accounts being used to pivot across a network.

ZTA relies on a number of existing technologies and processes to improve security; it leverages network micro-segmentation and granular access enforcement based on an entity's location and other factors to verify its trustworthiness. Figure 7-5 depicts the overall zero trust security model.

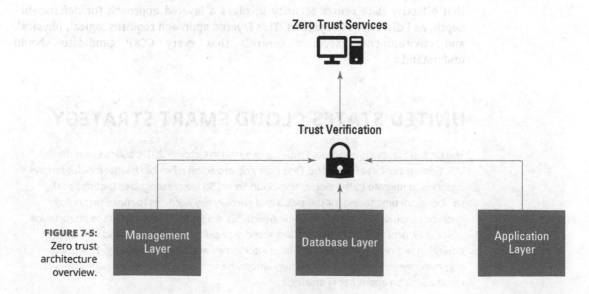

FIGURE 7-5: Zero trust architecture overview.

Physical design

The physical design of a data center includes the actual data center building and its contents, as well as the set of policies and procedures in place to prevent physical damage or compromise of the machines that store data. These policies and procedures should account for everything from natural disasters to nation-state attacks and other malicious actors.

Location, location, location!

Determining whether a data center is secure begins with its geographic location. A secure data center design should consider the following:

>> Geographical features of the area (tall trees, for example, are a wonderful and free barrier)

>> Risk of natural disasters and weather events

>> Geopolitical risk (it's worth noting if you're building in a warzone, for example)

>> Access to and costs of telecommunications infrastructure

>> Availability of utilities and other essential resources

>> Labor costs and availability

While you can prevent or mitigate some of these concerns, it's best to avoid any unnecessary risk when building a multibillion dollar facility to store your customers' sensitive information.

Buildings and structures

After you select the ideal location for your shiny new building, it's important that you design the actual building structure to reduce access control and other physical risks. Some important considerations include

>> Materials and thickness of the building's walls

>> Number of ingress and egress points

>> Type of perimeter fencing

>> Types of locks and alarms used on external and internal doors

>> Redundant electrical and telecommunications suppliers

The preceding list is just a start, but can help you begin to focus your attention on the most important building security concerns. A *Building Management System*

(BMS) is a hardware and software control system that is used to control and monitor a building's electrical, mechanical, and HVAC systems. A BMS is an important part of the physical design of any data center and helps data center personnel monitor plumbing, power, lighting, ventilation, fire suppression, and other critical building systems.

Physical security monitoring

It may seem obvious, but one of the most important aspects of physical security is ensuring that only authorized people can access the building and its critical areas. A secure data center should have a list of all authorized personnel and monitor their access to building resources. Visitors, such as vendors, should be appropriately verified, logged, and monitored as well.

Don't forget about tried and true security measures, such as video surveillance. All building entrances and exits should be monitored and recorded, and all internal doors to controlled areas (like areas with servers, HVAC systems, and so on) should be actively monitored by CCTV. As great as video surveillance is, it would be pretty useless without security staff on hand to respond to any alerts or suspicious activities; secure data centers have round-the-clock security patrols and personnel standing by to respond to potential threats.

Physical testing and auditing

No matter how great you design your physical controls, it is essential that you have a policy in place to periodically test them. Conduct physical penetration tests at least annually to ensure the ongoing effectiveness of your physical security mechanisms. In addition to testing you should do on your own, external audits (SOC, PCI, FedRAMP, and others) very often require that cloud data centers be physically audited by licensed or accredited auditors.

Environmental design

It's essential that as a cloud security professional you pay attention to the environment in which your systems exist. When designing a secure data center, consider a few key environmental concepts:

>> **Temperature:** If you've ever left your computer running for a long time, you might've felt it get pretty hot. Now imagine a few hundred thousand of those computers, each running multiple users' workloads — you've got your very own overheated data center! Temperature control is one of the absolute biggest concerns in a data center. Ensuring that servers don't overheat is critical, and failure to properly manage temperature can lead to massive availability issues. Pay attention to where servers exhaust their heat and how

you're monitoring rack temperatures and make sure your cooling systems are regularly maintained.

TIP

The American Society of Heating, Refrigerating and Air-Conditioning Engineers (ASHRAE) recommends data center thermal ranges stay between 64 and 81° F. This range has risen over the years, as computing equipment becomes more resilient and energy efficient.

>> **Humidity:** Humidity is water in the air, and water is bad for electronics. Humidity should be monitored and controlled within data centers, with 50 to 60 percent being a typical recommended range for relative humidity. (ASHRAE recommends absolute minimum and maximum humidity of 20 percent and 80 percent, respectively.)

>> **Electrical monitoring:** A secure data center should be designed to monitor electrical levels to not only trigger backup generators during outages, but also to watch for energy spikes that can damage sensitive equipment.

>> **Fire suppression:** Fire suppression systems are an absolute must in data centers. Not only do they keep data center personnel safe, but they're pivotal in preventing widespread outages and data loss should a fire occur. Hopefully, you never need them, but fire suppression systems are definitely "better safe than sorry" measures.

TECHNICAL STUFF

There are different types of fire suppression systems that depend upon on the asset type being protected and the type of fire it might be susceptible to. You should note that there are five classes of fire, based on the fuel source that the fire burns from:

>> **Class A:** "Ordinary" or common fires, fueled by paper, cloth, wood, and so on

>> **Class B:** Liquid fires, fueled by oil, grease, paint, and solvents

>> **Class C:** Electrical fires, fueled by electrical panels, connections, motors, and so on

>> **Class D:** Metallic fires, fueled by flammable materials like magnesium, aluminum, titanium, and other combustible metals

>> **Class K:** Commercial cooking fires, fueled by cooking oils, vegetable oils, and animal fats

Designing for resilience

As I discuss throughout this book, availability is one of the biggest selling features for organizations migrating to the cloud. A secure data center must be designed for *resilience*, which means being able to withstand and bounce back from possible issues or failures. Resilient cloud designs prioritize redundancy, fault tolerance, and scalability to minimize the impact of system failures or service interruptions. By spreading infrastructure resources across different areas or regions, organizations can reduce the risk of localized problems and keep services running smoothly.

The concept of multi-vendor pathway connectivity refers to the practice of establishing connectivity and communication pathways between cloud infrastructures and multiple CSPs that are sourced from different vendors. In a multi-vendor environment, organizations may utilize services and resources from various CSPs to meet their specific requirements or leverage specialized capabilities.

Multi-vendor pathway connectivity ensures that there are redundant and diverse network paths in place, allowing seamless data flow and interaction between your organization's infrastructure and the different CSPs you may use. By establishing multiple pathways, your organization can mitigate the risks associated with relying on a single CSP and minimize the impact of potential disruptions, such as network outages or failures. This approach enhances resilience by providing alternative routes for data transmission and enabling continuous access to critical services, even if one of your CSP experiences issues.

Analyzing Risks Associated with Cloud Infrastructure and Platforms

Any IT infrastructure you use comes with a certain level of risk, and it's always important to analyze those risks and determine the best ways to treat them. Many of the risks that come with cloud infrastructures are the same as traditional data center models, but some are unique to cloud environments. As a CCSP, you should know how to identify these unique risks, understand how to assess and analyze them, and be prepared with countermeasure strategies.

You should consider several categories of risk when evaluating cloud infrastructures. Some generally relevant categories are

>> Organizational risks

>> Compliance

>> Legal risks

>> Cloud infrastructure risks

>> Virtualization risks

I provide an overview of the first three categories in the next section, "Risk assessment and analysis." Cloud infrastructure and virtualization risks deserve sections of their own, which follow the next section.

Risk assessment and analysis

No matter what guidance you find in regulations, security blogs, or even this book, each cloud provider and cloud customer is ultimately responsible for performing their own tailored risk assessment and analysis. This section serves as a starting point for assessing organizational, compliance, and legal risks that cloud infrastructure presents for your organization.

Organizational risks

Organizational risks are inherently present whenever an organization outsources services to an external party — similar to third-party or vendor risk. These risks may potentially impact business processes, existing company policies, or anything else that a company views as important.

A few noteworthy organizational risks to be mindful of are

>> **Reduced visibility and control:** Customers who host and maintain their own infrastructure maintain complete control over their security (for better or for worse). If you run your own data center, you can change what you want when you want, and you have full visibility into your systems and services. Moving to the cloud means that you give up some of that control to the CSP. Customers must create a mature governance model prior to migrating to the cloud and find ways to mitigate or accept any residual risks related to control. Potential mitigations include SLA and contractual terms, as well as full utilization of monitoring tools available on your selected cloud provider.

>> **Staffing and operational challenges:** Cloud migration can introduce challenges for existing IT staff who are not properly trained on cloud computing and security. Managing and operating a cloud environment may require substantial training for existing staff or even require entirely new personnel to be hired. The skills gap that may exist creates the potential for security risks that go unnoticed or unmanaged. Cloud customers must proactively evaluate their current staff and identify training and/or hiring needs prior to cloud migration.

>> **Vendor lock-in:** Vendor lock-in becomes an issue when an organization has made significant investments in a cloud provider, but wants to move its data from that provider to another. The organization faces risks associated with greater time, effort, and cost to make the switch than planned. Vendor lock-in

risk increases when cloud providers use nonstandard formats and APIs or lots of proprietary tools. Cloud customers can mitigate vendor lock-in risk by carefully evaluating potential CSPs for interoperability and open-source support.

>> **Financial management:** Most organizations are accustomed to setting a strictly fixed IT budget every year; exceeding that budget usually means the CIO has some explaining to do. Even more confusing, though, some organizations actually have a use or lose policy that means if you fail to use all your IT funds this year, you can expect a lower budget next year. Moving to the cloud, where customers are billed for exactly what they use, can be a challenge for financial planning. Cloud utilization (and costs) can scale up and down on a monthly basis, rather than having a fairly consistent utilization from running your own data center. Further, on-demand self-service means that cloud customers must ensure that their users aren't abusing the cloud services at their disposal.

Compliance and legal risks

Customers in highly regulated industries, such as financial services and health-care, need to be concerned with data security and privacy regulations, like PCI-DSS and HIPAA. When moving to the cloud, it is still the customer's responsibility to ensure that their data meets those standards and regulations, as well as any contractual commitments they've made to their own customers. As part of these requirements, cloud customers may be required to know the following:

>> Where does their regulated data reside?

>> Who accesses (or may access) the data?

>> How is their regulated data protected?

When you move sensitive data to the cloud, you are relying on the CSP to protect it and help you meet your compliance obligations. Compliance and legal obligations are again where the Shared Responsibility Model comes into play, and cloud customers should look to their cloud provider for details on how they support compliance. By understanding a CSP's role in compliance, customers can identify what responsibility they have to ensure their data is compliant with relevant regulations.

REMEMBER

When moving to the cloud, you transfer some responsibility for protecting your infrastructure and systems. However, you're not transferring liability. Unless your contract with the CSP states otherwise, you're still legally responsible for ensuring compliance with legal regulations and requirements that impact your data.

Compliance is a huge point of contention for cloud customers, and it's insanely important that you, as a customer, perform your due diligence when moving to the cloud. Some CSPs offer customers a document called a *Customer Responsibility Matrix* (CRM), which delineates the CSP's responsibility from the customer's responsibility for each requirement in a given regulation. CRMs are formally required for FedRAMP authorized CSPs, but I've seen them available to support HIPAA and other regulations as well.

Cloud vulnerabilities, threats, and attacks

Cloud environments, at a high level, experience the same types of threats and vulnerabilities as their on-premises peers. Cloud environments run applications, those applications have vulnerabilities, and bad guys try to exploit those vulnerabilities to compromise systems and data.

The nature of cloud infrastructure, however, lends it to some very specific types of risks. I introduce a few earlier in this chapter, and I cover the following threats and risks in the next few sections:

>> Management plane compromise

>> Incomplete data deletion and sanitization

>> Insecure multitenancy

>> Resource exhaustion

>> Network, OS, and application vulnerabilities

Management plane compromise

The management plane is probably the most valuable attack target and the highest source of risk in a cloud environment. As a single interface with consolidated access to all your systems and resources, a management plane compromise can affect your entire cloud environment.

Because management planes are made available to customers through Internet-facing APIs, they're widely exposed to attackers for exploitation. Malicious actors look for weak APIs and can exploit vulnerabilities to gain access to an organization's cloud systems and data.

CSPs are responsible for securing their APIs — with special attention being given to management plane APIs. Cloud customers hold responsibility for ensuring that they use strong credentials and secure channels when accessing their cloud provider's management console.

Incomplete data deletion and sanitization

When cloud customers delete their data, they're relying on the cloud service provider to remove all traces of that data from the environment. Cloud customers have reduced visibility into where all components of their data resides, and they have very little ability to verify that all data has been securely deleted upon request.

Incomplete data deletion and sanitization can leave portions of your data available and potentially exposed to other CSP tenants who share the same infrastructure. This potential data leakage is particularly concerning for customers managing sensitive information like PII, PHI, and cardholder data.

WARNING

Incomplete data deletion in a cloud environment can lead to the compromise of data that you believed to be securely erased. I've seen companies experience data breaches in cloud platforms long after they had requested their data to be erased. While ensuring absolute data deletion from a cloud environment can be challenging, seeking a data destruction certificate can serve as an assurance that your data has been removed. Although this may not safeguard against data theft, it does establish a layer of accountability for the CSP or vendor, providing some degree of legal, compliance, and reputational safeguards.

Whereas an organization operating their own data center is able to physically shred, incinerate, or pulverize storage media to ensure its destruction, cloud customers do not have this level of control. Instead, customers rely on SLAs, contracts, and data agreements in which CSPs commit to certain processes and timelines for secure data deletion. Customers must be mindful that data deletion and sanitization processes and terms differs from one CSP to another and must ensure that their selected CSP provides terms that meet the organization's business needs, regulatory requirements, and legal commitments.

Insecure multitenancy

Multitenancy is a core property of public cloud, and it allows large CSPs to provide resources and services to thousands of customers in a scalable fashion. This architecture requires the cloud provider to use isolation controls to physically or logically separate each tenant from other tenants in the environment. Risks exist when these controls either do not exist or fail to function as intended.

Without proper separation between cloud tenants, an attacker can leverage one tenant's resources to compromise another tenant's environment. This compromise can include unauthorized access to data, Denial of Service, or other tenant-to-tenant attacks.

Securing multitenant infrastructures and ensuring effective separation between organizations is entirely the responsibility of the CSP. Logical controls, like strong encryption, are minimally required. In some cases, customers may require actual physical separation from other tenants and may request it through products like AWS Dedicated Hosts, Azure Dedicated Hosts, and Google's sole-tenant nodes.

Resource exhaustion

Resource exhaustion is another risk related to multitenancy and resource pooling (see Chapter 3). Resource exhaustion presents itself when an organization is denied resources because the resources are being completely consumed by another tenant or tenants; resource exhaustion may be malicious or not. If one or more tenant within the shared environment provisions a large amount of CPU, RAM, or network bandwidth, it can leave other organizations lacking sufficient resources to process their workloads. Reservations, shares, and limits can be used to mitigate this risk.

Network, host, and application vulnerabilities

As with any computing system, cloud environments are made up of hardware and software that may contain security vulnerabilities. In terms of cloud infrastructure, CSPs are responsible for routine scanning and patching of hosts, network devices, databases and applications under their control.

Unpatched vulnerabilities present a risk to organizations and their data; unlike in traditional data centers, customers may not be aware of this risk because of the lack of insight they have into the CSP's vulnerability management practices.

Chapter 9 provides examples of common cloud vulnerabilities.

Virtualization risks

In the "Virtualization" section of this chapter, I basically explain why virtualization is the greatest thing since sliced bread. No, I'm not going to take it all back — virtualization really is a phenomenal technology, without which we wouldn't have the cloud computing we know and love today. What I do want to do is highlight some of the key risks that virtualization technology presents.

The complex nature of virtualization technologies means you have more things to understand (or misunderstand) and more room for things to go wrong. In 2015, the Cloud Security Alliance (CSA) published "Best Practices for Mitigating Risks in

Virtualized Environments" — it's old but has aged gracefully. In the whitepaper, CSA identifies 11 virtualization risks that are broadly classified into three categories:

>> Architectural

>> Hypervisor software

>> Configuration

I list those risks and discuss some of the most prevalent risks in each of the following sections.

Architectural risks

Architectural risks are directly related to the abstraction between physical hardware and virtualized systems. This abstraction creates an added layer of complexity that presents risks to virtual machines stored or running in a cloud environment.

Per CSA, some key architectural risks include:

>> **Lack of visibility into and control over virtual networks:** Virtualized traffic is not easily monitored with existing physical network monitoring tools.

>> **Resource exhaustion:** This topic is discussed in the "Resource exhaustion" section earlier in this chapter.

>> **Workloads of different trust levels on the same host:** This risk is due to multitenancy and resource pooling. If sensitive data shares resources with less sensitive information, appropriate controls must exist to separate and appropriately categorize and secure each classification of data.

>> **Risk due to CSP APIs:** This topic is discussed in the "Management plane compromise" earlier section in this chapter.

Hypervisor software risks

As an essential component of virtualized systems, any vulnerabilities that exist in the hypervisor presents significant risk.

Per the CSA whitepaper, some key hypervisor risks include:

>> **Hypervisor security:** If not managed throughout its entire lifecycle, the hypervisor may contain exploitable vulnerabilities.

>> **Unauthorized access to the hypervisor:** Because it's the Holy Grail of virtualization, weak access control mechanisms present immense risk to cloud customers and their data.

>> **Account or service hijacking through the management portal:** This topic is discussed in the "Management plane compromise" section earlier in this chapter.

Configuration risks

Virtualization significantly speeds up the creation of computing environments. Without careful attention to secure configurations, large environments can be developed quickly and without proper security controls in place.

According to the CSA whitepaper, configuration risks include, but are not limited to the following:

>> **VM sprawl:** *VM sprawl* is the uncontrolled growth of VMs to the point where the cloud administrator can no longer effectively manage and secure them.

>> **Sensitive data within a VM:** Because VMs are just files that can be moved from place to place, lack of strong security controls (like encryption and access control) poses a risk to any sensitive data contained in the VM.

>> **Security of offline and dormant VMs:** This topic is discussed in the "Virtualization" section earlier in this chapter.

REMEMBER

While these risks are largely centered around virtual machines and the hypervisor, you should keep in mind that containers come with related virtualization risks. For example, a container's underlying host OS may be compromised and pose risk to data within that container (or within the broader containerized environment).

Risk mitigation strategies

After you understand the common risks present in cloud infrastructure, the next step is to identify some things you can do to mitigate those risks. It's important that you develop and employ countermeasure strategies that are based on a defense-in-depth approach to combating risk. Your strategy should include logical, physical, and environmental protections — and layered controls for each of those categories. For example, physical protection of your data centers should include reinforced walls, strong locks, video cameras, security guards, and a tall perimeter, among other controls.

Another part of your countermeasure strategy should be to use not only preventative controls, but also detective measures. You should certainly try your best to prevent 100 percent of compromises from occurring, but more importantly, you must have mechanisms in place to detect any of those compromises that you're not able to proactively stop. A strong combination of prevention and detection is key to an effective countermeasure strategy.

A key component of a strong countermeasure strategy is automation. Implementation, configuration, and management of security controls should be automated wherever possible. This automation helps ensure thorough coverage and also allows quicker validation of their effectiveness. Perhaps even more important, automation removes the human from the loop and prevents the killer effects of human error. When in doubt, automate, automate, automate!

As a cloud customer, focusing all your attention on protecting virtual machine instances and the data in your environment is easy. However, an effective strategy must include due diligence in determining whether your cloud provider is effectively protecting the underlying infrastructure, including the hypervisor. Although you have less direct insight into infrastructure security than you would in a traditional server model, it is your right and responsibility to request and review your CSP's security and compliance documentation.

Chapter **8**

Domain 3: Cloud Platform and Infrastructure Security, Part 2

I n this chapter, you learn about many of the key security controls that protect your cloud infrastructure and platforms. You also dive deep into the world of business continuity and disaster recovery (BCDR) planning. Domain 3 represents 17 percent of the CCSP certification exam, and this chapter covers roughly the second half of Domain 3.

Planning and Implementing Security Controls

Domain 3 covers the core capabilities of cloud infrastructures and many of the risks associated with migrating your data to one of them. I touch on some of the things you can do to mitigate those risks in Chapter 7, and this section dives deeper into how you should design and plan security controls for your cloud infrastructure and platforms. This chapter digs further into some of the topics covered in Chapter 7 and helps you understand the most important controls you can implement to ensure physical and environmental protection, as well as things you can do to secure your virtualized infrastructure.

Physical and environmental protection

Physical and environmental protection is focused on securing the actual data center by implementing security controls on its buildings, the physical infrastructure within them, and their immediate surroundings. Specific assets that require physical and environmental protection include

- Servers and their racks
- Networking equipment (routers, switches, firewalls, and such)
- HVAC systems
- Fire suppression systems
- Power distribution lines
- Telecommunications cables
- Backup generators

This list could go on and on, which goes to show the extreme importance behind physical security for a technology that is easy to view as strictly virtualized. In addition to the data center and its physical assets, physical protection must also extend to the end-user devices used to connect to the cloud environment. These devices can include desktops, laptops, mobile devices, and any other endpoint devices used by the customer. As a CCSP, you must remember that even physical protections have a shared responsibility.

The protections you need should be largely based on an assessment of the risks present in your specific situation. Among these risks, compliance risk should always be considered. Several regulations provide requirements for managing physical and environmental security; HIPAA, PCI-DSS, and FedRAMP, among others, include relevant guidance for CSPs. In addition, cloud providers have recently been increasingly considered critical infrastructure by countries around the world. As such, CSPs are being further monitored and regulated by critical infrastructure regulations, like the North American Electric Reliability Corporation Critical Infrastructure Protection (NERC CIP) in the United States.

For physical and environmental protection, security controls should minimally include

>> Policies that address the purpose, scope, roles, and responsibilities for physical and environmental protection

>> Procedures that detail how to implement and address relevant policies

>> Mechanisms to restrict access to data centers, server rooms, and other sensitive locations to authorized personnel and visitors (following the principle of least privilege)

>> Background screening for any staff with access to critical systems or highly sensitive information

>> Physical controls like fences, walls, trees, security guards, and badge readers to deter unwanted access

>> Fire suppression, water damage protection, temperature and humidity control, and other mechanisms to prevent natural disasters from causing preventable harm

>> Backup power and redundant telecommunications capabilities

System, storage, and communication protection

Despite being highly virtualized, cloud infrastructures are still a collection of physical systems that communicate with each other and with the outside world — much like within the traditional server model. Protecting these systems and communication channels again comes down to understanding the risks present in a particular environment, as well as evaluating the data being protected. Remember: Security follows the data!

Because following the data is so important when designing security controls, you should start by aligning your thinking with the cloud data lifecycle (see Chapter 5). By focusing on the state of the data you're securing, you can better develop security controls that address the specific risks that exist at any given point. Take a look at some common controls for data at rest, data in transit, and data in use:

>> **Data at rest:** The primary security controls available for protecting confidentiality at rest are encryption and tokenization. Protecting integrity and availability can be achieved through hashing controls and redundant storage, respectively.

>> **Data in transit:** For data in transit, encryption is again a useful control for ensuring confidentiality; this type of data relies on encrypted transport protocols like HTTPS and TLS. Traffic isolation through VLANs and other network isolation controls can also help protect confidentiality, integrity, and availability for data in transit. DLP is another fantastic security control to consider for data in transit, as it helps prevent data leakage through a variety of channels.

>> **Data in use:** Data in use can be protected through a combination of encryption, digital signatures, and access management controls across all APIs.

Some additional system and communications controls to consider include

>> Policies and procedures (again)

TIP

It's really hard to know what to do and how to do it if none of that is documented. You should have a policy and set of procedures for any meaningful security function that must be enforced and/or repeated. Not only is this good security hygiene, but it's also a compliance requirement for many regulations and industry certifications.

>> Isolation of security functions from nonsecurity functions

>> Logging and monitoring of traffic through boundary protection devices, including firewalls and Intrusion Detection/Protection Systems (IDS/IPS)

REMEMBER

You must have a firm grasp of where the responsibility for protecting cloud systems ends for the cloud service provider and where it begins for the cloud customer. Seek out documentation from your CSP regarding the Shared Responsibility Model and ensure that you understand what your responsibility is for your given service model and the specific cloud products and services you're using.

Virtualization systems protection

As I mention throughout this book, virtualization is the foundational technology behind cloud infrastructure, and it allows compute, storage, and network resources to be shared among multiple cloud tenants. Considering how critical virtualized infrastructure is, it makes sense that the systems behind virtualization are primary sources of cloud-specific risk that require specific controls and protection.

Protecting virtualization systems starts with the hypervisor, and you can find out about many controls for hypervisor protection in this chapter. Another important area to focus on when planning security controls is the management plane. The management plane has full visibility and control over all virtualized resources, and it is exposed to cloud customers through Internet-facing APIs. Protecting those APIs and all associated CLIs or web front-ends is of the utmost importance. As a CCSP, it's your job to break down all these components and understand the specific risks present in each before designing and implementing your security controls.

Virtualization security is a broad topic and includes many of the concepts discussed throughout this chapter. Key security controls that protect virtualization systems can be broadly grouped into three categories:

>> Vulnerability and configuration management

>> Access management

>> Network management

Vulnerability and configuration management

Software vulnerabilities in the management plane and hypervisor are particularly concerning because of what we know about virtualization. In short, a vulnerability in one of these components may not only impact one customer, but potentially all tenants that share the underlying physical systems. For example, in a *breakout attack*, a hypervisor security flaw might allow one guest to break out of their VM and manipulate the hypervisor in order to gain access to other tenants.

To prevent breakout attacks and other software exploits, you must ensure that virtualization systems are hardened in accordance with vendor security guidelines and best practice recommendations. These best practices include disabling unnecessary services and applications that can increase the attack surface of your systems and building comprehensive processes and controls for vulnerability remediation and patch management. You should automate as much of these processes as possible.

TIP

Pulling asset inventory information from your cloud APIs can help automate your vulnerability management and can ensure that you're scanning and remediating your entire cloud environment.

REMEMBER

The terms vulnerability management and patch management are sometimes used interchangeably, but they are not the same. *Patch management* is the part of configuration management that includes all processes for finding, testing, and applying software patches (or code changes) to your systems. *Vulnerability management* is the process of identifying, classifying, and fixing vulnerabilities that exist in your system. While some software patches may indeed result in vulnerabilities being fixed, many are related to product stability or other nonvulnerability related areas. Further, not all vulnerabilities can be fixed or mitigated by applying a patch. For example, some software weaknesses require disabling services or other manual configuration changes.

Access management

When it comes to access privileges, less is more — especially when controlling access to the hypervisor and management plane. Role-based access control (RBAC) should be enforced, and ideally only you (if you're the CCSP responsible for your cloud environment), your cloud administrator, and very few others should have access to your CSP's management console. The principle of least privilege means that you should set tight access restrictions that prevent unauthorized parties from modifying VM settings and accessing your sensitive resources and data.

Even with strict access controls in place, it's important that you log, monitor, and audit the effectiveness of these controls. Any administrative access to virtualization systems should be tracked in very detailed logs that identify the following, at a minimum:

>> Whether the access is successful or denied (multiple access denials is an indicator of foul play)

>> Who originates the access (username, IP address, and so on)

>> Where they are located (geolocation data can help identify misuse, especially if your management systems are generally accessed from specific locations)

>> What access path was used (CLI or web console, for example)

>> What privileged actions are taken (especially important to identify any pivots from one system to another)

Logging the proper details is a crucial control for detecting security compromises; preserving and analyzing those logs is just as important. Logs should be securely transported to and maintained on a separate system, where they are encrypted and tightly access controlled. Keeping your logs on a system that is separate from the systems being monitored adds a layer of protection against the logs being deleted or manipulated if the virtualization systems themselves are compromised.

Network management

Because network intrusions can affect hypervisors and management planes, proper network design is a fundamental requirement to protect virtualization systems. Secure network management includes suitable implementation and configuration of firewalls, IDS/IPS, and other security controls that prevent and detect anomalous or malicious network activity.

Connections to the management plane should occur over encrypted network sessions, for both cloud providers and cloud customers. Some regulations even mandate that specific encryption protocols or mechanisms be used for these connections. For example, U.S. government agencies are required to use FIPS 140-3 validated cryptographic modules when connecting to the cloud, per FedRAMP requirements. I cover FedRAMP and FIPS 140-3 (and the older FIPS 140-2) in Chapter 4.

In the traditional data center model, network perimeters are pretty easily defined. You draw an imaginary line around your important internal stuff, and that's your internal network. Another line drawn identifies the *demilitarized zone* (DMZ), which contains your perimeter devices that connect to the scary Internet. You may have some other zones in there, but the architecture at its core is this simple. In virtualized environments, the allocation of risk among systems differs from on-prem environments. When virtualization systems are not sufficiently protected by other controls, you can use additional trust zones as an added layer of protection.

TIP I discuss the topic of zero trust in the "Logical design" section of Chapter 7. While zero trust is a more recent security concept that provides a great deal of protections for virtualized environments, the concept of trust zones has been around for a long time and must be understood for the CCSP exam.

A *trust zone* is a network segment that includes systems and assets that share the same level of trust. The DMZ and internal network in the preceding paragraph are common examples of trust zones. Network traffic within a trust zone can move freely, with fewer limitations. However, traffic into and out of a trust zone is closely monitored and tightly restricted. There are many strategies for developing trust zones, and it's up to each CSP to identify the strategy that works best for their cloud.

Figure 8-1 depicts one common example of a trust zone architecture that includes a web zone, data zone, and management zone. Using trust zones allows a cloud provider to plan security controls for each zone that meet the individual security needs of the systems in that particular zone.

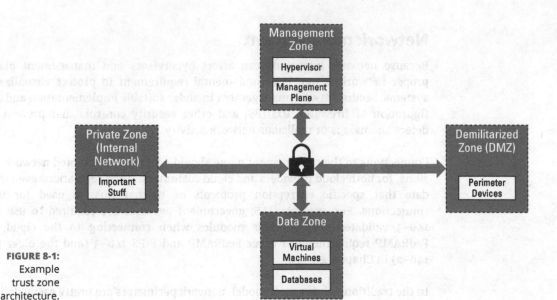

Management
Zone

Hypervisor

Management
Plane

Private Zone
(Internal
Network)

Important
Stuff

Demilitarized
Zone (DMZ)

Perimeter
Devices

Data Zone

Virtual
Machines

Databases

FIGURE 8-1:
Example
trust zone
architecture.

As the preceding example shows, keeping your data zone (which may include customer VMs, databases, and so on) separate from your management zone (which includes the hypervisor and management plane) is a great idea. This segmentation helps ensure that a compromised customer VM cannot affect other systems on the shared infrastructure.

TECHNICAL
STUFF

When connecting into a management zone from another zone, you should connect from a bastion (or jump) host. A *bastion host* is a system that runs outside your security zone that is generally designed to serve a single-purpose (like connecting to the management zone) and has been extremely hardened for enhanced security. A bastion host might reside in your DMZ and be used to allow administrators access to the management zone via a virtual private network (VPN). Because they are often the single connection into the highly sensitive management zone, bastion hosts must be stripped down of unnecessary functionality, protected with multifactor authentication, and monitored with auditing tools. You should pay close attention to failover plans for your bastion host, as they tend to be single points of failure. This means that you should have an alternate means of connecting to your management plane, in the event that your bastion host is ever inaccessible.

Identification, authentication, and authorization in cloud infrastructure

Any IT system requires you to manage identification, authentication, and authorization. Cloud infrastructure and platform environments are no exception, but you need to be aware of some cloud-specific nuances. I provide some background on these topics in Chapter 2, but this section takes a closer look.

Identification

Identification is essentially the act of giving a unique name or identifier to every entity in your environment; entities include users, servers, networking hardware, and other devices — you need to identify anything that needs to be granted some level of permission to resources. A username is the most basic form of identification.

REMEMBER

Keep in mind that cloud services, themselves, have identities and permissions that you need to manage. For example, AWS Lambda, a serverless compute service, has its own service identity that allows it to authenticate and interact with other AWS services. This identity ensures that only authorized actions are performed, providing a granular level of control and security in your cloud environment.

Just about every organization has an existing identity system or service, with Microsoft Active Directory being the most common in large organizations. Many smaller companies, academic institutions, and nonprofits choose open source identity standards instead of proprietary ones like Active Directory. Because large cloud providers must appeal to the masses, open standards like OpenID and OAuth have become the standards for cloud identity management.

TIP

You should be familiar with the OpenID and Oauth standards for your exam, and understand what they're used for at a high level. The nitty-gritty details are outside the scope of this book, but are worth investigating further.

TECHNICAL STUFF

Cloud-based identity services, like Auth0 (acquired by Okta in 2021), are designed to simplify your management of user identities and access control in your cloud environment. These services offer a centralized and scalable solution for identification, authentication, and authorization across your cloud applications and APIs, saving you from the complexities of building these functionalities from scratch and the challenges of relying on non-cloud-based services for user management.

One thing customers don't want is to be forced to manage two (or more) separate identity systems when they move to the cloud. *Federation* is the process of linking an entity's identity across multiple separate identity management systems, like on-prem and cloud systems. Federation enables a cloud provider's identity system to trust an organization's existing identity profiles and attributes and use that identity information to manage access to cloud resources. Figure 8-2 shows a typical federated identity structure, where each party has its own identity provider, and each system that accepts identity information is known as a *relying party*. I cover federated identity in Chapter 10.

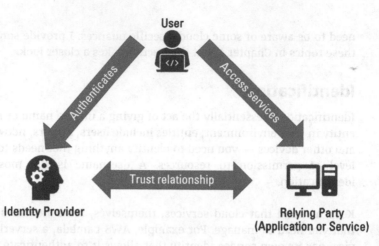

User

Authenticates

Access services

Trust relationship

FIGURE 8-2:
Federated
identity
overview.

Identity Provider

**Relying Party
(Application or Service)**

Authentication

If identification is the act of uniquely naming an entity, authentication is the process of confirming that an entity is who they say they are. The password that is associated with your username is the most common mechanism used for authentication. Your password is something that only you should know (ask Netflix), which gives an authentication system reasonable confidence that it can confirm your identity when you enter it. Multifactor authentication (MFA) enforces stronger validation of a user's identity, by requiring more than just a password (like a badge or fingerprint, for example). Using MFA is advisable whenever feasible, but should be considered a strict requirement for all privileged and high-risk access.

Authorization

Once your unique identity has been established and your credentials have been used to validate your identity, authorization is the process by which appropriate access privileges are granted. The relying party receives information about the entity from the identity provider and then makes the determination about what type of access to grant the entity, if any. The relying party determines this based on pre-set policies that govern which users and roles can access which resources.

TIP

You may come across tools and platforms like Okta, OneLogin, Azure Active Directory, and Duo. These (and many others) are examples of cloud-based identity management and active directory services that are growing increasingly popular.

Audit mechanisms

Auditing plays a major role in ensuring that IT systems comply with legal, regulatory, security, and other requirements. In a cloud environment, where many different customers share a single infrastructure, there is no way for an individual customer to do their own audits of a cloud environment. I dive into audits in Chapter 14, but in this section, I cover two specific audit mechanisms: log collection and packet capture.

Log collection

Log collection within a cloud environment can be a mixed experience if you don't know what to expect. While most cloud environments provide capabilities that enhance your ability access some logs and automate log management, your mileage will vary based on your service model and other factors.

On one hand, cloud environments make it super easy for customers to locate and centrally aggregate log data for all their assets via the management plane. Some CSPs even offer dedicated services for monitoring, storing, and analyzing your log files. AWS CloudWatch Logs, for examples, centralizes your DNS logs, EC2 logs, and log data from your other cloud-based systems. So, you can see how leveraging the power of the cloud can be a plus when it comes to log collection.

On the other hand, the types of logs you have access to in cloud environments never completely match what you can get when operating your own data center. Because of virtualization, you're not able to access hypervisor logs, which would expose too much about other tenants in the shared environment. You are largely out of luck when it comes to collecting logs for the underlying infrastructure, and the types of log data available to you decrease as you move up the service category stack (from IaaS to PaaS to SaaS). With IaaS, you'll get all the platform- and application-level logs, as well as logs for your virtual hosts (VMs) and virtual network. The PaaS service model generally has access to the same log data minus the virtual host and network logs. SaaS customers capture the least amount of log data and are usually limited to access information and logs that capture data about application usage.

When organizations migrate to the cloud, they benefit by giving up lots of the management responsibilities that come with operating a data center. Along with this benefit, cloud customers are making the decision to let go of some of the control that they may be used to. As a CCSP, it's your job to ensure that your organization understands what they're gaining and losing as it pertains to log collection.

Packet capture

Cloud-based packet capture faces many of the same challenges mentioned for log collection (see the preceding section) and is again dependent on the cloud service category being deployed. IaaS customers can conduct packet capture activities on their virtual machines, but PaaS and SaaS customers are limited to what their CSP is willing to share. As a CCSP, you must ensure that your organization understands what data is available in a given cloud and make an informed decision as to whether it meets your company's risk tolerance and business needs.

Planning Business Continuity (BC) and Disaster Recovery (DR)

I introduce business continuity and disaster recovery (collectively referred to as BCDR) in Chapter 2, and this section goes into the specific risks, requirements, and activities that go into creating, implementing, and testing your BCDR plans.

Certain characteristics and considerations of cloud infrastructures lend themselves very well to business continuity and disaster recovery; broad network access means that your organization can retrieve your critical data from just about anywhere, and large, geographically dispersed infrastructures provide you with levels of availability and resiliency that you just can't match on-prem. As great as these features are, we are cloud security professionals, and as usual, we must consider risks and other factors as we plan for BC and DR in the cloud.

Business continuity and disaster recovery strategy

In this section, I cover two categories of risk as they pertain to business continuity and disaster recovery in cloud environments. Understanding these risks is your first step toward defining your business continuity and disaster recovery strategy.

The first category is related to the risks that organizations face in traditional IT infrastructures that make cloud-based BCDR attractive, and the second category is focused on the risks involved in conducting BCDR in the cloud. For the latter, I also discuss some things you can do about those risks in order to create and implement a comprehensive and secure BCDR plan.

Risks to traditional IT

Risk exists in every form of computing, traditional server model and modern cloud computing alike. Whenever a risk can potentially disrupt an organization's ability to access their important data or conduct critical business activities, the company's business continuity and disaster recovery plan should address it. BCDR is an important set of activities that is required to minimize the business impact during and after potential disastrous events occur.

Many risks to traditional IT infrastructures can be completely solved or at least partially mitigated by migrating to the cloud. Those risks include, but are not limited to

>> Natural disaster risks, including damage from

- Flood
- Fire
- Earthquake
- Hurricane
- Tornado

>> Deliberate human risks

- DDoS attacks
- Ransomware
- Arson
- Terrorist attacks
- Employee strikes

>> Accidental human risks

- Fire
- Explosion
- Human errors

>> Indirect human risks

- Equipment failures
- Power outages
- Telecommunication outages
- Outage due to provider going out of business

While all these risks can potentially impact a cloud provider, the risk is substantially lower in cloud environments due to the vast nature of cloud infrastructures and the key characteristics of cloud.

Risks to cloud-based BCDR

Aside from risks that may trigger the use of a business continuity and disaster recovery plan, you must consider risks to a BCDR plan itself. The following risks impact any BCDR plan, including cloud-based:

>> **Cost and effort to maintain redundancy:** Any BCDR plan requires some level of redundancy, which comes with a level of financial and operational risk. If you're operating in a hot-hot configuration, you'll need to ensure that both the primary and secondary sites are fully staffed, configured, and updated at all times. Maintaining this type of configuration requires that the primary and secondary locations remain in sync, which can be operationally challenging. Syncing primary and secondary locations is made easier with cloud infrastructures because the cloud allows near real-time syncing between regions, and you can have your data maintained in multiple regions automatically. This convenience does, however, come at a cost; the higher level of redundancy not only increases availability, but also your usage fees.

>> **Performance hit due to location change:** If an outage to one cloud data center or region forces your resources to failover to another region, you can be faced with latency issues. Despite cloud infrastructures being developed and configured to run your workloads from multiple geographic regions, the way the Internet works means that the closer you are to your data, the faster you'll be able to access it. Say that you're a Texas-based company, your primary cloud region is in Oklahoma (very close to Texas), and your secondary region is in New York (kinda far from Texas). The latency and performance that you get when failing over to a region across the country may very well be noticeable (or even problematic, depending on the applications you're running). This risk can impact the cloud customer's perception of the CSP and may trickle down to affect any customers that use the cloud customer's hosted services. You can mitigate these risks by selecting a cloud provider with multiple regions available to support your geographic needs.

>> **Decreased operations during/after failover:** If you experience a complete outage of your primary site and must fully failover to your secondary site, you should be mindful of a couple potential risks:

- The speed at which you recover may present a risk to your business operations. This risk is generally less of a concern for cloud environments because of rapid elasticity, but full failover and recovery is dependent upon you properly maintaining backups of data and virtual machine instances. Again, cloud can help automate much of this risk, but it is your responsibility to configure these things according to your organization's needs.

- If your applications contain custom code or API calls to/from external services or IP addresses, you run the risk of not maintaining proper functionality post-failover. This risk can be mitigated by ensuring primary configurations are saved and readily accessible should a BCDR event occur. You should test your ability to effectively fail over to your saved configurations in a controlled manner prior to an actual event occurring.

In addition to these risks, you need to consider certain risks that depend on the particular BCDR use-case. Three common BCDR use-cases leverage cloud:

>> **Scenario 1:** Organizations use their existing IT infrastructure to run their primary workload and have a cloud provider serve as their BCDR site. This scenario is a hybrid deployment.

- **Primary:** On-premise; **Secondary:** CSP
- **Concerns:** Cloud migration can be a complex process. If any organization procures a cloud provider strictly for BCDR purposes, they must ensure that their workloads are able to migrate to the cloud and operate seamlessly in a failover situation. Use of containers within the on-prem solution can provide added portability and help ensure compatibility when migrated.

>> **Scenario 2:** Organizations run their infrastructure in a cloud environment and use a separate region of the same cloud for BCDR.

- **Primary:** CSP; **Secondary:** CSP
- **Concerns:** This scenario generally comes with the least amount of risk. The organization must evaluate the CSP to ensure multiple cloud regions exist that will support their requirements. CSPs sometimes do not operate all cloud services in every region. Make sure that you select a secondary region that offers the functionality and performance that your organization needs to continue operating smoothly.

>> **Scenario 3:** Organizations run their infrastructure in one cloud environment and use a completely separate cloud company for BCDR.

- **Primary:** CSP1; **Secondary:** CSP2
- **Concerns:** This scenario adds another potential risk, and that is the second provider's compatibility and ability to execute as required. Depending on your service model and the types of services in use, you may have to accept minor differences in functionality during failover due to the two CSPs potentially offering different capabilities. Containers are very helpful in mitigating some of these risks in a multicloud solution.

No matter what your use-case is, BCDR is an important topic that deserves a lot of attention and planning. A full assessment of potential risks is a prerequisite to designing an appropriate BCDR plan for your organization.

Business requirements

BCDR planning should be based on business requirements that are collectively generated by management from several parts of the organization (including security). Your business must establish three important requirements for BCDR, whether on-premises, hybrid, or cloud-only. I introduce Recovery Time Objective (RTO) and Recovery Point Objective (RPO) in Chapter 2; those are the most commonly used BCDR business requirements.

The third major concept is Recovery Service Level (RSL). *Recovery Service Level* is the percentage of total computing power, performance, or functionality needed during business continuity. In other words, RSL answers the question "What is the minimum percentage of my normal production that I need to maintain during a disaster?"

When determining your business requirements, it's important that you do so without regard to any potential BCDR solutions. In other words, don't derive these business requirements from the capabilities of potential CSPs. Instead, your organization must conduct a cost-benefit analysis and determine the potential cost (financial or reputational) to your business that is tolerable. This cost will translate into acceptable downtime (RTO), acceptable loss of data (RPO), or acceptable loss of functionality (RSL).

Creating, implementing, and testing BC and DR plans

After your organization has evaluated all potential risks, and you identify BCDR requirements that meet your business needs, it's time to develop your BCDR plans. Your strategy and plans should consider everything I cover earlier in this section and should help take you from concept through implementation. You can break down BCDR planning in a number of ways, but I like to use four phases:

>> Scoping and assessment

>> Creating/designing

>> Implementing

>> Testing and reporting

Scoping and assessment

The first phase in BCDR plan development is scoping and assessment. During this phase, your organization's primary goal is to establish the scope of your plan, generate your complete list of BCDR requirements and objectives, and assess any known risks. To help you understand, I break each of these out to better explain each step within scoping and assessment.

DEFINING YOUR SCOPE

When defining your BCDR scope, your organization should consider BCDR planning as an essential business function that is part of your Information Technology capability. Senior leadership from IT, Information Security, and other business areas should be included as you define key stakeholders, roles, and responsibilities, and as you continue to develop your plan. Scoping these components at the very beginning of your strategy can help you create a more comprehensive strategy with less need to gain stakeholder support down the line.

GENERATING YOUR REQUIREMENTS AND OBJECTIVES

Generating your BCDR requirements starts with identifying your critical business processes, systems, and data that need to be protected by BCDR. You must have a holistic inventory of your assets and should conduct threat and risk assessments on those assets to determine the business impact of losing access to them for a given period of time. Once you have this information, you should identify the RPO, RTO, and RSL, discussed earlier in the "Business requirements" section.

REMEMBER

Getting caught up in the dollars and cents of business requirements is easy, but remember to consider any regulatory and contractual obligations that your organization has to satisfy. If your company has built cloud-based applications and sells to other companies or operates in certain industries or countries, you may very well have external requirements to consider.

So, after you have a comprehensive matrix of your critical assets and the risks to those assets and you have a thoroughly documented list of internal and external business requirements, you can start thinking about potential types of solutions that might meet your BCDR needs.

Don't get too far ahead, though! During this step, you want to identify some key capabilities that a BCDR solution should have, but you don't want to architect your solution just yet. Start by analyzing your current hosting environment and identifying critical capabilities that need to be maintained during business continuity or replicated during disaster recovery. Combine this analysis with your understanding of critical business processes and assets and the risks they face. With all this information in hand, you should have the framework for your BCDR plan and can start assessing risks that may be exposed during a BCDR event.

ASSESSING RISK

I talk about risk throughout this chapter and cover different areas of risk through-out this book. Risk assessment is an immensely important topic to understand, and you should recognize the nuances between different risk discussions. In the previous section, I talk about identifying risks that your critical assets face; these risks inform your prioritization of BCDR features and selection of a BCDR provider. In this step, your focus should be on assessing risks associated with your potential BCDR providers (rather than on your assets themselves). Some common risks and challenges to consider include

>> **Service migration:** You must seek to understand the process a BCDR provider will use to migrate your services and data during failover. You may face longer than expected outages if the CSP lacks sufficient network infra-structure and bandwidth to migrate your workload within your desired RTO. You should also consider potential risks of getting data from your primary (on-prem or CSP) to the secondary (CSP) site. Not only must the BCDR site have sufficient bandwidth to support your recovery objectives, but you must have enough bandwidth between your primary and secondary sites to avoid length business outages.

>> **BCDR capacity:** You must ensure that the secondary site can handle the same load as your primary. Secondary site capacity is generally less of a concern with an on-prem to CSP architecture, as CSPs almost always have more available resources than on-prem hosted solutions do. However, it's important to consider capacity with CSP-CSP architectures, particularly when your BCDR site is a separate cloud provider altogether. Make sure that you understand and manage any risks associated with different SLAs between multiple cloud providers.

>> **Legal and compliance issues:** Compliance with regulatory requirements and contractual obligations is a shared responsibility between CSP and cloud customer, but the liability ultimately falls on you as the data owner. When a BCDR event occurs, you need to assess potential risks as you move from one environment to another. For example, say that you manage HIPAA-regulated PHI. If your BCDR provider does not support HIPAA regulations, then you could be in serious trouble. Risks even exist when you stay within the same cloud provider for BCDR. For example, many regulations include data location and data sovereignty requirements. If your data is required to remain in a particular country, you must be aware of your BCDR provider's ability and commitment to meeting these obligations, even during failover.

OUTCOME

The expected outcome of the scoping and assessment phase is for your organization to

>> Identify all stakeholders, including management from IT and other parts of the business

>> Assign initial roles and responsibilities for the development and approval of your BCDR plan

>> Identify and document all critical business processes and the systems and data necessary to support those processes

>> Assess and document the risk to critical business processes, systems, and data

>> Define business requirements, including RPO, RTO, RSL, and external requirements (legal, compliance, and so on)

>> Identify controls and features necessary for a BCDR provider to mitigate business risks

>> Assess the risk of all potential BCDR providers and identify initial mitigations

Creating, implementing, and testing your plan

After scoping your requirements and conducting a risk assessment of your initial BCDR plan, you're ready to create, implement, and continuously test your plan. These phases rely heavily on the research, analysis, and planning that is conducted during the first phase of BCDR plan development.

CREATING YOUR PLAN

The creation or design phase is where your organization identifies and fully evaluates BCDR options against the technical and business requirements you developed during the prior phase. It's here that you dig into the details of each potential solution and identify the one that best fits your organization's needs.

In addition to selecting a BCDR architecture that meets your technical requirements, your plan must also establish clear procedures to follow before, during, and after a BCDR event. You should establish the following items at a minimum:

>> Technical requirements for the BCDR solution, including required services, features, and capacity

» Support requirements that must be included in SLAs and contracts with BCDR provider

» Definition of events, situations, and scenarios that trigger BCDR

» Procedures necessary to invoke the BCDR solution for Business Continuity

» Policies and procedures to test the BCDR, including the frequency of testing and step-by-step process required to ensure functionality

To be effective, all policies and procedures should include a RACI (Responsible, Accountable, Consulted, Informed) matrix that identifies all relevant teams and personnel and their associated roles and responsibilities. The specific personnel required will vary based on your organization structure, but examples of key business units to include are

» Information technology (including the CIO for approvals, at least)

» Legal

» Compliance

» Administrative support

» Operations

» Facilities management

» Physical security

» Crisis management

» Human resources

TIP

Lots of teams and people get involved during a crisis or disaster. It's important that you have clear owners identified before the crisis hits so that you're not left figuring out who's responsible for what when tensions are high.

IMPLEMENTING YOUR PLAN

Okay, you've got a plan — that's great! If you haven't already, you need to make sure that your plan is fully vetted and approved by appropriate leadership in your organization. Once that's done, you're ready to bring your strategy to life and implement your plan.

Implementing your BCDR plan usually involves performing work on both your primary infrastructure and your BCDR infrastructure. The latter is pretty easy to understand, but many customers struggle with the notion that their on-prem or primary cloud implementation may need additional configurations or modifications to support BCDR preparedness. As a CCSP, you know better, and it's partially up to you to help your organization see the rationale.

Typical implementation activities required on your primary infrastructure include

>> Configuring necessary connections into the BCDR site, which may include programming API calls or even physical interconnects in some situations

>> Implementing and configuring continuous or routine backup and replication activities that support your defined business requirements

>> Implementing mechanisms that monitor for defined events and scenarios that should trigger BCDR

>> Modifying change management procedures to ensure ongoing alignment between the primary and secondary infrastructures

For your BCDR infrastructure, you're likely in a position that requires complete procurement and building out of capabilities to match your primary site. You must ensure that your BCDR site includes all the products and services that you need to ensure a near-seamless transition during failover. As a new environment, your BCDR infrastructure will need to be thoroughly tested after initial configuration.

TESTING YOUR PLAN

Once you create your BCDR plan and fully implement the required mechanisms and processes, you must test your plan to ensure that it'll work during an actual BCDR event. The objective of BCDR testing is to ensure that the plan, as implemented, meets the RPO, RTO, and other business requirements your organization defined during initial planning. Testing is not a one-time event, but rather an ongoing activity that should ensure your plan stays relevant as your systems, processes, and risks change over time.

TIP

Most regulations and standard practices recommend BCDR testing at least annually, but some regulations and contractual commitments require more frequent testing. It's also highly recommended that you do some form of BCDR testing any time your environment sees a significant change that may impact your existing BCDR procedures.

You can conduct several different exercises to test the efficiency of your BCDR plan, and each requires a different level of vigor and effort to execute. The four most common testing methods include:

>> **Tabletop exercise:** A *tabletop exercise* is a formal walkthrough of the BCDR plan by representatives of each business unit involved in BCDR activities. The

walkthrough includes reviewing the plan itself, discussing each step in the process, and clarifying roles, responsibilities, and any open questions from stakeholders. As the simplest BCDR testing method, this is not preferred for actual testing, but is better suited as a training exercise to get all stakeholders on the same page.

>> **Simulation exercise:** A *simulation exercise* is an enhanced version of a tabletop exercise that leverages a predefined scenario. Participants again walk through the steps in the BCDR, this time adding specific actions that should be followed during the imaginary scenario. These exercises generally involve some form of simulated notifications and mobilization activities, but stops short of actual physical mobilization to alternate sites.

>> **Parallel test:** A *parallel test* takes things to the next level and involves bringing the secondary site up to full operational capacity, while maintaining all operations in the primary site. Staff is mobilized to the alternate site along with any equipment and resources they'd bring during an actual event. This test is essentially a full drill that stops just shy of shutting off the primary infrastructure.

>> **Full-scale test:** Here, it's all systems go — well, actually it's one system goes down and another goes up. During a *full-scale test*, all operations are shut down at the primary location and shifted to the BCDR site. This test is the only one that provides a complete view of what would happen during an actual BCDR, but it is very expensive to accomplish.

Regardless of the testing method you select, once testing is complete, a comprehensive report must be generated and published for all stakeholders to review the testing results, including what worked, what didn't work, and any lessons learned. The report should include action items based on the lessons learned, with each action item being assigned an owner and tracked through completion. This report should serve as an input to revise the BCDR plan and the next BCDR testing exercise.

Chapter **9**

Domain 4: Cloud Application Security, Part 1

I n this chapter, you explore many of the most important application security concerns that exist in cloud environments. I provide an overview of the secure software development lifecycle process and then move into specific technologies for managing your cloud applications securely and effectively. Domain 4 represents 17 percent of the CCSP certification exam. This chapter covers the first half of Domain 4.

Cloud application development is a rapidly growing field thanks to the number of organizations that continue to migrate their applications and data to cloud-based infrastructures. As these migrations happen, it's up to the well-informed cloud security professional to guide organizations through requirements definition, policy generation, and application development. Although the process of securing cloud-based applications shares many similarities with on-premise solutions, as a CCSP candidate, you must be mindful of techniques and methodologies that are specific to cloud application security.

Advocating Training and Awareness for Application Security

While you may be surprised to see a section on training and awareness in the Cloud Application Security chapter, think for a minute about how critical application development and deployment is in cloud environments and keep in mind the potential impacts associated with insecure code being deployed across a vast cloud infrastructure. As a CCSP candidate, it's important that you're familiar with the basics of cloud application development and that you have a strong understanding of common pitfalls and vulnerabilities that exist throughout the software development lifecycle.

Cloud development basics

The key difference between application development in the cloud and in traditional IT models is that cloud development relies heavily on the use of cloud APIs. While it may almost sound like a type of beer, an *API*, or *Application Programming Interface*, is a software-to-software communication link that allows two applications (like a client and a server) to interact with one another over the Internet. APIs include the set of programming instructions and standards necessary for a client application to interact with some web-based server application to perform actions or retrieve needed information.

Because cloud environments are strictly web-accessible, CSPs make APIs available to cloud developers to allow them to access, manage, and control cloud resources. There are several types of API formats, but the most commonly used are Simple Object Access Protocol (SOAP) and Representational State Transfer (REST).

SOAP and REST both work across HTTP, and both rely on established rules that their users have agreed to follow — but that's just about where the similarities end; they are quite different in approach and implementation.

SOAP is a protocol that was designed to ensure that programs built in different languages or platforms could communicate with each other in a structured manner. SOAP encapsulates data in a SOAP envelope and then uses HTTP or other protocols to transmit the encapsulated data. A major limitation of SOAP is that it only allows usage of XML-formatted data. While SOAP was long the standard solution for web service interfaces, today it is typically used to support legacy applications, or where REST is not technically feasible to use.

REST is a standard that addresses SOAP's shortcomings as a complicated, slow, and rigid protocol. REST is not a protocol, but rather a software architecture style applied to web applications. REST is a flexible architectural scheme that can use SOAP as the underlying protocol, if desired, and supports data formats such as JSON, XML, or YAML. Part of the convenience behind REST is that RESTful services use standard URLs and HTTP methods (like GET, POST, and DELETE) to manage resources.

TECHNICAL STUFF

Five architectural constraints are required for a system to be considered RESTful: client–server architecture, statelessness, cacheable, layered system, and uniform interface. These constraints restrict the ways in which clients and servers communicate and ensure the appropriate scalability, performance, and interoperability.

Understanding the basics of APIs is important for every cloud professional and is especially important when preparing for the CCSP exam. Make sure that you understand which types of APIs your cloud provider offers and thoroughly consider any limitations and impact to your organization's cloud application security.

Common pitfalls

Being able to prepare for, identify, and understand cloud-based application issues is a tremendous skill that every cloud security professional should develop. As a CCSP, it's your responsibility to help your organization maintain awareness of potential and actual risks when migrating to or developing applications in the cloud. Failure to do so may result in application vulnerabilities that ultimately lead to unsuccessful projects, unnecessary expenses, reputational damage for your company, or worse. The issues I discuss in this section are some of the most common cloud application development pitfalls.

Migration and portability issues

Traditional on-premise systems and applications are designed, implemented, and optimized to run in traditional data centers. These applications have likely not been developed with cloud environments or services in mind, and so when migrating to the cloud, application functionality and security may not be exactly the same as what you're used to in your on-prem environments. As a cloud security professional, you must assess your on-prem applications with the expectation that they have not been developed to run in the cloud. This expectation helps ensure that proper precautions are taken when designing (or redesigning) application security controls during the migration.

In many instances, on-premise applications are developed in such a way that they depend on very specific security controls as implemented in your organization's data centers. When these applications are migrated to the cloud, some of these controls may need to be reconfigured or redeveloped to accommodate your new cloud-based solution. Remember that many CSPs offer modern security technologies that are routinely updated to remain cutting-edge. It's very likely that an application that's been hosted on a 30-year-old data center infrastructure is not properly configured for a simple lift and shift to the cloud.

REMEMBER

Lift and shift is the process of taking applications and workloads from one environment and seamlessly placing them in another, usually cloud-based, environment. It's important that you be mindful of the fact that not all applications can be lifted and shifted to the cloud due to the many technical interdependencies that exist in on-prem solutions. It's almost always necessary to modify existing configurations or change the way an application interacts with other applications and systems. Further, remember that lifting and shifting from one cloud provider to another (e.g., moving from Azure to AWS) is also likely to come with a need to modify various configurations and controls.

Integration issues

In a traditional IT environment, your organization maintains full control over the entire infrastructure — you have complete access to servers, networking devices, and all other hardware and software in your data center. When moving to a cloud environment, your developers and administrators no longer have this level of control, and in some cases, the difference can be drastic. Performing system and application integrations without full access to all supporting systems and services can be very complicated. Cloud customers are left to rely on the CSP for assistance, which may not only extend integration timelines but also increase project costs. Using the cloud provider's APIs, where possible, can help minimize integration risk and reduce the overall complexity of development. APIs are a CSP's way of providing just enough control to the customer to facilitate integration and management of their cloud-based applications.

Cloud environment challenges

When developing cloud-based applications, it is essential that developers and system administrators understand the nuances of cloud environments and the potential pitfalls that these nuances may present during application development. The following list identifies some key factors that organizations should consider before cloud-based application development:

>> The deployment model (i.e., public, private, community, or hybrid) being leveraged determines the level of multitenancy and may impact application development considerations related to privacy.

>> The service model (e.g., IaaS, PaaS, or SaaS) being leveraged is most often PaaS for pure application development projects, but may also include IaaS deployments. The service model determines how much access to systems, logs, and information your development team has.

The preceding items ultimately come down to considerations around multitenancy, shared responsibility, and customer control/access. It's important that you consider these factors to avoid common pitfalls, such as lack of required isolation (for example, as required by certain compliance frameworks) and lack of sufficient control over supporting resources. Fully understanding what deployment model and service model your application is being developed for is a critical step toward planning for and addressing potential development challenges in your cloud environment.

WARNING

Make sure that your development environment matches the production environment that you intend to use! Organizations sometimes use a development environment that has a different deployment model than their production environment — it's not uncommon to see development being done in a private cloud (or even on-premise) environment before moving to a public cloud infrastructure. Some organizations even use a separate CSPs for development and production, often for cost purposes. It's important to keep in mind that not all CSPs offer the same APIs or functionality, which may cause portability issues if you're using dissimilar environments for dev and prod.

Insufficient documentation

As a field, application development has evolved over the years into some generally accepted best practices, principles, and methodologies. Mature organizations maintain well-documented policies and procedures that guide their development teams through the SDLC. Following these policies and procedures helps developers efficiently create their applications while minimizing security risks.

As developers move to different environments, like the cloud, some of their tried-and-true methodologies don't work the way they always have. As such, organizations often find themselves with a lack of thorough documentation focused on secure development in cloud environments. Although many CSPs provide guidance to their customers, documentation often lags their speed of innovation — service updates and new releases may make existing documentation obsolete or incomplete. Ultimately, it's up to each organization (led by their fearless CCSPs) to understand how cloud architectures influence their SDLC and to accurately document policies, procedures, and best practices that take into account the additional concerns and considerations associated with cloud development.

Common cloud vulnerabilities

As discussed throughout this book, cloud environments demonstrate certain essential characteristics (on-demand self-service, resource pooling, broad network access, and so on) that help provide the benefits of cloud computing when properly understood and utilized. Having a firm understanding of these characteristics and the vulnerabilities inherent in cloud computing is critical for developers building cloud-based applications.

TIP

The OWASP Top 10 (discussed later in this chapter) and the CWE/SANS Top 25 are two of the most comprehensive collections of common software vulnerabilities.

The following categories of common cloud vulnerabilities are each associated with one or more of the key cloud computing characteristics I discuss in Chapter 3.

>> Access control vulnerabilities

>> Internet-related vulnerabilities

>> Data storage vulnerabilities

>> Misuse vulnerabilities

The following sections discuss each of these in detail.

Access control vulnerabilities

The cloud characteristic *on-demand self-service* means that cloud users can access cloud services whenever they need them. This sort of ongoing access makes identity and access management a critical concern for developers. It is essential that applications are developed and implemented with the principle of *least privilege* in mind, providing each user access to only the resources that they need to do their job.

In addition to managing users' roles and access within applications, developers should be mindful of using weak authentication and authorization methods that allow users to bypass built-in security measures, such as least privilege. Developers should enforce strong authentication by requiring periodic re-authentication and multifactor authentication where possible. For even more assurance, developers and cloud architects should consider implementing a zero trust architecture, as introduced in Chapter 7.

Another (even scarier) vulnerability is that of unauthorized access to the management plane. Some level of access to a management interface is usually required for cloud users to access their cloud resources. Without proper configuration, this access presents a higher risk in cloud environments than in traditional IT infrastructures with very few management interfaces. Cloud developers and administrators must ensure that management APIs are tightly secured and closely monitored.

Internet-related vulnerabilities

The cloud characteristic *broad network access* means that cloud resources are accessible by users via a network, using standard network protocols (TCP, IP, and so on). In most cases, the network being used is the Internet, which must always be considered an untrusted network. As such, common Internet-related vulnerabilities like Denial of Service and man-in-the-middle attacks are major considerations in cloud computing. A well-designed system (and applications) include controls that detect and prevent misconfigurations that can lead to these types of vulnerabilities being exploited.

TIP

Many CSPs offer native protections against common Internet-related vulnerabilities; for example, AWS offers managed DDoS protection via the AWS Shield service, and Google offers the Cloud Armor service for protection against a host of web-based attacks. Using cloud-native protection mechanisms is often a good way to simplify your approach to securing cloud-based application development.

Data storage vulnerabilities

The cloud characteristic *resource pooling* and the related term multitenancy mean that the data of one cloud customer is likely to share resources with another, unrelated cloud customer. Although CSPs generally have strong logical separation between tenants and their data, the very nature of sharing physical machines presents some level risk to cloud customers. In many cases, legal or regulatory requirements can be satisfied only by demonstrating appropriate separation between tenants' data. Developers can help enforce logical separation between tenants by encrypting data at rest (and in transit) using strong encryption algorithms. Where encryption is not possible, developers should explore data tokenization and other obfuscation techniques.

The cloud characteristic of *rapid elasticity* means that systems scale up and down as necessary to support changing customer demand. In order to provide this functionality, CSPs build large, geographically dispersed infrastructures that support users where they are. With this dispersion comes another legal and compliance vulnerability related to data location. While some cloud providers allow you to restrict your data to certain geographic locations, most CSPs do not currently provide this ability for all their services. When certain regulations require that data remains in specific regions, developers must ensure that their applications store and process regulated data only in compliant cloud services.

Misuse vulnerabilities

The cloud characteristic *measured service* means that you pay for what you use — nothing more and nothing less. Where this approach can go wrong is when system and application vulnerabilities allow unauthorized parties to misuse cloud resources and run up the bill. An example is *crypto jacking*, which is a form of malware that steals computing resources and uses them to mine for Bitcoin or other cryptocurrencies. Proper monitoring should be built into all systems and applications to detect cloud misuse as soon as possible.

Describing the Secure Software Development Lifecycle (SDLC) Process

Streamlined and secure application development requires a consistent methodology and a well-defined process of getting from concept to finished product. The SDLC is the series of steps that is followed to build, modify, and maintain computing software.

Business requirements

Your organization's business requirements should be a key consideration whenever you develop new software or even when you modify existing applications. You should make sure that you have a firm understanding of your organization's goals (overall and specific to your project) and knowledge of the end-user's needs and expectations.

It's important to gather input from as many stakeholders as possible as early as possible to support the success of your application. Gathering requirements from relevant leaders and business units across your organization is crucial to ensuring that you don't waste development cycles on applications or features that don't meet the needs of your business.

These business requirements are critical inputs into the SDLC.

Phases

While the SDLC process has multiple variations, it most commonly includes the steps, or phases, shown in Figure 9-1:

>> Planning

>> Defining

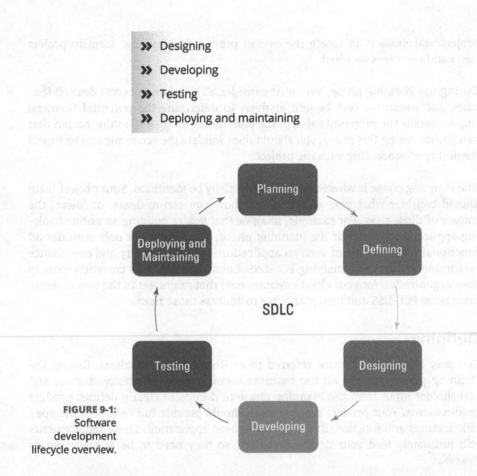

» Designing

» Developing

» Testing

» Deploying and maintaining

Planning

Defining

Deploying and Maintaining

SDLC

Testing

Designing

Developing

TIP

There's a good chance that you will see at least one question related to the SDLC on your exam. Remember that the titles of each phase may vary slightly from one methodology to the next, but make sure that you have a strong understanding of the overall flow and the order of operations.

REMEMBER

Although none of the stages specifically references security, it is important that you consider security at each step of the SDLC process. Waiting until later stages of the process can introduce unnecessary security risks, which can add unforeseen costs, extend your project timeline, or lead to avoidable security issues down the line.

Planning

The Planning phase is the most fundamental stage of the SDLC and is sometimes called Requirements Gathering. During this initial phase, the project scope is established and high-level requirements are gathered to support the remaining lifecycle phases. The project team should work with senior leadership and all project stakeholders to create the overall project timeline and identify project costs and resources required.

During the Planning phase, you must consider all requirements and desired features and conduct a cost-benefit analysis to determine the potential financial impact versus the proposed value to the end-user. Using all the information that you gather during this phase, you should then validate the economic and technical feasibility of proceeding with the project.

The Planning phase is where risks should initially be identified. Your project team should consider what may go wrong and how you can mitigate, or lower, the impact of those risks. For example, imagine that you're building an online banking application. As part of the Planning phase, you should not only consider all functional requirements of such an application, but also security and compliance requirements, such as satisfying PCI-DSS. Consider what risks currently exist in your organization (or your cloud environment) that might get in the way of demonstrating PCI-DSS and then plan ways to address those risks.

Defining

You may also see this phase referred to as Requirements Analysis. During the Defining phase, you use all the business requirements, feasibility studies, and stakeholder input from the Planning phase to document clearly defined product requirements. Your product requirements should provide full details of the specific features and functionality of your proposed application. These requirements will ultimately feed your design decisions, so they need to be as thorough as possible.

In addition, during this phase you must define the specific hardware and software requirements required for your development team — identify what type of dev environment is needed, designate your programming language, and define all technical resources needed to complete the project.

TIP

This phase is where you should specifically define all your application security requirements and identify the tools and resources necessary to develop those accordingly. You should be thinking about where encryption is required, what type of access control features are needed, and what requirements you have for maintaining your code's integrity.

Designing

The Designing phase is where you take your product requirements and software specifications and turn them into an actual design plan, often called a *design specification document*. This design plan is then used during the next phase to guide the actual development and implementation of your application.

During the Designing phase, your developers, systems architects, and other technical staff create the high-level system and software design to meet each identified requirement. Your mission during this phase is to design the overall software architecture and create a plan that identifies the technical details of your application's design. In cloud development, this phase includes defining the required amount of CPU cores, RAM, and bandwidth, while also identifying which cloud services are required for full functionality of your application. This component is critical because it may identify a need for your organization to provision additional cloud resources. Your design should define all software components that need to be created, interconnections with third-party systems, the front-end user interface, and all data flows (both within the application and between users and the application).

At this stage of the SDLC, you should also conduct threat modeling exercises and integrate your risk mitigation decisions (from the Planning phase) into your formal designs; in other words, you want to fully identify potential risks. I cover threat modeling in the aptly titled "Threat modeling" section in this chapter.

Developing

Software developers, rejoice! After weeks or even months of project planning, you can finally write some code! During this phase of the SDLC, your development team breaks up the work documented in previous steps into pieces (or *modules*) that are coded individually. Database developers create the required data storage architecture, front-end developers create the interface that users will interact with, and back-end developers code all the behind-the-scenes inner-workings of the application. This phase is typically the longest of the SDLC, but if the previous steps are followed carefully, it can be the least complicated part of the whole process.

During this phase, developers should conduct peer reviews of each other's code to check for flaws, and each individual module should be unit tested to verify its functionality prior to being rolled into the larger project. Some development teams skip this part and struggle mightily to debug flaws once an application is completed.

In addition to conducting functional testing of each module, the time is right to begin security testing. Your organization should conduct static code analysis and security scanning of each module before integration into the project. Failure to do so may allow individual software vulnerabilities to get lost in the overall codebase, and multiple individual security flaws may combine to present a larger *aggregate risk*, or combined risk.

Testing

Once the code is fully developed, the application enters the Testing phase. During this phase, application testers seek to verify whether the application functions as desired and according to the documented requirements; the ultimate goal here is to uncover all flaws in the application and report those flaws to the developers for patching. This cyclical process continues until all product requirements have been validated and all flaws have been fixed.

As a completed application, security testers have more tools at their disposal to uncover security flaws. Instead of relying solely on static code analysis, testers can use dynamic analysis to identify flaws that occur only when the code is executed. Static analysis and dynamic analysis are further discussed in the "Security testing methodologies" section of Chapter 10.

TIP

The Testing phase is one of the most crucial phases of the SDLC, as it is the main gate between your development team and customers. Testing should be conducted in accordance with an application testing plan that identifies what and how to test. Management and relevant stakeholders should carefully review and approve your testing plan before testing begins.

Deploying and maintaining

Once the application has passed the Testing phase, it is ready to be deployed for customer use. There are often multiple stages of deployment (Alpha, Beta, and General Availability are common ones), each with its own breadth of deployment (for example, alpha releases tend to be deployed to select customers, whereas general availability means it's ready for everyone).

Once applications have been tested and successfully deployed, they enter a maintenance phase where they're continually monitored and updated. During the Maintaining phase, the production software undergoes an ongoing cycle of the SDLC process, where security patches and other updates go through the same planning, defining, designing, developing, testing, and deploying activities discussed in the preceding sections.

Many SDLC models include a separate phase for disposal or termination, which happens when an application is no longer needed or supported. From a security perspective, you should keep in mind that data (including portions of applications) may remain in cloud environments even after deletion. Consult your contracts and SLAs for commitments that your CSP makes for data deletion and check out Chapter 6 for more on secure data deletion.

Methodologies

Although the steps within the SDLC remain largely constant, several SDLC methodologies, or models, exist, and each approaches these steps in slightly different ways. Two of the most commonly referenced and used methodologies are waterfall and agile.

Waterfall

Waterfall is the oldest and most straightforward SDLC methodology. In this model, you complete one phase and then continue on to the next — you move in sequential order, flowing through every step of the cycle from beginning to end. Each phase of this model relies on successful completion of the previous phase; there's no going back, because . . . well, because waterfalls don't flow up.

Some advantages of the waterfall methodology include

» It's simple to manage and easy to follow.

» Tracking and measuring progress is easy because you have a clearly defined end state early on.

» The measure twice, cut once approach allows applications to be developed based on a more complete understanding of all requirements and deliverables from the start.

» The process can largely occur without customer intervention after requirements are initially gathered. Customers and developers agree on desired outcomes early in the project.

Some challenges that come with waterfall include

» It's rigid. Requirements must be fully developed early in the process and are difficult to change once the design has been completed.

» Products may take longer to deliver compared to more iterative models, like agile (see the next section).

» It relies very little on the customer or end-user, which may make some customers feel left out.

» Testing is delayed until late in the process, which may allow small issues to build up into larger ones before they're detected.

Agile

Agile is sort of the new kid on the block, having been introduced in the 1990s. In this model, instead of proceeding in a linear and sequential fashion, development and testing activities occur simultaneously and cyclically.

Application development is separated into *sprints* that produce a succession of releases that each improves upon the previous release. With the agile model, the goal is to move quickly and to fail fast — create your first release, test it, fix it, and create your next release quickly!

Some advantages of the agile methodology include

>> It's flexible. You can move from one phase to the next without worrying that the previous phase isn't perfect or complete.

>> Time to market is much quicker than waterfall.

>> It's very user-focused; the customer has frequent opportunities to give feedback on the application.

>> Risks may be reduced because the iterative nature of agile allows you get feedback and conduct testing early and often.

Some challenges that come with Agile include

>> It can be challenging to apply in real-life projects, especially larger projects with many stakeholders and components.

>> The product end-state is less predictable than waterfall. With agile, you iterate until you're happy with the result.

>> It requires a very high level of collaboration and frequent communication between developers, customers, and other stakeholders. This challenge can be a pro, but sometimes has a negative impact on developers and project timelines.

Applying the SDLC Process

Applying the SDLC to your cloud application development requires an understanding of common application vulnerabilities, cloud-specific risks, and the use of threat modeling to assess the impact of those risks. This section guides you through securely applying the SDLC process to your cloud development initiatives.

Common vulnerabilities during development

The Open Web Application Security Project (OWASP) is an online community with a wealth of helpful projects and resources. I cover some of its helpful logging-related resources in Chapter 6, but one of the most famous projects is the OWASP Top 10, which identifies the most critical security risks to web applications. This list is particularly relevant to cloud applications, which are inherently web-based.

As of this writing, the OWASP Top 10 was last updated in 2021. The top ten web application security risks outlined by OWASP are

>> Broken access control

>> Cryptographic failures

>> Injections

>> Insecure design

>> Security misconfigurations

>> Vulnerable and outdated components

>> Identification and authentication failures

>> Software and data integrity failures

>> Security logging and monitoring failures

>> Server-side request forgeries (SSRFs)

The following sections describe these risks in detail.

Broken access control

I introduce access control in Chapter 3, and you learn about it in detail throughout this book. In short, access control is the set of policies and mechanisms that ensures users can't act outside of their intended permissions. *Broken access control* is, of course, failure of access control mechanisms to properly limit or control access to resources. Broken access control includes things like unauthorized privilege escalation, bypassing access controls by modifying the URL or other settings, and manipulating metadata to gain unauthorized access.

Prevention of broken access control begins during the Testing phase, but continues well into the Maintaining phase. Static and dynamic analysis techniques can help identify weak access control mechanisms, but security teams should also conduct penetration tests on systems that process sensitive information. In addition, enforcing a deny by default policy, validating application inputs, and performing periodic checks of a user's privilege can all help mitigate risks associated with broken access control. Finally, do not forget that detection is just as important as prevention; you must log and continually monitor access to your application to enable quick detection and remediation of broken access control.

Cryptographic failures

Many web applications collect, store, and use sensitive user information — data like user credentials, PII, and credit card data. You should always determine the data protection needs of your information, based on its sensitivity and any legal or regulatory requirements (GDPR, PCI, HIPAA, and so on). Your most sensitive data most certainly warrants the use of encryption at rest and in transit. Cryptographic failures include things like storing or transmitting data in cleartext (without encryption), using weak encryption algorithms, or not enforcing encryption (e.g., allowing HTTP instead of requiring HTTPS).

Protecting against cryptographic failures begins with properly classifying your data and identifying encryption requirements based on your business needs. Make sure you encrypt sensitive data at rest and in transit by using strong algorithms and protocols, and stay away from legacy protocols and functions like FTP, SMTP, SSL, MD5, and SHA1.

REMEMBER

Much attention is paid to properly protecting sensitive data at rest and in transit, and rightfully so! However, you should keep in mind that data that is not stored cannot be stolen. The principle of data minimization means that you should always collect, store, and use only the data that is necessary to achieve the intended purpose. Following this principle helps reduce the amount of data that you're responsible for protecting, which gives you fewer areas to focus on, while also reducing the impact of a successful attack.

Injection

Injection attacks refer to a broad class of attacks in which a malicious actor sends untrusted commands or input to an application. Vulnerable applications process the untrusted input as part of a valid command or query, which then alters the course of the application's execution. In doing so, injection attacks can give an attacker control over an application's program flow, grant an attacker unauthorized access to data, or even allow full system compromise. It's no wonder that this type of vulnerability ranks close to the top of the OWASP Top 10.

Common injection attacks include SQL injection, code injection, and cross-site scripting. These attacks are not only dangerous, but also very widespread. Many freely available tools make exploiting these common vulnerabilities simple, even for inexperienced hackers.

TECHNICAL STUFF

Cross-site scripting, or *XSS*, is a specific variant of injection attacks that target web applications. XSS enables an attacker to inject untrusted code (like a malicious script) into a web page or application. When an unsuspecting user navigates to the infected web page, the untrusted code is then executed in the user's browser using their permissions. XSS acts as a vehicle for an attacker to deliver malicious code to anyone who navigates to the infected application. The infected code can manipulate the output of the original website, redirect the user to a malicious site, give the attacker control over the user's web session, or even leverage the browser's permissions to access information on the user's local machine. As you can imagine, the potential damage caused by XSS vulnerability is huge, and it remains one of the top security concerns for cloud developers.

Applications can be protected against injection attacks by restricted privileges for high-risk actions and by performing input validation. *Input validation* is the process of ensuring that all input fields are properly checked and approved by the application prior to processing the input. Input validation requires locking down your application code to allow only expected input types and values and filtering any suspicious or untrusted inputs. As a cloud security professional, make sure that your applications check all input for malicious code or unintended input.

Insecure design

Insecure design is a new category in the 2021 OWASP Top 10 update that addresses risks related to design and architectural flaws. Insecure design refers to various vulnerabilities arising from "missing or ineffective control design," distinguishing it from insecure *implementation*. A key factor contributing to insecure design is the absence of business risk profiling during software or system development, leading to a failure to determine the level of security required for the system.

REMEMBER

A secure design can still have vulnerabilities resulting from faulty implementation, while an insecure design cannot be fixed solely by perfect implementation — said differently, insecure designs were never architected with the required security controls in the first place.

Addressing insecure design requires increased utilization of threat modeling, secure design patterns, and reference architectures. Accordingly, OWASP calls on the developer community to go beyond "shift-left" in coding, and focus on pre-code activities to achieve the principles of Secure by Design.

TECHNICAL STUFF

Shift-left and Secure by Design are two software engineering principles that you'll want to know. *Shift-left* is the concept of moving certain activities or processes earlier in the SDLC. The goal of shift-left is to identify and address issues, such as bugs, vulnerabilities, and quality issues, as early as possible in the development process. *Secure by Design* is a related concept that emphasizes building systems, applications, and products with security considerations baked in from the very beginning of the design phase; in essence, Secure by Design means that security is a fundamental and inherent part of the entire development process, rather than being bolted on as an afterthought.

Security misconfiguration

Security misconfiguration is pretty straightforward; it's when systems or applications are not properly or securely configured. Examples of security misconfiguration include

>> Use of default credentials (for example, admin:admin)

>> Use of insecure default configurations (for example, leaving firewalls in a default allow configuration)

>> Unpatched or outdated systems

>> Error messages that share too much information (for example, your application should never say "wrong username" or "incorrect password," because this phrasing gives attackers a clue as to which might be right or wrong — login failures should be reported as "incorrect username/password" or similar)

Preventing security misconfiguration starts with unit testing that you conduct in the Designing phase and continues through testing and into the Maintaining phase. It's essential that you have strong configuration management practices in place to monitor and manage configurations across all your systems and applications.

Vulnerable and outdated components

This vulnerability occurs when your application is built on one or more vulnerable framework, module, library, or other software component. While each component may have limited privileges on its own, the potential risk increases once it is integrated into your application. Using components with known vulnerabilities may indirectly impact other parts of your application and may even compromise sensitive data.

The best protection from this vulnerability is vigilant updating and patching of all components in your application. Your application is only as secure as its weakest link; failing to patch one component's security flaws makes your entire application vulnerable to attack.

Identification and authentication failures

Identification and authentication failures allow an attacker to capture or bypass an application's identification and authentication mechanisms, allowing the attacker to assume the identity of the attacked user, thus granting the attacker the same privileges as that user.

Identification and authentication failures can occur in several ways. It can be as obvious as an application allowing weak passwords that are easily guessed or as obscure as an application not terminating an authenticated session when a browser is closed. In the latter example, imagine that you're using a public computer to check your bank account (generally not advised, but bear with me). Instead of clicking the Sign Out button, you simply close your browser. If the banking site is not programmed to time out upon browser closure, then the next user of that machine could potentially open the same browser and still be authenticated to your account.

Developers can do a few things to protect applications from identification and authentication failures. Some recommendations include

>> Avoid using default credentials for any users, especially those with privileged access.

>> Enforce multifactor authentication, wherever possible, and enforce password length and complexity everywhere else.

>> Implement a session timeout for sessions that have been inactive longer than a predetermined amount of time.

>> Monitor for and deter brute force login attempts by disabling accounts after an organization-determined number of failed logins (five is a common number, but you should check your compliance obligations as well).

>> Use SSL to encrypt data in transit, wherever possible.

>> Properly encrypt and/or hide session IDs and session tokens. Do not place session IDs in URLs because users often share links.

>> Consider using a web application firewall (WAF). WAFs filter all traffic into your web application and can also support multifactor authentication. Many CSPs now offer built-in WAF services, though some come at an additional cost.

TECHNICAL STUFF

BEWARE INSECURE DESERIALIZATION

Jargon alert! Jargon alert! In computer science, *serialization* is the process of breaking down an object (like a file) into a stream of bytes (0s and 1s) for storage or transmission. *Deserialization* is, of course, the inverse operation of reconstructing a series of bytes into its original format.

Insecure deserialization occurs when an application or API takes an untrusted stream of bytes and reconstructs it into a potentially malicious file. One of the ways that malware masks itself is by breaking itself down to avoid signature detection and then relying on some later process to reconstruct it. Insecure deserialization can be used to perform a wide array attacks and can also lead to remote code execution.

Developers should ensure that applications and APIs accept only serialized data from trusted sources, if at all.

Software and data integrity failures

Software and data integrity failures occur when code and infrastructure lack the necessary safeguards to prevent integrity violations. An illustration of this is when applications depend on plugins or libraries from untrusted sources or repositories. Insecure CI/CD pipelines can introduce risks of unauthorized access, malicious code, or system compromise. Moreover, with the prevalent use of auto-update functionality in many applications, updates may be downloaded without sufficient integrity verification and applied to previously trusted software. This opens up the possibility for attackers to upload their own updates and distribute them across all installations. Another example lies in encoding or serializing data into a structure that can be seen and manipulated by attackers, making it susceptible to insecure deserialization.

Protecting against software and data integrity failures requires validating your software supply chain, ideally through a combination of automated mechanisms (such as an OWASP Dependency Check) and through manual review processes. You should review code updates and configuration changes to reduce the likelihood of introducing malicious code and always retrieve libraries, updates, and other code from trusted sources only. You can also use digital signatures to verify that software or data is coming from the intended source and has not been altered.

Security logging and monitoring failures

Insufficient logging exists when systems and applications fail to capture, maintain, and protect all auditable events. Events that should be logged include privileged access, login failures, and other events I discuss in Chapters 6 and 8. The auditable events must be captured in logs and stored in a system separate from the system being audited to ensure that the logs are not compromised if the system itself is compromised. Also, be sure to maintain log data in accordance with any regulatory and contractual requirements.

Insufficient monitoring occurs when logged events are not sufficiently monitored or integrated into incident response activities. This vulnerability may allow attackers to maintain persistence, pivot to other systems, and cause additional harm that may be prevented with early detection. The best prevention against insufficient monitoring is to develop and maintain a comprehensive strategy for monitoring logs and take action on important security events.

Server-side request forgery (SSRF)

Server-side request forgery (SSRF) is a type of attack that targets applications that accept data from URLs or allows data retrieval from URLs. SSRF occurs when a web application fetches a remote resource without validating a user-supplied URL, allowing an attacker to force the application to send a request to an unexpected destination. A successful SSRF attack can allow an attacker to gain unauthorized access to your organization's internal resources and sensitive information.

WARNING

SSRF was recently added to the OWASP Top 10 based on feedback in OWASP's community survey, despite data suggesting a relatively low incidence rate. Fetching URLs is a common occurrence in modern web applications, leading to a rise in SSRF incidents. Additionally, the growth of cloud services and the complexity of application architectures continues to increase the severity of these attacks. Given these factors, the security community considers SSRF to be a major concern.

As with injection attacks (discussed earlier in this section), input validation and sanitization is critical in preventing SSRF exploits; your developers should ensure that all user-supplied data, including URLs, are validated to prevent malicious or unexpected inputs from being processed. You can also use allow lists to restrict the range of URLs and IP addresses that your application will accept. Fundamentally, you should assume that your applications are vulnerable to SSRF (and other vulnerabilities) and implement thorough logging and monitoring to detect and respond to potential compromises as quickly as possible.

Cloud-specific risks

You probably realize that a great deal of overlap occurs between application security in the cloud and application security in traditional data center environments. Despite the similarities, it's important that you take note of the nature of cloud computing and how cloud architectures contribute to a unique risk landscape. The

Cloud Security Alliance (CSA) routinely publishes a fantastic guide that outlines the top risks in cloud environments. I cover the CSA's 2022 "Pandemic Eleven" in Chapter 4.

I won't go into the specifics of each risk again, but you should definitely check out Chapter 4, if you haven't already. What's important to remember is that your risks change depending on your cloud service category. For PaaS, risks like insufficient identity, credential, access, and key management and limited cloud usage visibility are bigger concerns because you, as a cloud customer, have a lower level of access and control than you do in IaaS environments. For application developers in IaaS environments, your risk is skewed more toward misconfiguration and inadequate change control and insider threat because your users and applications generally have a higher level of access, which poses a higher level of risk if misused. When considering cloud-specific risks, make sure that you take into account how your service category affects your application's risk posture.

Threat modeling

Threat modeling is a technique by which you can identify potential threats to your application and identify suitable countermeasures for defense. Threats may be related to overall system vulnerabilities or an absence of necessary security controls. You can use threat modeling to help securely develop software or to help reduce risk in an already deployed application.

There are numerous approaches to threat modeling, but three of the most commonly used are called STRIDE, PASTA, and ATASM.

TIP

In addition to STRIDE, PASTA, and ATASM, you may come across the DREAD threat modeling approach. DREAD is a mnemonic for five categories that require risk rating under this threat model: Damage, Reproducibility, Exploitability, Affected users, and Discoverability. Although the DREAD approach is not commonly used in practice, you should know what it is, in case it shows up on your exam.

STRIDE

STRIDE is a model developed by a team at Microsoft in 1999 to help identify and classify computer security threats. The name itself is a mnemonic for six categories of security threats. STRIDE stands for

>> Spoofing

>> Tampering

>> Repudiation

>> Information disclosure

>> Denial of Service

>> Elevation of privilege

TIP

STRIDE is an important acronym that helps you remember six categories of known threats to evaluate at every system or application endpoint. Remember what the STRIDE acronym stands for, as it may show up on your exam.

>> **Spoofing:** *Spoofing* is an attack during which a malicious actor assumes the identity of another user (or system) by falsifying information. A common example of identity spoofing occurs when email spammers modify the From: field to show the name of a sender that the target recipient is more likely to trust. Within applications, spoofing can occur if an attacker steals and uses a victim's authentication information (like a username and password) to impersonate and act as them within the application. Digital signatures and strong identification and authorization controls (like MFA) are good technical controls to protect against spoofing attacks, but security awareness training is a very helpful non-technical mechanism. It can help your users spot the signs of spoofing and avoid falling victim to attempts.

>> **Tampering:** *Data tampering* is an attack on the integrity of data by intentionally and maliciously manipulating it. Tampering can include altering data on disk, in memory, over the network, or elsewhere. Within cloud and other web-based applications, tampering attacks generally target the exchange between your application and the client. Tampering with a cloud application can lead to modification of user credentials or other application data by a malicious user or a third party conducting a man-in-the-middle attack. You should ensure that your applications properly validate user input to prevent malicious users from modifying values for personal gain (decreasing the price of an item in their shopping cart, for example) or manipulating data stored and used by your applications.

>> **Repudiation:** I introduce the concept of nonrepudiation in Chapter 6. The opposite concept, *repudiation*, is the ability of a party to deny that they are responsible for performing some action. Repudiation threat occurs when a user claims that they did not perform an action, and no other party is able to prove otherwise. In the real world, signing for a package delivery is a common form of nonrepudiation — the delivery company maintains physical record that you received and accepted the package on a specific date. In applications, an example of repudiation threat is a user claiming that they did not make an online purchase. Your organization may have just given away a free item if your application does not have controls to prove that the user did indeed

complete the purchase. It is essential that your applications maintain comprehensive logs of all user actions that face this threat. Controls like digital signatures and multifactor authentication can be integrated into certain applications to provide additional nonrepudiation for high-risk actions.

>> **Information disclosure:** Information disclosure is what happens during a data breach — information is shared with someone who should not have access to it. This threat compromises the confidentiality of data and carries a great deal of risk depending on the sensitivity of the leaked data. You should focus a great deal of attention on protecting against this threat in applications that store PII, PHI, financial information, or other information with high privacy requirements. Data encryption, strong access control, and other data protection mechanisms are the keys to protection here.

>> **Denial of Service:** I talk about DoS throughout much of this book. A DoS attack denies access by legitimate users. Any application is a potential DoS target — and, even with the high availability provided by cloud infrastructures, cloud developers must still remain aware of this threat. Controls should be put in place to monitor and detect abnormally high resource consumption by any single user, which may be an indication of either malicious or unintentional resource exhaustion. As a principle, applications should be developed with availability and reliability in mind.

>> **Elevation of privilege:** Elevation of privilege (or privilege escalation) comes last in the STRIDE acronym, but is one of the highest risk items on this list. Elevation occurs when an unprivileged (or regular) application user can upgrade their privileges to those of a privileged user (like an administrator). Elevation of privilege can give an untrusted party the keys to the kingdom and grant them access to and control over sensitive data and systems. Strong access control is critical to protecting against this threat. Applications must require reverification of a user's identity and credentials prior to granting privileged access, and multifactor authentication should be used, wherever possible.

PASTA

Most people would be surprised to hear that spaghetti and linguini can help secure their cloud environments. I would be surprised, too — that's just silly! The *Process for Attack Simulation and Threat Analysis* (PASTA) is a risk-based threat model, developed in 2012, that supports dynamic threat analysis. The PASTA methodology integrates business objectives with technical requirements, application risks, and attack modeling. This attacker-centric perspective of the application produces a mitigation strategy that includes threat enumeration, impact analysis, and scoring.

The PASTA methodology has seven stages:

1. Define objectives.

During this step, you define key business objectives and critical security and compliance requirements. In addition, you perform a preliminary business impact analysis (BIA) that identifies potential business impact considerations.

2. Define technical scope.

You can't protect something until you know it exists and needs protecting. During this step, you document the boundaries of the technical environment and identify the scope of all technical assets that need threat analysis. In addition to the application boundaries, you must identify all infrastructure, application, and software dependencies. The goal is to capture a high-level, but comprehensive, view of all servers, hosts, devices, applications, protocols, and data that need to be protected.

3. Perform application decomposition.

This step requires you to focus on understanding the data flows between your assets (in other words, the application components) and identify all application entry points and trust boundaries. You should leave this step with a clear understanding of all data sources, the parties that access those data sources, and all use cases for data access within your application — basically, who should perform what actions on which components of your application.

4. Complete a threat analysis.

In this step, you review threat data from within your environment (SIEM feeds, WAF logs, and so on) as well as externally available threat intelligence that is related to your application (for example, if you run a banking app, numerous resources are available to learn about emergent cyber threats to financial services companies). You should be seeking to understand threat-attack scenarios that are relevant to your specific application, environment, and data. At the end of this stage, you should have a list of the most likely attack vectors for your given application.

5. Conduct a vulnerability analysis.

During this step, you focus on identifying all vulnerabilities within your code and correlating them to the threat-attack scenarios identified in Step 4. You should be reviewing your OS, database, network, and application scans, as well as all dynamic and static code analysis results, to enumerate and score existing vulnerabilities. The primary output of this stage is a correlated mapping of all threat-attack vectors to existing vulnerabilities and impacted assets.

6. Model attacks.

During this stage, you simulate attacks that could exploit identified vulnerabilities from Step 5. This step helps determine the true likelihood and impact of each identified attack vector. After this step, you should have a strong understanding of your application's attack surface (for example, what bad things could happen to which assets within your application environment).

7. Conduct a risk and impact analysis.

During this final stage, you take everything you've learned in the previous stages and refine your BIA. You also prioritize risks that need remediation and build a risk mitigation strategy to identify countermeasures for all residual risks.

ATASM

Here's yet another important acronym — just in case you haven't had your fill yet! The *Architecture, Threats, Attack Surfaces, and Mitigations* (ATASM) threat modeling methodology highlights the importance of understanding the underlying architecture for the system or application that you're threat modeling. This methodology involves breaking apart (or decomposing) your architecture into logical and functional components to help find all potential attackable surfaces (e.g., system inputs and outputs) and evaluating your defenses to determine where you need new mitigations.

Secure coding

Secure coding is the foundation of building strong and robust software that can stand up against cyber threats. It's all about following the best coding practices and industry standards to keep nasty software vulnerabilities at bay and reduce the risk of successful hacker exploits.

Your organization should reference reputable resources like the OWASP Top 10 (discussed earlier this chapter), as well as ASVS and SAFECode, discussed here:

>> The Application Security Verification Standard (ASVS) is an OWASP project that sets a standard for secure coding practices for web apps and web services — particularly useful for cloud-based application development. According to OWASP, "the standard provides a basis for designing, building, and testing technical application security controls, including architectural concerns, secure development lifecycle, threat modeling, agile security including continuous

integration/deployment, serverless, and configuration concerns." Developers can use the ASVS to validate the security of their applications against a comprehensive checklist of requirements.

>> The Software Assurance Forum for Excellence in Code (SAFECode) is a global non-profit organization that shares industry-leading practices and guidance on secure software development. SAFECode offers publications on threat modeling at scale, DevSecOps, and a host of other secure coding topics.

Software configuration management and versioning

The final phase of the SDLC involves maintaining an application after deployment for the full lifetime of the application. A big part of ongoing software maintenance is configuration management and application versioning. *Configuration management* is the process of tracking and controlling configuration changes to systems and software. *Versioning* is the process of creating and managing multiple releases of an application, each with the same general function but incrementally improved or otherwise updated.

Configuration management is a major consideration for any development team in any environment. Ensuring that systems and applications remain properly configured and in harmony with one another is an important challenge. In cloud environments, where systems freely spin up and down and resources can be rapidly provisioned on the fly, configuration management becomes an even greater concern for developers and security professionals alike. Whereas traditional data center environments usually involve configuration updates being made directly on each server, cloud environments operate at massive scale that makes this task nearly impossible — and cloud customers typically lack the access or control to directly manage these systems anyway. Instead, in cloud environments, cloud developers should address configuration management by building and managing software images that are updated, tested, and deployed throughout the customer's cloud environment. To maintain consistent configuration management and software versions, cloud developers should generally seek to use automated tools and processes.

TIP

For tracking source code changes throughout the SDLC, developers can use version-control tools like Git (https://git-scm.com) or Apache Subversion (https://subversion.apache.org). Both of these tools are open source version-control systems that are used by large and small organizations to manage their code development and releases.

A bevy of open source and commercial tools are available for maintaining system configurations and software versions. Aside from the tools and features built into most CSP offerings, developers often flock to solutions like Ansible (www.ansible.com), Puppet (https://puppet.com), and Chef (www.chef.io). These tools enable a process known as *Infrastructure as Code* (IaC) that allows developers to view and manipulate their IT environments directly from lines of code using a programming or configuration language. Developers can use these tools to monitor and maintain system and application configurations, which allows centralized configuration management across their entire environment.

Many other code and configuration management tools (both open source and commercial) are available, including options offered directly by some CSPs. Your organization should carefully consider your business and technical needs to determine which tool(s) work best for your software development.

Chapter **10**

Domain 4: Cloud Application Security, Part 2

In this chapter, you dive into the depths of integrating application security within the software development lifecycle. I introduce the most important application security methodologies that you should be familiar with, and I introduce identity and access management topics that help secure your applications. Domain 4 represents 17 percent of the CCSP certification exam. This chapter covers the second half of Domain 4.

Applying Cloud Software Assurance and Validation

Having a mature SDLC process is really important. Testing, auditing, and verifying that your SDLC process is producing secure applications that function as intended is just as important. In this section, you learn about functional testing and explore various application security testing methodologies.

Functional testing

Functional testing is a type of software testing that evaluates individual functions, features, or components of an application rather than the complete application as a whole. Functional testing is considered black box testing and works by feeding the tested function an appropriate input and comparing the output against functional requirements. This type of testing does not evaluate the actual source code or the processing within the application, but instead is concerned only with the results of the processing. Because functional testing is used to test various aspects of an application, the types of tests are wide-ranging. Examples of some functional tests include unit testing, component testing, integration testing, regression testing, user acceptance testing, and several others.

TECHNICAL STUFF

Black box testing is a software testing method in which the internal design of the component being tested is not known by the tester. *White box testing* is the opposite method and involves granting the tester complete knowledge of the tested component's inner workings. Black box tests are used in cases where knowledge of the internal design is not needed for testing or in situations where you seek test results that mimic those of a complete outsider. White box testing is more exhaustive and time consuming, but allows testers to expose more weaknesses because they're given information that allows them to design tests specifically for a given application.

Functional testing within cloud environments has all of the same considerations as traditional data center environments and then some. Because you're operating in an environment with shared responsibility (between the CSP and cloud customer), you must perform functional testing to evaluate the application's compliance with all legal and regulatory obligations. You must consider how multitenancy, geographic distribution, and other cloud-specific attributes impact your specific testing needs.

Security testing methodologies

Before deployment and on an ongoing basis, cloud developers should use several application security (appsec) testing methodologies to find and remediate weaknesses in their applications. For the most part, the methodologies described in the following sections align with security testing practices in traditional data center environments, but practical application of each methodology may differ due to the characteristics of cloud architectures.

Static application security testing (SAST)

Static application security testing (SAST), or static code analysis, is a security testing technique that involves assessing the security of application code without executing it. SAST is a white box test that involves examining source code or application binaries to detect structural vulnerabilities within the application. SAST tools and processes can help you detect things like memory overflows that are otherwise hard for humans to detect. Because they analyze source code, your development team must be sure to find and use a SAST tool that works with your particular development environment and your application's programming language.

WARNING

Since SAST relies on static code analysis instead of executing code, it is often prone to high false positive rates. Be prepared for some level of manual validation of your SAST findings.

Dynamic application security testing (DAST)

Dynamic application security testing (DAST), or dynamic code analysis, involves assessing the security of code during execution. DAST seeks to uncover vulnerabilities by running an application and sending various inputs to it, effectively simulating an attack against it. By examining the application's reaction to select inputs, you can determine whether the application is vulnerable. For cloud applications, DAST scanners run against web URLs or REST APIs and search for vulnerabilities like injections, XSS flaws, and so on. DAST scanners use applications in a similar manner as a typical user and often require application credentials in order to run.

DAST is considered a black box test because testing is performed strictly from outside the application, with no intimate knowledge of the application's code or inner workings.

WARNING

DAST may impact the performance of your applications, given that it inserts itself into the execution of your application code.

Interactive application security testing (IAST)

IAST is the new kid on the appsec block, and it combines the static and dynamic analysis methods. *Interactive application security testing* (IAST) is an approach to security testing that identifies an application's vulnerabilities during runtime (like DAST), but does so from within the application code. IAST has access to the source code and the runtime environment, whereas DAST only accesses the runtime environment This enhanced access allows IAST to provide more detailed information about the security vulnerabilities in your applications.

TIP

Like DAST. IAST may impact application performance. So it works best when deployed in a QA environment, though you'll need to make sure that the same code tested in QA is what makes it to production.

Software composition analysis (SCA)

Software composition analysis (SCA) is an application security methodology that focuses on open source software. Development teams can use SCA to track and analyze open source components in your software to evaluate security, code quality, and license compliance. Like SAST, software composition analysis is also programming language dependent.

TIP

SCA is not new, but the rise in open source software in the cloud era has made it a pillar of appsec programs. It is now a key component of mature DevSecOps programs.

Vulnerability scanning

Vulnerability scanning is the process of assessing an application or system for known weaknesses. This process usually involves using a tool to run tests on servers, networks, or application that look for signatures that match known malware, misconfigurations, and other system vulnerabilities. Vulnerability scan tools typically generate reports that list all discovered vulnerabilities, rated by severity (for example, high, moderate, or low). In cloud environments, your service category (IaaS, PaaS, or SaaS) impacts your responsibility for scanning. For all service categories, the CSP is responsible for scanning (and patching) the underlying cloud infrastructure. For IaaS deployments, customers are typically responsible for vulnerability scanning their virtual machine instances and database instances. SaaS customers generally leave the vulnerability management activities up to their cloud provider, while PaaS customers' responsibilities vary based on the types of PaaS services in use. You should consult your CSP's customer responsibility matrix, user guide, or other relevant documentation to determine what responsibility you have for conducting vulnerability scans.

Penetration testing

Penetration testing (or *pentesting*) is the process of conducting a simulated attack on a system or application in order to discover exploitable vulnerabilities. A pentest may be either a black box or white box test, during which the tester uses tools and procedures similar to those of a malicious attacker. The objective of a penetration test is for the good guys to discover exploitable vulnerabilities before the bad guys do. In doing so, pen tests provide insights into high risk security flaws within an application and highlight the potential impact of those flaws.

WARNING

Do not confuse vulnerability scans with penetration tests; I've seen this done, and it's a big red flag for me whenever a security professional uses them interchangeably. Vulnerability scans are generally automated (or at least simple to execute with a few configurations), whereas penetration tests are typically manually performed by a security professional with expertise in conducting cyber-attacks. Conducting a vulnerability scan requires you to use your selected scanning tool to search your application for vulnerabilities. Vulnerability scanning is typically an early part of conducting a penetration test, but the pentest takes it further by actually trying to exploit the discovered vulnerabilities to determine how much damage can be done; a pentester will try to steal data, shut off services, and more.

Quality assurance (QA)

Quality assurance, or QA, is the process of ensuring software quality through validation and verification activities. The role of QA in software development is to ensure that applications conform to requirements and to quickly identify any risks. QA is not testing, but rather an umbrella field that includes testing, guidance, and oversight activities throughout the entire SDLC.

QA professionals are an integral part of any application development project and should work with developers, cloud architects, and project managers to ensure a quality product is designed.

Abuse case testing

Considering use cases is a common part of software development — product managers identify use cases so developers write code that meets the intended business outcomes. Use cases help you define a path of least resistance for users to get what they want. Unfortunately, this doesn't account for security risk, and so you need the opposite of use cases to define a path of high resistance for bad guys to get what *they* want. Enter *abuse cases*, which describe how a malicious user might misuse or exploit weaknesses in software to trigger outcomes that the software creator did not intend.

Abuse cases complement use cases, and you should consider having one abuse case for every use case you have. Ask yourself questions like "what happens if I feed the application unexpected input — perhaps the wrong data type or size?" or "what negative outcomes might happen if I click this button repeatedly?" A simple way to think of abuse case testing is to consider it almost like penetration testing the code itself; you're considering all the things that could go wrong and trying to find them before your code is deployed.

Using Verified Secure Software

A key aspect of software development is understanding your development environment and the components that make up your software application. Using verified secure software is critical in any environment, but even more important in cloud environments that are often comprised of or connected to many different components that are not completely within your control. In this section, you explore the use of approved APIs, management of your cloud development supply chain, and the benefits and risks associated with open source software.

Securing application programming interfaces (APIs)

In cloud computing, APIs are powerful mechanisms by which cloud providers expose functionality to developers. APIs provide cloud developers an interface they can use to programmatically access and control cloud services and resources. With great power comes great responsibility, and APIs are a major example of that. The security of APIs plays a big role in the overall security of cloud environments and their applications. Consuming or leveraging unapproved APIs can lead to insecure applications and compromised data.

As a CCSP, you must ensure that your organization builds a formal process for testing and approving all APIs prior to use. Any significant changes to an API, whether vendor updates or security vulnerabilities, should prompt additional review of the API before further use. API testing should ensure that the API is secured appropriately depending on the type of API it is. Testing an API's security includes ensuring that the REST or SOAP API uses secure access methods, enables sufficient logging, and encrypts communications where applicable.

Here are some additional API security best practices:

>> **Input validation:** Validate and sanitize all incoming data to prevent injection attacks and data manipulation.

>> **Rate limiting:** Enforce rate limiting to prevent excessive requests and protect against API abuse or DOS attacks.

>> **API tokens and keys:** Where possible, use secure API tokens or keys for authentication instead of using sensitive user credentials.

>> **Logging and monitoring:** Maintain comprehensive audit logs to monitor API activity and help detect potential malicious behavior.

>> **Error handling:** Implement proper error handling to avoid revealing sensitive information through errors.

>> **Parameterized queries:** Use parameterized queries to prevent injection attacks on APIs that access databases.

>> **Security testing:** Conduct regular security testing, including code reviews and penetration tests, to identify and address vulnerabilities.

TECHNICAL STUFF

Parameterized queries refer to a method of executing database queries in applications using placeholders for user-provided data instead of directly embedding the data into the query string. Using parameterized queries separates the query structure from user inputs, which forces the database to treat input values as data rather than executable code.

Supply-chain management

It is increasingly common for companies to integrate pieces of code or entire applications from other organizations into their own applications. Cloud applications, in particular, tend to be composed of multiple different external components and API calls. They often leverage software or data sources from one or more cloud provider as well as other external sources (including open source software, discussed earlier). It is essential that organizations consider the security implications whenever they use software components outside of their organizational control.

In many cases, developers rely on third-party software components that they don't have complete understanding of; they may need the functionality that an external component offers, but haven't validated that the component has been securely developed and tested in accordance with the organization's policies and requirements. It is critical that your organization assess all external services, applications, and components to validate their secure design and proper functioning before integrating into your own applications.

Third-party software management

While supply-chain management is focused on securely managing your use of third-party applications, you should also assess your organization's use of third parties to manage parts of your software. Examples include third-party patch management, third-party encryption software, and third-party access management solutions. Third-party software management goes both ways: You must carefully assess your organization's implementation of external software and perform due diligence on your use of third-party providers who help manage your own software, including cloud providers.

The principle of "trust, but verify" is rarely more relevant than it is with third-party software management. It's essential that your organization has third-party risk management processes that allow you to govern your use of vendors, partners, and other third parties. Remember that you're only as strong as your weakest link.

Validated open source software

Open source software is widely used by individuals and organizations alike. In cloud environments, developers heavily rely on open source applications, libraries, and tools to build their own software. Open source software is often considered to be more secure than closed source software because its source code is publicly available and heavily reviewed and tested by the community. Popular open source software often garners so much attention and scrutiny that security bugs are found and patched much quicker than their proprietary software peers.

Despite the popular belief that open source software offers many security benefits, some organizations (government agencies, for example) are a little more skeptical and cautious when it comes to open source software. Every organization should carefully assess any software component — open source and proprietary — and determine its suitability for application development and use.

Software composition analysis (SCA), discussed earlier in this chapter, is a major factor in validating the security and compliance of your open source software.

Comprehending the Specifics of Cloud Application Architecture

Developing cloud applications involves more than a development environment and your application code. Cloud application architecture requires supplemental security components from your cloud infrastructure and a combination of technologies like cryptography, sandboxing, and application virtualization. You can explore these concepts throughout this section.

Supplemental security components

I introduce the topic of defense-in-depth in Chapter 2, and it's a critical theme throughout much of this book. When developing applications, it's important not to rely solely on the application itself for security. Following a defense-in-depth approach, your application architecture should include multiple layers of security controls that protect different aspects of your applications in different ways. The additional layers of security components serve to supplement the security already built into your application development.

Firewalls

Firewalls are a core security component in both traditional IT environments and cloud infrastructures. These foundational components are traditionally physical devices located at strategic points throughout a network to limit and control the flow of traffic for security purposes. In cloud environments, however, customers aren't able to just walk into a CSP's data center and install their own firewalls. As such, cloud customers rely on virtual firewalls to manage traffic to, from, and within their networks and applications. Most CSPs offer virtualized firewall functionality, and many vendors of traditional firewall appliances now produce software-based firewalls for cloud environments. These virtual firewalls can be used with any cloud service model (IaaS, PaaS, or SaaS) and can be managed by the customer, CSP, or a third party.

TECHNICAL STUFF

Security groups are the cloud-based equivalent to firewalls. You'll find security groups in AWS and GCP, and they're called network security groups in Azure.

Web application firewalls (WAFs)

A *web application firewall* (*WAF*) is a security appliance or application that monitors and filters HTTP traffic to and from a web application. Unlike regular firewalls, WAFs are layer-7 devices that are actually able to understand and inspect HTTP traffic and can be used to apply rules to communication between clients and the application server. WAFs are typically used to protect against XSS, SQL injection, and other application vulnerabilities listed in the OWASP Top 10 (discussed in the "Common vulnerabilities during development" section of Chapter 9).

WAFs are highly configurable, and their rules must be carefully developed to fit your specific application and use case; an overly sensitive WAF can inadvertently block legitimate traffic, while weak WAF rules may not filter bad traffic. Cloud security professionals and application developers must work together to ensure that WAF rules are configured for security without loss of functionality.

Malware and threat protection

Malware protection dates back to the earliest days of the Internet when every business and personal computer needed a good antivirus program to keep it safe from the latest Trojan horse or backdoor virus. Things have evolved quite a bit since then, but the fundamental purpose of malware protection remains the same.

In modern computing, malware protection is often coupled with threat intelligence and protection. Together, malware and threat protection help intelligently discover zero day vulnerabilities and other threats to cloud applications before they become exploited. A good malware and threat protection solution correlates your cloud environment's existing log infrastructure with other data sources, including externally provided threat intelligence. In doing so, these solutions help organizations proactively identify high-risk users, actions, and configurations that could lead to data loss or compromise if undetected. Companies like Palo Alto Networks, CrowdStrike, and others offer malware and threat protection solutions for cloud-based applications.

TECHNICAL STUFF

A *zero day vulnerability* is a security flaw that is so new that the software developer has yet to create a patch to fix it.

Cryptography

Encryption is a central component of every cloud security strategy, as you read throughout this book. In cloud application architectures, encryption plays a huge role in securing data at rest and data in transit.

Application encryption at rest involves encrypting sensitive data at the file/object, database, volume, or entire instance level. Encryption at the file/object or database level allows customers to encrypt only their most sensitive information or data that has specific regulatory requirements around encryption. Volume encryption is similar to disk encryption in noncloud environments and involves encrypting the entire volume (or drive) and all of its contents. Instance encryption protects the entire virtual machine, its volumes, and all of its data; instance encryption protects all of an application's data, both at runtime and when the instance is at rest on disk.

Encryption in transit typically involves either TLS or VPN technologies; both are discussed in Chapter 2. TLS encrypts traffic within an application and between an application server and a client's browser. Using TLS helps maintain the confidentiality and integrity of data as it moves across a network. A VPN can create a secure network tunnel between the client and the application, effectively bringing the client's machine into the trusted boundary of the application. VPNs may use the TLS protocol, but take security a step further by creating a private channel for all communications rather than merely encrypting individual data components.

Sandboxing

Sandboxing is the process of isolating an application from other applications and resources by placing it in a separate environment (the *sandbox*). You can think of sandboxing as similar to placing a rotten apple in a bag separate from healthy apples; by doing so, you prevent the rotten apple from spoiling the healthy ones. Similarly, by sandboxing an application, errors or security vulnerabilities in that application are also isolated within the sandbox, thus protecting the rest of the environment from harm. Sandboxes can either mirror the full production environment or be limited to a stripped-down set of resources and are commonly used to run untrusted (or untested) code and applications in a safe manner. Sandboxing is tremendously important in cloud environments, where customers don't have the ability to physically separate resources.

TIP

As you may imagine, virtual machines serve as a great mechanism for cloud customers to create sandboxes. Just be mindful that your virtual firewalls, access controls, and other configuration settings appropriately isolate traffic from your sandbox VM to the rest of your environment.

Application virtualization and orchestration

Application virtualization and orchestration are key concepts that center on bundling and using application components, but with different purposes.

Application virtualization

Application virtualization is the process of encapsulating (or bundling) an application into a self-contained package that is isolated from the underlying operating system on which it is executed. This form of sandboxing allows the application to run on a system without needing to be installed on that system, which enables running the target application on virtually any system — even ones with operating systems that the application wasn't built to run on. From the user's perspective, the application works just as if it were running on its native OS, much like hypervisors trick virtual machines into thinking they're running directly on hardware.

Application virtualization benefits cloud users by providing the ability to test applications in a known environment without posing risk to the rest of the environment. In addition, application virtualization allows applications to run in environments that they couldn't function in natively — for example running Windows applications in Mac, or vice versa. Another notable benefit to cloud customers is that application virtualization uses fewer resources than virtual machines, as only the bare minimum resources needed to operate the application are bundled in the virtualized application.

It should come as no surprise that where there are benefits, there are also drawbacks or things to consider. Developers should be aware that applications that require heavy integration with the OS or underlying hardware are not suitable for virtualization. Additionally, application virtualization adds considerable software licensing challenges — both the virtualized application and its host system must be correctly licensed.

Application orchestration

Application (or service) *orchestration* is the process of bundling and integrating two or more applications or services to automate a process. Orchestration involves configuring, managing, and coordinating a workflow between multiple systems and software components in an automated fashion. The objective of orchestration is to use automation to align your technology stack with a particular set of business needs or requirements. By automating the configuration and management of disparate applications and services, orchestration allows organizations to spend less time managing important, yet time intensive, tasks.

REMEMBER

Orchestration may sound like it's simply the same as automation, but the terms are not synonymous. Automation generally refers to a single task, whereas orchestration is how you automate an entire workflow that involves several tasks across multiple applications and systems.

Orchestration can be used to automate many different processes. In the cloud, orchestration can be used to provision resources, create virtual machines, and handle several other tasks and workflows. Several CSPs offer cloud orchestration services, with AWS CloudFormation being among the most popular.

Designing Appropriate Identity and Access Management (IAM) Solutions

Managing and controlling access to your application and its data is front and center when it comes to application security. Identity and access management (IAM) solutions help you uniquely identify users, assign appropriate permissions to those users, and grant or deny access to those users, based on their permissions. Several components make up an IAM solution. I introduce the foundations of identification, authentication, and authorization in Chapter 8. In this section, you explore these topics further.

Federated identity

The concept of identity federation (discussed in Chapter 8) is pivotal in cloud environments, where customers often manage user identities across multiple systems (on-prem and cloud-based). *Federated identity* means that a user's (or system's) identity on one system is linked with their identity on one or more other systems. A federated identity system allows reciprocal trust access across unrelated systems and between separate organizations.

Federated identity management is enabled by having a common set of policies, standards, and specifications that member organizations share. This common understanding forms the basis for the reciprocal trust between each organization and establishes mutually agreed-upon protocols for each organization to communicate with one another. Organizations use multiple common standards (or data formats) to meet their federated identity goals. SAML, OAuth, and OpenID are the most common, and they are discussed in the following sections.

Security Assertion Markup Language (SAML)

Security Assertion Markup Language, or *SAML*, is an XML-based open standard used to share authentication and authorization information between identity providers and service providers. In short, SAML is a markup language (that's the ML) used to make security assertions (there's the SA) about a party's identity and access permissions. In a federated system, the service provider (or the application being accessed) redirects the user's access request to an identity provider. The identity provider then sends SAML assertions to the service provider that include all the information needed for the service provider to identify and authorize the user's access.

SAML is managed by a global nonprofit consortium known as OASIS (or the Organization for the Advancement of Structured Information Standards), which adopted SAML 2.0 in 2005.

OAuth

OAuth is an open standard that applications can use to provide clients with secure access delegation. In other words, OAuth works over HTTPS (secure) and issues access tokens rather than using credentials (like usernames and passwords) to authorize applications, devices, APIs, and so on. You might see OAuth in action with applications like Google or Facebook, which use OAuth to allow you to share certain information about your account with third parties without sharing your credentials with that third party.

OAuth 2.0 was released in 2012 and is the latest version of the OAuth framework. It's important to note that OAuth 1.0 and OAuth 2.0 are completely different, cannot be used together, and do not share backward compatibility.

OpenID

OpenID is an open standard and a decentralized authentication protocol that allows users to authenticate to participating applications (known as *relying parties*). OpenID allows users to log in to multiple separate web applications using just one set of credentials. Those credentials may be username and password, smart cards, or other forms of authentication. Relying parties that participate in the OpenID community can then manage user identification and authorization without operating their own IAM systems.

Cloud developers can leverage the OpenID standard as a free identification and authentication mechanism for their applications. In doing so, developers allow users of their application to sign in using an existing account and credentials.

The OpenID Foundation is a nonprofit standards development organization that oversees and promotes the OpenID framework. The most recent OpenID standard is OpenID Connect (OIDC), which was published in 2014. OIDC is an identity layer built on top of the OAuth 2.0 framework, providing a standardized way for applications to authenticate and obtain identity information about users. OIDC enables single sign-on (SSO) and secure user authentication across different websites and applications.

Identity providers (IdPs)

In a federated system, an *identity provider* is a trusted third-party organization that stores user identities and authenticates your credentials to prove your identity to other services and applications. If you've ever visited a retail website and been prompted to "Sign in with Facebook," then you have seen a real-life identity provider in action. In this example, Facebook serves as the online store's trusted identity provider and uses your Facebook account info to authenticate you on behalf of that retailer. Instead of Facebook passing your account info to the retailer, it uses your verified Facebook credentials to tell the retailer that you are who you say you are. This verification saves you the trouble of creating a new account just to buy that pair of jeans and saves the retailer the trouble of storing and securing your account information; everybody wins!

Tons of identity providers work on-prem and in the cloud. Some popular identity providers include (in no particular order)

>> Ping Identity
>> Okta Identity Management
>> OneLogin

>> Google Cloud Identity

>> Azure Active Directory

>> AWS IAM

Using a trusted identity provider can offer a lot of security benefits. Not only does it offload the need for your application to manage user identities, but it also provides a centralized audit trail for all access to your application; reliable identity providers keep historical records of all access events, which is a major benefit when demonstrating compliance with various regulatory requirements. In addition, a good identity provider provides robust security around its identity management systems, allowing your development team to focus more on creating great applications and less on foundational access security. Whether your organization uses an identity provider or manages identities internally, it's important that you give strong consideration to application identity management as part of your cloud security strategy.

Single sign-on (SSO)

Single sign-on, commonly referred to as *SSO*, is an access control property that allows a single user authentication to be used to sign on to multiple separate, but related applications. SSO allows a user to authenticate a single time to a centralized identity provider and then use tokens from that authentication to access other applications and systems without repeatedly signing in.

REMEMBER

SSO sounds a lot like federated identity — and while they're related concepts, they are not the same! SSO enables a single authentication to allow access to multiple systems within a single organization. Federated identity extends this principle by enabling a single set of credentials to allow access to multiple systems across multiple different organizations; with federated identity, you may have to enter your credentials more than once, but it will be the same set of credentials across all participating systems. Both SSO and federated identity function by using identity tokens, but federated identity relies heavily on the principle of mutual trust between separate organizations.

In the bad old days of the early Internet, it was common for organizations to require users to manage separate accounts for their desktops, email accounts, time-keeping systems, and so on. In many cases, each system would have different password complexity or password rotation requirements. This system not only wasted users' time, but also led to forgotten passwords — and even worse, written down passwords! SSO is a saving grace for users and help desks alike.

Google applications are a great demonstration of SSO in action. When you sign in to your Google account, you're able to access Gmail, Drive, YouTube, and all other Google services, without having to sign in again and again. Google apps are a pure example of single sign-on.

Multifactor authentication (MFA)

Multifactor authentication (MFA) is an authentication method requiring a user to present two or more factors (which are forms of evidence) to the authentication mechanism; the factors can come in the form of knowledge, possession, or inherence.

>> **Knowledge** is something you know. This factor almost always comes in the form of a password or PIN. It should not be something that is easily guessed or researched, such as the user's birthdate.

>> **Possession** is something you physically have with you. It can come in the form of a mobile phone with an authentication app installed, an RFID badge, an RSA token with a rotating code, or another tangible asset that can verify a user's identity.

>> **Inherence** is something you, and only you, are. Think of biometric methods like fingerprints, retina scans, voice recognition, or anything else that uniquely physically identifies you.

>> **(Bonus) Location** is the user's physical location. As devices and applications continue to become more location-aware, a user's physical location is increasingly being used as a fourth potential factor for authentication.

REMEMBER

The term multifactor specifically requires that multiple factors be used for authentication. Use of two things you know (like two passwords), for example, is not MFA and is not more secure. The security benefit of MFA comes from the fact that each factor has a separate attack vector. Make sure that you remember that you must have at least two separate types of factors in place for your implementation to be considered multifactor.

Two-factor (2FA) is the standard application of MFA and should really be the standard access method for sensitive systems and applications, as well as all privileged access. Most cloud providers and many third-party access management platforms support 2FA. In addition to passwords, they usually require "something you have," such as

>> **SMS message to a mobile device:** For this method, the target application sends the user an SMS with a numerical code; the user then inputs that code

into the target application. This method is probably the oldest on this list, and it is gradually being phased out due to the ease with which SMS can be intercepted.

>> **Software one-time password (OTP):** This method involves using a mobile application like Google Authenticator and initially configuring it with a secret key. The secret key configures the app to generate a one-time password that changes every few seconds based on the algorithm in the secret key; the algorithm is time-synced with the target application. Whenever authenticating to the target application, you use this software-based OTP as a second factor. Thanks to the time-sync, the target application is able to associate the OTP with your mobile device (and your identity).

>> **Hardware device:** This method involves carrying and using a physical device that generates a rotating one-time password.

Cloud access security broker (CASB)

There was a time not long ago when popular belief was that the cloud was inherently insecure. That belief has mostly been dispelled, as mature CSPs have demonstrated an ability to secure systems and data better than many other organizations. The one issue that continues to haunt security professionals, including those in cloud security, is user error. Enter the CASB!

A *cloud access security broker*, or *CASB* (pronounced kaz–bee), is a software application that sits between cloud users and cloud services and applications, while actively monitoring all cloud usage and implementing centralized controls to enforce security (see Figure 10-1). A CASB may be used to mitigate high-risk security events or to prevent such events altogether by enforcing security policies, stopping malware, and alerting security teams of potential security events.

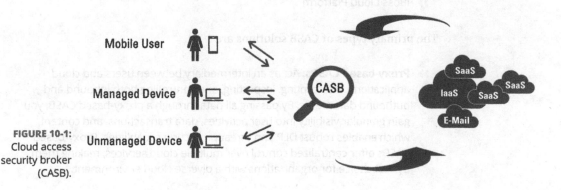

FIGURE 10-1:
Cloud access security broker (CASB).

A CASB can serve many purposes, but at a minimum, a CASB has four pillars:

>> **Visibility:** Provide visibility into an organization's cloud usage, including who uses which cloud applications and from what devices. CASBs also enforce BYOD policies and can help detect, monitor, and secure Shadow IT.

>> **Data security:** Monitor the security of data owned and operated by the organization. CASBs can help prevent data exfiltration through cloud services and can enforce specific security policies based on the user, data, or activity.

>> **Threat protection:** By providing a comprehensive view of cloud usage, CASBs can help guard against insider threats, both malicious and accidental.

>> **Compliance:** Help organizations demonstrate compliance with regulatory requirements like HIPAA, PCI-DSS, and GDPR.

From a security perspective, most CASBs are able to enforce policies related to authentication and authorization (including SSO), logging, encryption, malware prevention, and more.

The CASB market has exploded in recent years. Some popular names in the space (in no particular order) include

>> Cisco Cloudlock

>> Netskope Cloud Security Platform

>> Palo Alto Networks Next-Gen CASB

>> Proofpoint Cloud App Security Broker

>> Forcepoint CASB

>> Oracle CASB

>> iBoss Cloud Platform

The primary types of CASB solutions are

>> **Proxy-based CASBs:** Act as an intermediary between users and cloud applications, intercepting, inspecting, and controlling both inbound and outbound data traffic. By passing all data through a proxy-based CASB, you gain granular visibility into user activities, data transactions, and content, which enables robust DLP and threat protection capabilities. Proxy-based CASBs offer centralized control over multiple cloud services, making them a great choice for organizations with a diverse cloud environment.

>> **API-based CASBs:** Integrate directly with CSPs through APIs and allow organizations to enable CASB protection for any user on any device from any location. API-based CASBs monitor data within the cloud itself, rather than on a proxy at the perimeter. There's no need to install anything on user devices, and it's also much more performance-friendly than both proxy-based methods. A major limitation, however, is that not all cloud applications provide API support. API-based CASBs are particularly well-suited for SaaS applications, but not as good as proxy-based CASBs at securing complex, multicloud environments.

Secrets management

The best way to keep a secret safe is to never tell anyone. Of course, in the software world, developers use secrets (like passwords, API and encryption keys, tokens, and other digital credentials) all the time. *Secrets management* is the set of processes and tools used to securely create, store, and manage all of your digital secrets. Secrets management is all about protecting your critical secrets from unauthorized access, misuse, or exposure.

Managing secrets is fairly straightforward for smaller software projects. However, the complexity of handling secrets increases as your teams and codebases grow. In a typical application ecosystem, various secrets may be distributed across microservices, development tools, containers, orchestrators, and API connections — making managing these secrets incredibly challenging.

Many cloud providers offer secrets management services — AWS and Google both aptly call theirs "Secrets Manager," and Microsoft offers Azure Key Vault. There are also several other vendor options available for securely managing your secrets. Regardless of your choice, it's essential that you pick a tool to manage your secrets and build secrets management into your software development lifecycle.

WARNING

It's not uncommon to find secrets hardcoded in scripts, source code, or configurations. This is one of the biggest security risks in application development, and you should ensure your development teams avoid this practice. Training and awareness goes a long way to ensure that your developers use sound secrets management practices and tools to keep your organization's secrets. . . secret.

TIP

See Appendix B for a helpful Secrets Management Cheat Sheet from OWASP.

Chapter **11**

Domain 5: Cloud Security Operations, Part 1

I n this chapter, you focus on building, implementing, operating, and maintaining a physical and logical cloud infrastructure from beginning to end. Domain 5 represents 16 percent of the CCSP certification exam, and this chapter covers the first part of Domain 5.

Cloud security operations is all about the day-to-day tasks necessary for you to protect the confidentiality, integrity, and availability of cloud systems and the data that reside on them. In this domain, I cover planning, designing, implementing, and operating your cloud's physical and logical infrastructure.

Building and Implementing a Physical and Logical Infrastructure for a Cloud Environment

Securely operating a cloud environment begins with building and implementing your physical and logical infrastructure with security in mind. This step starts with careful planning and implementation of physical components, such as servers, networking equipment, and storage devices, and also requires thorough consideration of the logical infrastructure aspects that separate cloud environments from traditional data centers.

Hardware-specific security configuration requirements

As with traditional data centers, a cloud data center's infrastructure begins with its physical hardware — all the servers, networking devices, and storage components that you'd find in the on-premise world. While these environments have many similarities, there are some unique points to consider when implementing and building a cloud infrastructure. There are many types of hardware components, each with countless combinations of configuration requirements and settings. This variety becomes even more pronounced in a cloud environment due to the sheer size of cloud infrastructures and the often diverse set of hardware devices that need to be configured and secured.

Basic Input Output Systems (BIOS)

Basic Input Output System, or BIOS, is firmware that initializes and tests computer hardware before booting the operating system. BIOS is the first piece of code to run on a machine when it is powered on. All physical computing devices, including those used in cloud infrastructures, have BIOS settings that configure the hardware and manage the data flow between the device's OS and other components.

Because it is the first code a computer sees, the BIOS is incredibly powerful and important to protect. A successful compromise of the BIOS can be difficult to detect and have a major impact on your system's security. In cloud environments, the BIOS can impact the functioning and security of the hypervisor, Trusted Platform Module (discussed in the next section), and other critical virtualization hardware. It's important that the CSP tightly restrict access to BIOS settings and limit the ability for settings to be accessed and/or modified by unauthorized parties. The principle of least privilege should be followed, and only a select few privileged CSP personnel should be able to access the BIOS of any system. Even still, this limited access should be closely monitored for any malicious misuse or accidental damage. Each hardware vendor has its own methods for BIOS management. CSP security personnel should check with the vendor for any recommended BIOS security and general physical device management recommendations.

TECHNICAL STUFF

I should note that most modern computing devices replace the traditional BIOS with its successor, the UEFI. *Unified Extensible Firmware Interface* (UEFI) is a backwards-compatible specification that improves on legacy BIOS functionality and security. UEFI can theoretically address hard drives with capacities up to 9.4 zettabytes (1 zettabyte is equal to 1 billion terabytes — so, yeah, that's a lot), supports systems with more than four partitions, enables faster booting, and other modern computing features. Despite these improvements, most systems that run a UEFI still refer to its configuration as BIOS settings.

Trusted platform module (TPM)

A *trusted platform module* (TPM) is a microcontroller (computer chip) that is designed to provide hardware-based security functions to a system. A TPM is a secure crypto processor, which is a dedicated chip that carries out cryptographic operations. In other words, a TPM securely stores credentials in the form of passwords, certificates, or encryption keys and can be used to ensure that a platform or system is what it claims to be (in other words, it provides authentication). The chip is physically secured to make it tamper-resistant and logically secured to protect against software interfering with its security functions. By being hardware-based and physically secured, a TPM can help protect against compromised operating systems, privileged account misuse, and other software-based vulnerabilities.

TIP

Trusted platform module was standardized by the International Organization for Standardization (ISO) and International Electrotechnical Commission (IEC) in 2009 as ISO/IEC 11889. Refer to that standard for additional architectural and security information related to TPMs.

A trusted platform module can be used for a variety of security-related functions. Some common uses include

>> **Platform integrity:** A TPM performs checks to ensure that a platform (whatever computing device you've secured with the TPM) boots into a known-good state and is behaving as intended. When a platform is powered on, the TPM validates that a trusted combination of hardware and software is in place before fully booting the OS. A UEFI uses this feature, which is considered establishing a root of trust.

>> **Drive encryption:** Full disk encryption (FDE) tools like BitLocker leverage this functionality to protect disk encryption keys. When encrypting a drive or disk, you can seal the encryption keys within a TPM. Doing so ensures that the drive cannot be decrypted unless the operating system has securely booted into a known-good state. In other words, if an attacker compromises your OS, it's not able to regain control over your system after a reboot because the compromised OS will not pass the integrity checks of the TPM.

>> **Password protection:** Passwords that are stored and authenticated using only software mechanisms are prone to dictionary attacks and other software-based vulnerabilities. By storing passwords in a TPM, passwords are protected from such attacks and allow more secure authentication.

You may be thinking that the concept of a trusted platform module sounds amazing, but maybe you don't quite see how it can help secure cloud environments or cloud customers. Well, for one, many CSPs leverage TPMs to protect their critical infrastructure from unauthorized changes and to ensure that their complex infrastructures maintain a high level of integrity as things rapidly change. Even more exciting, many CSPs now provide customers with additional security by providing virtual trusted platform modules that perform the same functions as hardware-based TPMs using software.

I introduce the topic of virtualization and discuss hypervisors in Chapter 4. As you learn throughout this book, cloud computing's reliance on virtualized hardware often requires security features that are similar to traditional IT, but slightly nuanced and tailored to cloud environments. A *virtual TPM* (vTPM) is provided by the hypervisor and brings the security goodness of physical TPMs to virtual machines and guest operating systems. vTPMs rely on the hypervisor to provide an isolated environment that is segregated from the actual virtual machines in order to secure the TPM code from the VM's OS and applications. When properly implemented, a vTPM can provide the same level of security as a hardware or firmware-based TPM.

While a physical TPM can store its secrets in what's called *nonvolatile secure storage* (basically a hardware-based storage unit), a virtual TPM does not have that luxury. Instead, when a virtualized component writes secrets to a vTPM, it actually stores it in a file that is separately encrypted at rest, outside of the virtual machine, to provide its own form of tamper-resistance. Additionally, CSPs must encrypt this sensitive information in transit between machines, to ensure comprehensive protection of sensitive vTPM data.

Hardware security module (HSM)

A *hardware security module (HSM)* is a specialized hardware device designed to act as a secure environment for generating, storing, and managing cryptographic keys, as well as performing cryptographic operations (encryption and decryption). HSMs allow cloud users to generate secrets and perform operations on secrets, without giving the cloud users access to those secrets. By using an HSM with your cloud infrastructure, you can ensure that your organization's most sensitive operations, such as authentication, digital signatures, and data encryption, are carried out within a controlled and isolated environment.

In cloud environments, HSMs offer a critical layer of protection for sensitive data and cryptographic keys by preventing unauthorized access to cryptographic materials in a tamper-resistant hardware device. Even gaining physical access to an HSM does not offer access to the secrets. In fact, many HSMs automatically destroy keys if the HSM is tampered with.

TECHNICAL STUFF

As you can tell, HSMs share some similarities with TPMs (discussed in the previous section), but there are some noteworthy differences. Most glaringly, HSMs are designed to be used in data centers, while TPMs are designed to support a single system. A TPM is closely integrated with its host computer, operating system, and booting sequence. On the flip side, an HSM is a more generic device that can typically be made available to any application in an environment. Additionally, HSMs are more powerful than TPMs. In fact, a high-end HSM is often faster than a CPU when performing cryptographic operations.

Storage controllers

A *storage controller* (also sometimes called a *disk array controller*) is a device that manages and controls storage arrays. It virtually integrates multiple physically storage units into a single logical pool of storage and dynamically determines where to write and read data.

Many storage controllers are equipped with security features, such as controller based encryption. With this technology, the storage controller encrypts data at the controller-level before being sent to disk, which helps protect the confidentiality and integrity of data that moves across the storage controller. Available security features and options vary depending on the vendor of your particular storage controller. Cloud security professionals should evaluate all vendor-specific security features and determine which are suitable for their cloud environment. It's also important to consult vendor documentation for recommended best practices in implementing and configuring storage controllers securely.

For virtualized environments, storage controllers and associated traffic should be segregated on its own network on the data plane, which allows designated security controls to be applied to the highly sensitive operations of reading, writing, and control data flow. Whenever storage controllers offer the built-in encryption functionality discussed earlier in this section, you should use it. When built-in encryption isn't supported, then it becomes important to use other compensating security controls (like network segregation) to protect data in transit through the storage controller.

Storage controllers may operate with one of several interfaces and protocols. Cloud environments often rely on the iSCSI protocol for virtualized, network-based storage. *iSCSI* stands for *Internet Small Computer Systems Interface* and is an IP-based storage standard that enables the use of SCSI over TCP/IP networks. iSCSI essentially enables block-level data storage over LANs, WANs, or the public Internet — giving virtualized storage the look and feel of physical storage via Storage Area Networks. iSCSI supports security protocols and features, such as the Challenge-Handshake Authentication Protocol (CHAP) and Kerberos (for authentication) and IPsec (for encrypted communications). It's important that cloud security professional use these and other security mechanisms to secure storage controllers and their associated protocols.

Network controllers

A *network controller* is a centralized point of control used to configure, manage, and monitor a physical and virtual network infrastructure. A network controller assists in automated management of vast networks and eliminates the need for manual configuration of network components. In cloud environments, network controllers are an integral part of Software-Defined Networking (SDN), which I discuss in Chapter 7.

Installing and configuring management tools

From hypervisors to Software-Defined Networks, and everything in between, virtualization is the backbone of cloud infrastructures. *Virtualization management tools* interface with virtualized components as well as the underlying physical hardware to oversee and manage the operations of the virtualized environment. With such a heavy reliance on virtualization, cloud security professionals must ensure that careful attention is given to securely installing and configuring these management tools. The tools that manage the hypervisor and management plane are incredibly sensitive and must be protected at all costs! Successful attacks against virtualization management tools can compromise the confidentiality and integrity of cloud user data or even jeopardize the availability of the entire infrastructure.

There are many types of virtualization technologies, and even more virtualization vendors that supply them. Each vendor generally has its own tools and guidelines for managing and securing their products. As with any third-party product, you should first consult your particular virtualization vendor's documentation and support team for installation and configuration guidance. In my experience, the best cloud providers form strong relationships with their vendors, and I'd recommend that any organization with a highly virtualized environment establish similarly strong relationships with their vendors. If possible, you should form these relationships early in the development of your cloud solution and leverage your vendors' guidance throughout the entire development lifecycle.

Management tools, when properly configured, provide you with greater awareness and automation of your cloud environment:

>> **Awareness:** Configure your management tools to capture a unified view of your entire virtualized environment and all associated components. Using virtualization management tools provides the unique ability to see and understand your whole environment at a glance.

>> **Automation:** Configure your virtualization management tools to automate standard infrastructure management tasks, including workload management, performance monitoring, and resource optimization. These tools can be used to automate the less strategic tasks so that your IT resources can focus on more impactful and innovative projects.

Aside from properly installing and configuring virtualization management tools, it is crucial that you take a comprehensive approach to the security of these tools. Vendor guidelines go a long way to ensuring a secure installation and configuration — but, that's only the beginning. Effective security of these tools generally follows best practices for effective security of any highly sensitive system.

Starting with our friend, the principle of least privilege, you should ensure that the fewest people possible have access to your virtualization management tools. Such high-impact access should be limited to personnel with an absolute business need for such access, and they should be sufficiently background checked to help ensure their suitability for such roles. You may want to rethink giving that intern access to your virtualization management tools (sorry, interns!). For users with a proper business need, RBAC and strong authentication mechanisms are a must. Use multifactor authentication. Period.

Network isolation is a major control in safeguarding your virtualization management tools, and all virtualization management should occur on its own segregated management network. Segregating your critical management tools from customer environments ensures that vulnerabilities in a tenant environment cannot affect other tenants (by pivoting through the management tools) or even impact your entire infrastructure. I discuss network management further in Chapter 8.

In addition to these preventative mechanisms, make sure that you thoroughly log and monitor all access to these management tools, including logging access denials, which may alert you to brute force attempts or other foul play.

Virtual hardware specific security configuration requirements

Configuring virtual hardware requires awareness and consideration of the underlying physical hardware. For example, you'd have a problem if you had a physical host with 100TB of storage, but you configured your virtual hosts to use a total of 150TB of storage. This trivial example demonstrates just how in sync the virtual and physical worlds must be. Each vendor generally documents a set of required and recommended configuration settings for its virtualization products. As the cloud provider goes through the process of generating and configuring virtual images for customer use, it's important that they consider those requirements in order to ensure functional and secure management of virtual resources for all cloud customers.

Network

In a cloud environment, physical networking devices and a virtualized networking infrastructure support multitenancy. While physical network security controls (discussed in the next section) are important, they are not sufficient in protecting your virtual hardware and the data that moves across your virtual networks. Appropriate virtual network security requires that you have designated virtualized tools — virtual firewalls, network IDS/IPS, logging systems, and so on — in place to monitor and manage your virtualized network hardware. You should be using tools that are purpose-built for virtualized networks and configure these tools to have proper awareness of relevant underlying physical components (physical switches, for example). A strategy that includes physical and virtual network security provides comprehensive data protection at the network layer.

Storage

Secure configuration of virtual storage hardware again starts with adhering to vendor-specific recommendations and configuration guidelines. In addition, you should follow many of the security practices throughout this chapter and the rest of the book:

>> Ensure strong credentials (and no default credentials) are in use.

>> Apply MFA for privileged access to virtualized storage clusters.

>> Disable unnecessary protocols and APIs.

>> Make sure that you log and monitor all access to your virtualized storage hardware.

Memory

Securing virtual memory in cloud environments requires a multi-pronged approach, with responsibilities shared between the cloud provider and cloud user. The following list identifies some key considerations for memory security:

>> Because cloud infrastructures rely heavily on APIs, cloud providers should implement secure API access controls to prevent unauthorized manipulation of memory resources through APIs.

>> Cloud providers commonly offer encryption services, and it's the cloud user's responsibility to leverage memory encryption services that the CSP makes available.

>> Cloud providers should ensure that the hypervisor layer is secure by regularly applying patches and utilizing trusted boot processes.

>> Configuring proper isolation between virtual machines and containers is important. Cloud providers should employ hypervisor-level isolation to protect system compromise through shared physical memory.

>> Cloud users can use Cloud Security Posture Management (CSPM) tools to check for misconfigurations and other issues that might lead to data compromise (in memory or otherwise).

Installing guest operating system virtualization toolsets

Most of this section is focused on the virtualized hardware that serves as the underlying host for tenant VMs. The other side of this coin focuses on the virtualization toolsets that enable the guest OS to be installed and run from a VM; this toolset is essentially a set of technologies and procedures provided by an OS vendor that allow it to run in a virtualized environment rather than directly on a physical machine.

Virtualized environments can run any type of OS that provides a virtualization toolset (most popular operating systems do). Therefore, the variety of operating systems available to cloud customers is limited mainly by the cloud provider and what they've configured. When a CSP chooses to support a given guest OS, they should carefully configure and manage the associated virtualization toolsets in accordance with the OS vendor's guidelines and recommendations.

Operating and Maintaining Physical and Logical Infrastructure for a Cloud Environment

After you securely implement and build your physical and logical cloud environment, your attention must turn to securely operating and maintaining that environment throughout its lifetime. Operating and maintaining a physical and logical cloud environment involves implementing access control mechanisms, securing physical and virtual network configurations, building and deploying hardened OS baselines, and ensuring the availability of all physical and virtual hosts and resources. Many of these guidelines are vendor-specific, but the specific characteristics of your overall cloud environment must be considered as well.

Configuring access control for local and remote access

When thinking about access control for cloud environments, a lot of attention is usually given to controlling access to customer environments and data and rightfully so — that's important stuff. While much of this book is geared toward that user-centric access control, I use this section to focus on access control of the underlying cloud infrastructure. Many of the access control principles from traditional data center security apply here — things like limiting physical and logical access to sensitive data, physically securing buildings and rooms that store critical components, conducting personnel screening for data center employees, and so on.

There are three primary mechanisms to consider when securing local and remote access:

>> Keyboard video mouse (KVM)

>> Console-based access

>> Remote desktop protocol (RDP) and Secure Shell (SSH)

All of these access methods should require MFA and thorough logging and monitoring, at a minimum. You explore additional configuration recommendations in the following sections.

TIP

I discuss the principle of least privilege throughout this book. A set of slightly newer concepts — Just-in-Time (JIT) and Just-Enough-Access (JEA) — should be used to ensure that only the right amount of access is issued during only the right times. Tools like CyberArk and other Privileged Access Management systems can be used to enforce these concepts and ensure true least privilege.

Secure keyboard video mouse (KVM)

A *KVM switch* (KVM) is an input/output device that allows a user to access and control multiple computers from a single keyboard, video display, and mouse. These devices provide physical access to devices that can be located in multiple, separate physical locations.

In cloud environments, where a single administrator may access multiple devices of different security levels, a secure KVM can be used; secure KVM switches are designed to ensure data isolation between the systems connected to it.

Some basic requirements and features of a secure KVM include

>> **Isolated data channels:** A secure KVM must make it impossible for data to be transferred between its connected devices — one KVM-controlled server should not be able to access another server's data through the KVM.

>> **Restricted I/O function:** A secure KVM restricts USB and other input/output functionality to keyboards and mice. Other I/O devices like USB storage drives should be actively detected and prohibited in order to prevent insecure or unauthorized data transfer.

>> **Pushbutton control:** A secure KVM should require that a physical button be pressed in order to switch between connected devices. Pushbutton control requires physical access to the KVM and helps prevent remote compromises.

>> **Locked firmware:** The firmware of a KVM should be impossible to reprogram. Failure to securely lock KVM firmware can lead to an attacker altering the logic or operation of the KVM.

>> **Tamper-proof components:** The components within the KVM should be securely bonded/soldered to the circuit board in order to prevent component alteration or removal.

> » **Physical security and intrusion detection:** The KVM housing should be physically secured in a manner that makes it difficult to open. Tamper-evident labels should be installed along the device's enclosure to provide clear visual evidence if it has been opened or tampered with. For added security, a secure KVM should become inoperable if it has been successfully opened.

Secure terminal and console-based access mechanisms

Secure terminal and other console-based access support physical access to configuring and managing your environments. Because this involves physical access, compromise of console-based access can allow a malicious actor to achieve dangerous levels of control over the hypervisor and all hosts that reside on it. As a result, this type of access must be thoroughly protected just as you must secure any other form of hypervisor access. Hypervisors typically come with vendor-specific mechanisms to limit and control console-based access. It's very important that these mechanisms be fully implemented, monitored, and periodically audited for proper functionality. Additionally, physical security plays a huge role here. Cloud providers should ensure that their systems don't allow just anyone to plug in and gain console access to critical infrastructure.

Remote desktop protocol (RDP) and Secure Shell (SSH)

Remote desktop protocol (RDP) was developed by Microsoft to allow a user to connect to a remote computer (for example, over a network) and allow that user to interact with the remote computer via graphical interface. RDP requires that a user employs RDP client software, while the remote computer must run RDP server software. Though developed by Microsoft, RDP client and server software are available for Windows, macOS, and various flavors of Linux and UNIX.

As with any remote access method, RDP must be properly secured and monitored, especially when used to access critical systems. Many versions and configurations of RDP are prime targets for man-in-the-middle, remote code execution, and various other attacks. Ensure that you are actively scanning and patching all systems and make sure to keep an eye out for critical RDP vulnerabilities and patches. RDP should be configured with strong passwords, MFA, and role-based access controls to limit privileged access. You should also carefully log and monitor all RDP access in your environment.

WARNING

Remote desktop protocol is considered an insecure protocol and should only be used within closed or private networks, if at all. Do not expose RDP over the Internet, without VPN protection, at a minimum.

Secure Shell (SSH) is commonly used for remote access to Linux-based systems. Similar to RDP, SSH access requires strong passwords, multifactor authentication, network security through firewalls, and thorough logging and monitoring.

REMEMBER

Remote access comes with inherent risk, especially privileged access and when traversing the Internet. All remote access should be encrypted with TLS or a similar mechanism, and all privileged remote access should go through a secured system (like a bastion host or jump server). Multifactor authentication should be considered a requirement for all privileged access, and I highly recommend it for remote access, whenever possible. I introduce MFA in Chapter 2 and provide a deeper look in Chapter 10.

REMEMBER

Whether you're using RDP, SSH, or any other remote access mechanism, you should strongly consider using a bastion host (or jump box) for remote management of your cloud infrastructure. As mentioned in Chapter 8, a bastion host is a hardened device that sits between a lower-security zone (like your corporate network) and higher-security zone (like your cloud management plane). Bastion hosts give you a single point of entry, allowing you to tightly control and monitor all remote activity into your cloud.

Secure network configuration

Secure network configuration in the cloud involves the use and configuration of several technologies, protocols, and services. VLANs, TLS, DHCP, DNS, and VPN are some of the key concepts you must understand for the CCSP exam and for real world applications.

Virtual Local Area Networks (VLANs)

A *Virtual Local Area Network* (VLAN) is a set of servers and other devices within a LAN that are logically segmented to communicate with each other as if they were physically isolated on a separate LAN. Network isolation and segregation are two of the most pivotal concepts in securing cloud environments. When physical isolation isn't feasible (as it typically isn't in the cloud), cloud providers and customers rely on VLANs to enable virtual network segregation. A VLAN acts like a physical LAN, but allows devices to be grouped together regardless of what switch they're on; as such, you can use a VLAN to virtually group devices that are physically separate, as well as to virtually segregate devices that are physically located on the same switch. When properly configured, VLANs help cloud providers and users logically separate systems with different security and management needs. Common uses of VLANs include, but are not limited to

>> Separating production versus development environments

>> Separating tenant environments from one another

- » Separating different zones, planes, or tiers within your environment (management, application, and data tiers, for example)

- » Segmenting storage controllers from the rest of your environment

TECHNICAL
STUFF

In terms of the OSI model, VLANs are a layer 2 (or data link layer) technology.

Transport Layer Security (TLS)

I introduce TLS in Chapter 2, and it's a pivotal cryptographic protocol that you read about throughout this book. I don't go into great detail here, but it is worth examining this protocol further.

The TLS protocol replaced the long-used SSL (Secure Sockets Layer) protocol, which has since been deprecated. As such, TLS is now the de facto standard for encrypting network traffic. TLS is made up of two layers:

- » **TLS record protocol:** Provides the actual secure communications method for data in transit. Ensures data confidentiality by encrypting the connection with symmetric-key encryption and validates data integrity through the use of hashes and checksums. Used to encapsulate various upper layer protocols, most notably the TLS handshake.

- » **TLS handshake protocol:** Allows two parties (like a client and server) to authenticate each other and negotiate the parameters of the TLS connection, including the session ID and encryption algorithms to be used. The entire handshake process occurs before any secure data is transmitted.

As of this writing, TLS 1.3, released in August 2018, is the most current TLS specification.

Dynamic Host Configuration Protocol (DHCP)

The Dynamic Host Configuration Protocol is a network technology that doesn't always get enough love. Simply put, *DHCP* is a protocol that assigns and manages IP addresses, subnet masks, and other network parameters to each device on a network. Without this technology, administrators must manually configure network settings on every device under their control. It's easy to imagine how such manual network configuration would be a challenge in large, distributed cloud environments.

Whereas DHCP was commonly frowned upon in traditional data center environments, it is really a cloud network's best friend and can help securely automate orchestration and configuration of networks. Because DHCP allows central configuration of critical network parameters, it's essential that all DHCP servers are tightly secured and controlled. Failure to adequately protect these systems can allow a hacker to manipulate IP addresses and network settings to redirect traffic to malicious or compromised destinations.

Domain Name System (DNS) and DNSSEC

DNS, or Domain Name System, is arguably one of the parent technologies of the worldwide web, and it's what allows you to enter www.[*pickyourfavoritewebsite*]. com instead of an 8- to 12-digit IP every time. *DNS* is a decentralized naming system that translates domain names (like websites) to their IP addresses, and back.

Again, with great power, comes great responsibility. Protecting DNS is paramount in any environment, but particularly in cloud environments that tend to touch so much of the Internet. Hardening your DNS servers is a must, and *DNSSEC* is a technology that can help prevent DNS hijacking, DNS spoofing, and man-in-the-middle attacks.

DNSSEC is a set of security extensions to standard DNS that support the validation of the integrity of DNS data. In other words, DNSSEC provides DNS clients with a cryptographic signature that validates the origin and authority of a DNS server that responds to a DNS lookup.

TIP

The primary attacks against DNS target availability and integrity. DNSSEC is great for ensuring DNS integrity, but does nothing to protect the availability of DNS resources. Standard Denial of Service and other availability controls must be used to mitigate availability attacks on DNS services.

As with many Internet protocols, DNS wasn't built with security in mind. As such, it has several known design flaws and attack vectors that you must protect against. In addition to DNSSEC, DNS infrastructures should be over-provisioned to support far greater requests than expected — this helps protect against volume-based attacks that can compromise availability.

Virtual private network (VPN)

A *virtual private network*, or *VPN*, allows a private network to be securely extended over a public network (like the Internet) by creating a point-to-point connection between the private network and a device that sits outside that network. VPN is commonly used in organizations that allow employees to telework (work from home or outside the office), which became even more popular at the start of the COVID-19 pandemic. VPN is also recommended when connecting to the Internet from untrusted hotspots, like the WiFi in your favorite coffee shop. With a VPN, users can directly connect into a private network through a secure tunnel and experience that network just as if they were physically sitting with the rest of the devices on it. VPNs subject the remote device to all the same policies, monitoring, and restrictions as all other devices. It's a must-use technology whenever connecting to a sensitive network over the Internet or other untrusted network.

Network security controls

Securely managing the logical and physical infrastructure for a cloud environment requires security controls at multiple layers. (You can read about defense-in-depth in Chapter 2.) A layered approach to network security relies on several types of technologies, including firewalls, IDS/IPS, and more.

Firewalls

Firewalls are a core network security control that you're probably familiar with. It's important that you not only know what they do, but also how they fit into a cloud's network security stack. Firewalls are hardware or software systems that monitor and control inbound and outbound network traffic. Firewalls rely on customized rules to allow and deny traffic to, from, and within a network or device. Traditional data centers tend to use hardware firewalls, but the heavy reliance on virtualization in cloud environments makes software firewalls (or a mix of the two) more suitable.

TIP

Most modern firewall appliances are considered next-gen firewalls that include IDS/IPS, WAF, or other functionality all-in-one. When crafting your network security architecture, treat each of these components as if they are separate devices connected together (like the good ole days) and focus on each component's individual capabilities.

Firewalls play two main roles in cloud networks: perimeter control and internal segmentation. Cloud customers are generally exposed to firewalls in two ways: virtual firewalls and network Access Control Lists (ACLs). Virtual firewalls are logical equivalents of their physical brethren. Network ACLs allow you to define rules that control traffic into and out of a network without an actual firewall appliance. Most CSPs offer customers a feature called virtual private cloud, or VPC, which simulates virtual firewall functionality. By using VPCs and network ACLs, a cloud customer can manage their logical infrastructure similar to if it were their own data center.

Intrusion detection systems (IDS) and intrusion prevention systems (IPS)

An *intrusion detection system* (IDS) is a hardware appliance or software application that monitors networks and systems and alerts designated personnel of any malicious or unauthorized activity. An *intrusion prevention system* (IPS) performs very similarly, with one major difference: IPS is designed to actually block suspected attacks, in addition to alert on them.

Now you may be wondering why anyone would choose an IDS over IPS — it's better to block attacks than alert them, right? Well, one thing to keep in mind is that these devices are known for generating a high number of false positives, especially when first installed. Careful configuration and ongoing tuning help to reduce these false positives, but IPS is best used only when it will not create a Denial of Service for authorized traffic.

TECHNICAL
STUFF

Whereas firewalls operate by filtering traffic based on IP addresses, ports, and protocols, IDS and IPS systems use deep packet analysis to analyze network traffic and compare network packets against known traffic patterns or attack signatures. Some IDS/IPS devices can even operate in signature-less fashion and trigger on anomalous activity (for example, unknown activities that smell fishy). IDS/IPS devices are generally placed after a network firewall and act as a second line of defense. Additionally, IDS/IPS capabilities can often be found as part of next-generation firewalls (NGFWs).

WARNING

Because they rely on deep packet analysis, IDS/IPS cannot fully examine encrypted network traffic. As a cloud security professional, you must evaluate the tradeoffs between ubiquitous encryption and intrusion monitoring and consider where and when it makes sense to temporarily decrypt data for inspection.

The two categories of IDS are

>> **Host IDS (HIDS):** This type of IDS operates on a single host and monitors only network traffic that flows into and out of that host. In addition to monitoring a host's network traffic, HIDS are often able to monitor critical configurations and files on a host and can be configured to alert on suspicious modifications. Similar to other host-based security controls, HIDS are prone to compromise if an attacker gains root-level access on that host. To combat this, HIDS logs should immediately be sent a remote system (like your centrally managed SIEM), and HIDS configurations and settings should be locked down and managed on a remote system.

TIP

Consider installing a HIDS on your baseline images for your highly sensitive systems. Configure the HIDS to communicate with your SIEM or other centrally managed alerting dashboard. You can then deploy and manage those distributed HIDS in one fell swoop.

>> **Network IDS (NIDS):** This type of IDS is installed along the network and can monitor network traffic across multiple hosts, instead of just one. NIDS are traditionally installed after firewalls, on a network tap. By having broader

network visibility, NIDS can identify suspicious trends across hosts that may be too hard to spot on individual machines. The sheer volume of network traffic and the number of alerts these tools can generate is the primary challenge with NIDS. Instead of using NIDS to monitor entire cloud networks, they should be installed in strategic locations near high-value assets, such as your management plane subnet.

REMEMBER

In practice, most environments benefit from some combination of IDS and IPS; for that reason, and because of their structural similarities, the two are often mentioned together. Despite this, you should have a clear understanding of their differences, and you should know the differences between host-based and network-based IDS.

Honeypots

Here's a treat for you! A *honeypot* is a decoy system that mimics a sensitive system in order to lure attackers away from the legitimate target. Honeypots are typically designed to mirror your production environment, but they host dummy data instead of actual sensitive information. It's also common to leave a few known vulnerabilities in order to make a honeypot easier to find and more attractive to hackers. By using a honeypot, you can trap hackers in a fake environment and watch as they attempt to do damage. In doing so, you're able to learn the attackers' origins and techniques, which can help you better protect your actual network and systems. Sounds pretty sweet!

Network security groups

Most cloud providers use the notion of a *security group*, which is basically a network ACL that operates at the VM level rather than the network level. In many cases, security groups may not be as full-featured as network ACLs, but the core functionality is there. A *network security group*, however, is a feature popularized by Microsoft, that effectively combines the concepts of security groups with network ACLs; network security groups allow you to control traffic to and from either an OS or an entire network.

Hardening the operating system through the application of baselines, monitoring, and remediation

When securing any physical computing device, one of the first things you should focus on is its underlying operating system. Creating and applying baselines is a standard procedure for securing operating systems in traditional IT and cloud environments alike; it involves establishing and enforcing known good states of system configuration. OS baselines should be developed with least privilege in mind and configured to allow only services, features, and access methods that are absolutely required for system functionality — turn off and disable any unnecessary services, close unused ports, and disable access routes that aren't required.

Depending on your business requirements and technology implementations, your organization may develop a single baseline for each OS in your environment, or you may find it necessary to develop multiple baselines to cover specific use-cases. For example, it is very common to see a Windows baseline for webservers, another baseline for Windows-based database servers, and another one for employee desktops — each separate baseline must have its own policy that identifies what services and functions are required and which are prohibited.

No matter which OS you're securing, the process for creating baselines generally starts with taking a fresh OS install and disabling all unnecessary ports, protocols, and services. If nobody will be browsing the Internet, then go ahead and remove that vulnerability-prone browser. If only HTTPS traffic is allowed, then consider disabling port 80. Anything and everything that is not needed for system functionality should be shut down, deleted, and disabled. Doing so reduces the attack surface of not just one device, but every single device that gets this baseline configuration. Aside from this generic process, specific OS vendors have their own tools and best practices for baseline configuration and deployment. I explore Windows, Linux, and VMware baseline management in the following sections.

TIP

In addition to applying security best practices and ensuring least privilege, OS baselines can and should be used to enforce any OS-related legal and regulatory compliance obligations.

Applying baselines is an important step to toward ensuring consistent and secure operating systems, but it's far from a set-it-and-forget-it process. Once OS baselines are applied, it's important to ensure that systems remain in compliance with those baselines through continuous monitoring. Compliance can be accomplished by using configuration management tools with automated baseline scanning functionalities. You load these tools with your approved baselines for each OS and scan your infrastructure to detect any noncompliant systems. In doing so, you can spot systems with unexpected configurations, which may occur for several reasons:

>> Your baseline was not applied to all systems, either intentionally or accidentally.

>> A legitimate administrator made an unauthorized change to a system.

» A malicious outsider gained access to a system and made modifications — for example, discovering an unauthorized open port may be an indication that a hacker has set up backdoor communication.

» A system has an approved policy exception that the baseline scanner did not account for (for example, port 80 may be disallowed in your Linux baseline, but allowed on a handful of webservers that use HTTP instead of HTTPS).

Windows

Microsoft offers several tools and resources to support baseline configuration and management. Configuration Manager, Intune, and Microsoft Deployment Toolkit (MDT) all offer tools and processes for automating and deploying system configurations. Specifically, MDT enables you to deploy and manage system images and can be used to help you manage initial and ongoing security configurations of your baseline images.

Linux

Now, this is a fun one. Linux comes in many different flavors and distributions, and each includes its own set of default utilities and settings. As such, your process for creating secure baselines largely depends on which flavor you're using. Some Linux variants are offered as bare-bones distros that come with very few processes and utilities; these distros may require minimal hardening, whereas some of the more robust Linux distros may need to be heavily modified and restricted, depending on your particular use-case. All in all, when establishing and applying baselines for Linux, you should first start with general Linux guidelines and best practices before moving onto vendor-specific guidelines and recommendations.

TIP

Specific Linux best practices are outside the scope of this section. You should do additional research on common Linux security configurations if your specific implementation is Linux-based.

VMware

VMware is a historical leader in virtualization and cloud computing and has developed its operating systems with remote and automated baseline management features built in. VMware's vSphere Update Manager (VUM) utility allows you to create and manage host baselines, virtual machine baselines, and virtual appliance baselines all in one. VUM provides insights into your entire vSphere OS deployment and allows you to quickly identify and fix hosts that are not compliant with their respective baseline. The tool can also help ensure that all systems under a given baseline have been patched and received any other security configuration updates.

Patch management

Patch management is a subset of configuration management, which includes all processes for finding, testing, and applying software patches (or code changes) to your systems. Patch management includes more than just vulnerability management, although that is a huge component of it. Patches are released by software and firmware vendors and made available for their customers to install; the patches typically provide new functionality, improve stability, and, of course, fix known security vulnerabilities. Every organization should develop a patch management policy that identifies which assets require what type of patches on what schedule. In addition, your organization should create and maintain a set of patch management procedures that define what steps to take in order to acquire relevant patches, validate their appropriateness for your environment, apply them to all assets, and test their effectiveness.

Organizations approach patch management in several ways, but a typical patch management process may look something like the following:

1. Identify.

The first step is to identify that a required patch actually exists. This step entails gathering information from all relevant vendors about all outstanding patches for all your software and firmware. In most cases, vendors offer notification mechanisms or other means for customers to quickly identify when new patches are released. This step can be quite tedious for large public clouds with many systems and numerous types of software. All outstanding patch information should be aggregated into a database or patch management tool for consistent, automated, and streamlined deployment.

2. Acquire.

After identifying that patches exist for your environment, this next step is to actually obtain those patches by downloading the appropriate executables, scripts, or packages. Some software can phone home and download relevant patches directly within the software itself, while other software requires navigating to the vendor's website or other means. Your patch management procedures should include documented steps to procure patches for each vendor within your environment.

3. Test.

Many vendors provide hashes for you to validate the integrity of their patches after downloading — installing a compromised patch can wreak havoc on your systems, and hashes help prevent that. Regardless of whether you have a hash, you should first test patches in a development environment to ensure that they don't break your systems or introduce new risks. Once you confirm that a patch causes no harm, you can approve it for deployment/installation.

4. Deploy.

Now that you've found, acquired, and tested your patches, you can go ahead deploy them across your production environment. You should consult your patch management policy to determine the appropriate patching schedule. In many cases, organizations implement deployment windows during which patches and system updates can be made. Automation is critical here, especially in large cloud environments. In most cases, cloud infrastructures rely on patching baseline images and redeploying those baselines to impacted systems; patching images removes the need to individually patch thousands of systems and reduces the risk of one-off errors.

5. Validate.

This final step requires that you validate that your patches are installed properly and confirm that everything is in working order. In some cases, it can be as simple as a looking for a confirmation message, but others can be as involved as running tests to ensure the underlying host is operating as expected.

TIP

I cannot stress enough how important automation is for cloud patch management. Infrastructures with thousands (or even hundreds of thousands) of systems cannot be effectively managed individually or manually. I have seen some very sophisticated automation technologies used to streamline the entire patching lifecycle, and even then, patch management can still be a major headache. Doing your homework early on and developing a robust patch management plan and process can help tremendously.

On the cloud customer side, remember that your patch management responsibilities are dependent on your particular cloud service model (IaaS, PaaS, or SaaS) and what cloud services you're using. I've seen this be a major point of confusion for cloud customers who incorrectly believe that patching is 100 percent handled by the CSP, even for IaaS services. The cloud provider is completely responsible for patching the underlying infrastructure, but IaaS (and even PaaS customers, to an extent) must be aware of their patching duties. For example, if you're using AWS EC2, Amazon is responsible for patching the underlying physical hosts that run your EC2 instances, but you are wholly responsible for patching your OS images. Consult your CSP's documentation for information specific to your implementation.

Infrastructure as Code (IaC) strategy

Infrastructure as Code (IaC) is a practice that involves using code to define, deploy, and manage an entire IT infrastructure. Instead of manually configuring and provisioning hardware, networks, and software components, IaC supports automation by treating infrastructure as software. This code-driven approach allows developers and operations teams to create, modify, and scale infrastructure resources consistently and efficiently, promoting agility and reducing the potential for human error (including security misconfigurations).

With IaC, your infrastructure team defines infrastructure components and configurations in version-controlled code repositories. IaC tools then execute the code to provision and configure resources in a repeatable manner. Changes to infrastructure are made through code modifications, enabling versioning, collaboration, and auditing, similar to software development practices.

IaC offers benefits such as rapid provisioning, easier resource management, enhanced scalability, and improved consistency across environments. IaC is a core component of modern DevSecOps practices and cloud computing, and it enables you to treat infrastructure as a dynamic and flexible asset that can evolve alongside application development.

In cloud infrastructures, IaC plays an important role in enabling automated creation, configuration, and management of cloud resources. Cloud environments are inherently dynamic, and IaC's code-driven approach can help you simplify provisioning, orchestration, and security of virtual machines and other cloud resources.

WARNING

Protecting the integrity of your IaC code is crucial because any unauthorized changes or tampering with IaC scripts can lead to misconfigurations or security vulnerabilities in cloud environments.

Availability of stand-alone hosts

Within a computing environment, a stand-alone host is a physical machine that operates independently from other machines in the environment. Stand-alone hosts are commonly used in traditional data center models when it's desirable to isolate one system from others, whether for security, compliance, performance, or other reasons. Although less common, stand-alone hosts are still used in cloud environments.

CSPs generally make stand-alone hosts available to customers who want to streamline their cloud migration. By offering stand-alone hosts, customers can maintain their existing system architectures and configurations as they move everything to the cloud. Another great use case for stand-alone hosts is in providing physical separation between systems or datasets, often for compliance purposes.

TIP

The concept of stand-alone hosts is growing in popularity among CSPs, again with regulatory and compliance being a huge driving factor. AWS offers services like dedicated hosts and dedicated instances, while Google Cloud offers sole-tenant nodes. Be sure to familiarize yourself with each product's documentation to ensure they meet your technical and compliance needs.

Availability of clustered hosts

A *host cluster* is a group of hosts that are physically or logically connected in such a way that they work together and function as a single host. Each host's resources are pooled and shared among the cluster. Every host within the cluster is set to perform the same task, which is controlled and managed through software. Clustered hosts help protect against software and hardware failures of a single machine and can also be used for load balancing and parallel processing.

REMEMBER

Resource-sharing concepts like reservations, limits, and shares help orchestrate and manage resource allocation among tenants using the same host cluster. These topics are discussed in Chapter 7.

TIP

Every CSP is different, but more times than not, you're getting some form of clustered hosts when moving to the cloud. For the CCSP exam, you should know the differences between stand-alone and clustered hosts and when to use each.

Distributed resource scheduling (DRS)

Distributed resource scheduling (DRS) is a feature that enables clustered environments to automagically distribute workloads across physical hosts in the cluster — and yes, *automagically* is a word! In cloud environments, DRS helps scale workloads to maintain a healthy balance across physical hosts. DRS allows virtual hosts to move from one physical host to another, with or without the customer knowing (or caring).

TIP

The topic of DRS is really interesting to me, but instead of me going on about it here, check out VMware's DRS documentation at www.vmware.com/products/vsphere/drs-dpm.html for a look at one popular implementation of this technology.

Dynamic optimization (DO)

Dynamic optimization (DO) is the automated process of constantly reallocating cloud resources to ensure that no physical host or its resources become overutilized while other resources are available or underutilized. DO technologies use sophisticated algorithms and resource analysis to intelligently optimize resource utilization — reducing waste and cost, while improving service availability and performance. Dynamic optimization is one of the fundamental technologies underlying the fundamental cloud principles of autoscaling and rapid elasticity.

Storage clusters

The goal behind storage clustering is closely related to the principles of host clustering. *Storage clusters*, similar to their server peers, are a logical or physical connection of multiple storage systems in a way that allows them to operate as a single storage unit. In cloud environments, storage clusters support multitenancy, increases performance, and enables high availability (discussed in the following sections).

Maintenance mode

In many cases, a CSP needs to perform maintenance actions like patching or upgrading a server, or replacing a failed drive, for example; these types of actions often render a physical host temporarily unavailable. *Maintenance mode* allows a provider to gracefully move a tenant's workloads to another physical host while maintenance is being performed. In ideal situations, maintenance mode occurs automatically and gracefully, with little or no impact to the customer's ability to access their resources. I've seen maintenance mode in action, and the amount of automation that it requires is mind-blowing!

TIP

Not all CSPs are created equally, and some have more sophisticated maintenance procedures than others. Ask a potential CSP for details about how system maintenance activity may or may not impact uptime and other SLAs.

High availability

One of the core concepts of cloud computing — and one of the greatest reasons for cloud migration — is high availability; customers expect their cloud services and workloads to be available whenever they need them, and it's a CSP's responsibility to making sure that happens. Clustered hosts, and clustering of other resources (like storage systems, networking components, and so on) is a key approach that cloud providers use to provide their customers with high availability. Just about every component must be built with high availability and elasticity in mind. Aside from clustering, CSPs ensure high availability through redundancy and by replicating customer data across zones and regions.

Availability of guest operating systems

In the same way that clustered hosts and storage clusters increase the availability of physical resources, tools and processes to support redundancy increase the availability of guest operating systems. A cloud customer expects their guest OS to be available whenever they need it, and a cloud provider should really live up to that expectation if they want to keep customers in the crowded CSP market. A guest OS is little more than a file on the provider's physical hardware, and so ensuring its availability starts with protecting that file via standard data protection mechanisms discussed throughout this chapter and the rest of the book.

Performance and capacity monitoring

Performance monitoring is a critical task that every cloud provider must perform on a continuous basis to ensure that systems are running dependably, and customer SLAs are being met. *Performance monitoring* involves routine collection and analysis of performance metrics for key components of the cloud environment. Key components that should be monitored include network, compute, and disk, and memory. Most vendors offer performance metrics and recommend techniques for monitoring them, but some things to examine include

>> **Network:** Latency, dropped packets, and other standard network performance metrics

>> **Compute (for example, CPU):** Excessive utilization and response time

>> **Disk:** Read/write times and capacity limits

>> **Memory:** Excessive usage and capacity limits

REMEMBER

When conducting performance and capacity monitoring, it's important that CSPs consider their ability to support all current customers as well as their capacity to support autoscaling and future customer growth. Due to rapid elasticity, a cloud provider must have enough capacity to withstand an unexpected spike in resource utilization by one or more customers; capacity planning must take this into account.

Hardware monitoring

When talking about monitoring cloud environments, it's almost natural to jump straight to the virtual infrastructure and its resources. After all, cloud computing is all about virtualizing network, compute, and storage resources, right?! While that may be true, it's important not to forget that underneath all of that virtualized infrastructure lies actual physical hardware that must also be monitored. The same key components (network, compute, disk, and memory) must be monitored in the physical plane just as you do for virtual performance and capacity monitoring. In many cases, you can use the same processes and even similar tools to monitor physical hardware and virtualized infrastructure. As always, make sure to first check with each hardware vendor for recommended monitoring utilities and best practices.

In addition to the standard monitoring mentioned in the previous paragraph, hardware should also be monitored for things like fan speed, device and surrounding temperatures, and even voltage readings. This type of information can help you track the overall health of your hardware and can help you identify overworked or aging hardware before it fails.

Monitoring vast cloud infrastructures is a monumental task. Due to resource pooling, clustering, and other high availability features, it's often necessary to consider large sets of hardware rather than each machine individually. Consistent with a major theme of this chapter, automation should be used wherever possible to streamline these efforts. Most integrated hardware monitoring utilities provide dashboards with at-a-glance details of your hardware's health status and any important metrics or alerts.

Configuring host and guest operating system backup and restore functions

Whether in a traditional data center or a cloud environment, backup and restore are some of the most critical security functions. Ensuring that important data is backed up and easily restored, when needed, supports the core information security principle of availability. For cloud infrastructures, it's essential to configure physical hosts as well as guest operating systems so that important systems and data are available and functional after an incident or disaster.

You should be familiar with three main types of backup technologies:

>> Snapshots

>> Agent-based

>> Agentless

Snapshots

Snapshots are not a true backup, in the purest sense, but I'll get to that. Simply put, a *snapshot* is a copy of a virtual machine, its virtual disks, and any settings and configurations associated with the VM. The snapshot is saved to disk as a simple file.

Snapshots are often performed before deploying software patches or other potentially unsafe operations in a virtual machine. If something should fail, snapshots are a great way to roll back to a specific point in time. Snapshots should be differentiated from backups for a couple reasons. Snapshots are not complete, on their own and rely on the virtual machine's parent disk and filesystem; if the parent disk is deleted or corrupted, a snapshot cannot help you restore your system. Snapshots are saved on the same storage infrastructure as the VM itself. With true backups, it's important to keep the backup completely separate from the original data; VM snapshots are neither separate from the underlying physical host nor the virtual infrastructure of the VM.

Agent-based backups

Agent-based backup mechanisms were considered the gold standard when virtualization first became popular during the Stone Age (circa 1990s). Agent-based backup requires installing a component (the agent) on every system in your environment that handles the backup duties for you and sends it over to your desired backup storage. Being installed directly on a system gives agent-based backups an edge when particular systems or applications require direct access to perform complete backups.

The downside, as you've probably figured, is that agent-based backups can become unwieldly and hard to manage in large environments (like a public cloud). Enter agentless backups.

Agentless backups

Agentless backups are not truly agentless, but instead require a single agent be installed on any given network. This single agent provides centralized network-wide backup capabilities without you needing to somehow interact with every endpoint. Generally speaking, the more systems you have to backup, the more attractive agentless solutions become. So, for a cloud environment, agentless backup tends to offer greater control, simplified management, and lower cost than agent-based solutions.

It's not all rosy though. Agentless backup requires a fully virtualized environment, so networks with both physical and virtualized servers require an agent-based or hybrid approach. Further, agentless backup doesn't work with every system, and so it's important that you consider your architecture before choosing one backup solution over the other.

TIP

Agentless backups generally interact directly with your hypervisor to snapshot and backup your VMs. To use an agentless solution, first make sure that the backup product supports integration with your particular hypervisor.

Management plane

Managing the physical and logical infrastructure of a cloud environment requires effective task and operations scheduling, efficient orchestration of activities and resources, and comprehensive, yet minimally disruptive maintenance. All of these activities take place in the management plane.

Scheduling

Cloud infrastructures involve managing a large variety of virtualized resources, and cloud providers employ task scheduling to fulfill and manage customer requests related to those resources. Scheduling and resource allocation go hand in hand: *Scheduling* is the process of taking customer resource requests and prioritizing those requests (or tasks) in such a way that available resources are assigned and utilized most efficiently. When multiple customers request compute power, for example, the CSP's task scheduler considers the nature of each request (whether it's for CPU or GPU, for example), the size of the request (e.g., how much compute power is needed), the length of time the resource is needed, and the availability of suitable resources. Based on all of these factors and other metrics, the scheduler's algorithms determine which customers to supply with the appropriate resources, at what time, and for how long. Proper scheduling enables efficient resource utilization and keeps request pipelines moving smoothly.

Orchestration

Another essential component of cloud management, *orchestration* is the organization and integration of automated tasks between systems and services in a cloud environment. Cloud orchestration allows you to create a consolidated workflow from multiple interconnected processes. With orchestration, you can automate complex processes such as resource provisioning, allocation, and scaling. Orchestration is absolutely required to enable cloud providers to provide highly available, dynamically scaling services to customers with little to no human interaction.

WARNING

Orchestration is often confused with automation. The two concepts are very much related, but not the same. While *automation* refers to a single task or process, *orchestration* is the coordination and management of these automated tasks into a streamlined, automated workflow.

Maintenance

Yet another critical component of managing a cloud environment is conducting routine and emergency maintenance of the physical and logical infrastructure. In traditional data center environments, operators serve very few customers — maybe even a single customer, which may be themselves. This type of independence lets data center operations teams easily find the best time to conduct maintenance simply by coordinating with their users. Public cloud infrastructures that serve thousands of customers simply don't have this luxury. As such, cloud providers need to carefully consider potential customer impact when invoking maintenance mode (discussed earlier), and they should ideally leverage orchestration tools to minimize or even remove this impact altogether. Whenever possible, customer workloads should be (automatically) routed to stable systems while maintenance occurs on physical or logical resources. Anytime a CSP suspects that maintenance might impact customers' performance or availability, the provider should communicate this to all potentially impacted customers, as soon as possible, with details of the maintenance window and its expected impact.

IN THIS CHAPTER

» **Aligning with operational controls and standards**

» **Conducting digital forensics investigations in the cloud**

» **Communicating important details to stakeholders**

» **Learning how to run security operations for your environment**

Chapter **12**

Domain 5: Cloud Security Operations, Part 2

In this chapter, you dive deep into the nitty gritty areas within security operations. I cover many of the key topics involved in managing security operations for your cloud environment. I also explore various operational controls and standards and discuss how to communicate with relevant external parties. Domain 5 represents 16 percent of the CCSP certification exam, and this chapter covers the second part of Domain 5.

Implementing Operational Controls and Standards

Many processes need to be managed when it comes to cloud security operations. Fortunately, many of these processes are similar to traditional IT operations, and well-established standards can guide your understanding and application of those processes. ISO/IEC 20000 is a common international Service Management System (SMS) standard that defines requirements for service providers to plan, develop, operate, and continually improve their services. The standard was most recently updated in late 2018, and you can check out part 1 of it (ISO/IEC 20000-1) by visiting www.iso.org/standard/70636.html.

Another well-known standard is ITIL, which used to be an acronym for Information Technology Infrastructure Library. ITIL is a framework that establishes a set of detailed IT Service Management (ITSM) practices. You can find more information on ITIL by visiting www.axelos.com/best-practice-solutions/itil. The following list is primarily derived from the ITIL framework and aligns with the core practices identified in the CCSP exam outline:

>> Change management

>> Continuity management

>> Information security management

>> Continual service improvement management

>> Incident management

>> Problem management

>> Release and deployment management

>> Configuration management

>> Service level management

>> Availability management

>> Capacity management

The preceding list includes processes from ITIL's Service Design, Service Transition, and Service Operations stages, and you can find similar information in ISO 20000-1. You can learn about all 11 processes in the following sections.

Change management

Change management is an IT discipline focused on ensuring that organizations employ standardized processes and procedures to make changes to their systems and services. The overall objective of change management is to allow IT changes to be made in a structured and secure manner, while minimizing negative impacts to users.

You may hear the term change management used in project management circles and assume that it's strictly up to a PM to handle change management. Unfortunately, you're not quite off the hook. Changes to an IT environment may potentially impact the security posture of that environment, and so every cloud security professional has a responsibility to partner with their organization's Program Management Office (PMO) to securely manage these changes.

In a cloud environment, some activities that require change management include

>> Buying, building, or deploying new hardware or software

>> Upgrading or modifying existing hardware or software

>> Decommissioning hardware or software

>> Modifying the operating environment (for example, changing data center humidity levels)

>> Modifying IT documentation (yup, this needs to be considered an extension of the system itself and properly controlled)

What does an IT change management process look like?, you ask. Well. . . I'm glad you asked! ITIL, ISO, and other frameworks break change management down into a series of steps. These steps may vary from one framework to the next, but in general the process looks something like this:

1. Request a change.

During this step, a necessary change is requested or somehow otherwise identified. The person or team requesting the change typically creates an RFC (request for change) that documents the details of the request, including such details as the requestor's contact info, time requirements, business justification, and more.

2. Evaluate the requested change.

The RFC is reviewed for completion, appropriateness, and feasibility. During this step, you should evaluate the change to assess benefits and risks associated with it. You want to leave this step with a clear understanding of all pros, cons, and impact to your systems and business if you make the requested change. Who evaluates an RFC depends on the size and scope of the particular change. For larger or more impactful changes, your organization may rely on a Change Advisory Board (CAB) or Change Control Board (CCB) to evaluate the RFC. A CAB usually consists of stakeholders throughout the organization, while CCBs are most often limited to project-level stakeholders. Having an information security representative (like a CCSP) on both the CAB and CCB are important and often overlooked by organizations.

3. Approve the change.

Once the RFC has been thoroughly evaluated, a recommendation to authorize the change is sent to the appropriate authority, depending on the request.

Approval can be anything from getting a Senior Sys Admin to sign off on replacing a hard drive to requiring a VP to approve a data center expansion.

4. Plan the change.

Planning the change again depends on the size and scope of the effort. Smaller changes may require a quick writeup, whereas larger changes call for full project plans. Identify any resources you need and the steps you must follow to complete the change.

5. Implement the change.

With a plan in hand, go forth and make it happen!

6. Review the change.

During this final step, test that your change was implemented successfully and validate that no unintended consequences have occurred. For larger changes, a post-implementation review (PIR) should be developed to document the implementation results and any lessons learned.

Continuity management

Continuity management helps ensure that a CSP can recover and continue providing service to its customers, even amid security incidents or during times of crisis.

Continuity management involves conducting a business impact analysis (BIA) to prioritize resources, evaluating the threats and risks to each of those resources, identifying mitigating controls for each risk, and developing a contingency plan that outlines how to address potential scenarios. See Chapter 2 for full coverage of business continuity planning (BCP).

Information security management

Information security management codifies the protection of your environment's confidentiality, integrity, and availability as part of your overall IT management objectives. Information security management basically includes everything covered in Chapter 2 and in many places throughout this book being made an official part of your IT service management plan. This practice involves planning, building, and managing security controls that protect your systems and data against security risks. Having information security specifically called out as a management objective ensures that it's treated as an integral part of all IT decisions.

ISO/IEC 27001, mentioned a couple times in this book, is one of the leading standards for information security management.

REMEMBER

Continual service improvement management

Continual service improvement management is borrowed from ISO 20000-1, and is a lifecycle of constantly improving the performance and effectiveness of IT services by collecting data and learning from the past. The goal of this process is to perpetually search for ways to make your systems and services better than they currently are.

Incident management

Incident management is the process of monitoring for, responding to, and minimizing the impact of incidents. In this case, an *incident* is any event that can lead to a disruption in a service provider's ability to provide its services to users or customers. I introduce incident handling (the tactical part of incident management) in Chapter 2.

Problem management

Problem management is the process of managing any and all problems that happen or could happen to your IT service. The objective here is to identify potential issues and put processes and systems in place to prevent them from ever occurring. Achieving this objective requires analyzing historical issues and using that insight to predict potential future problems. Problem management does not always succeed at preventing issues, and so the process also involves putting processes and systems in place to minimize the impact of unavoidable problems.

Release and deployment management

The objective of *release and deployment management* is to plan, schedule, and manage software releases through different phases, including testing in development environments and deployment to a production environment, while maintaining the integrity and security of the production environment. Successful release and deployment management requires collaboration between developers, project managers, the release team, and those responsible for testing. A release management team is generally constructed during the early planning stages and oversees the release through development, testing, troubleshooting, and deployment.

Configuration management

I discuss application configuration management in Chapter 9, but I'm going to take a broader view for a second. *Configuration management* is the process of tracking and controlling configuration changes to systems and software. Configurations include information about all physical and logical components within the cloud environment, and proper configuration management encompasses all settings, versions, and patch levels for your hardware and software assets. Your organization should have a configuration management plan that identifies how you identify, plan, control, change, and maintain all configurations in your environment. Due to the sprawling and dynamic nature of cloud environments, cloud providers and their customers should seek to use automated tools and techniques to streamline the configuration management process.

Service level management

There are few acronyms I hear more than SLA when talking to cloud customers. It's discussed all over this book, and for good reason — service level agreements are contracts between a CSP and cloud customer that set the customer's expectations for the minimum level of service they'll receive. As such, *service level management* is a huge part of cloud business, and it involves negotiating, developing, and managing all CSP SLAs.

You can read more about SLAs in Chapter 3.

Availability management

Availability management is the process of ensuring that the appropriate people, processes, and systems are in place in order to sustain sufficient service availability. Availability management involves establishing your system's availability objectives (for example, SLAs) as well as monitoring, measuring, and evaluating your performance against those objectives. An underrated objective of an availability manager (unless you're a cloud provider) is achieving all these goals as cost-effectively as possible.

Capacity management

Capacity management is the process of ensuring that the required resource capacity exists, at all times, to meet or exceed business and customer needs, as defined in SLAs. Similar to availability management, cost-efficiency is paramount here. While having insufficient capacity can lead to poor service performance and loss of business, overspending on capacity can lead to less profit, lower margins, and potentially unsustainable business. It's certainly a fine line between provisioning too little capacity and too much, but it's a line your organization must spend time carefully defining.

Supporting Digital Forensics

Digital forensics, sometimes called *computer forensics*, is a branch of forensic science that deals with the recovery, preservation, and analysis of digital evidence associated with cybercrimes and computer incidents. Digital forensics is an intersection between law, information technology, and the scientific method.

While it is now an established field, the intersection of digital forensics and cloud computing is still unfolding in some ways. It's important that you, as a CCSP, recognize and understand how the uniqueness of cloud computing shapes the way you conduct digital forensics.

ISO/IEC offers several standards to guide you in your digital forensics activities (and incident response, in general):

>> **ISO/IEC 27037:2012:** Guidelines for Identification, Collection, Acquisition and Preservation of Digital Evidence

>> **ISO/IEC 27041:2015:** Guidance on Assuring Suitability and Adequacy of Incident Investigative Method

>> **ISO/IEC 27042:2015:** Guidelines for the Analysis and Interpretation of Digital Evidence

>> **ISO/IEC 27043:2015:** Incident Investigation Principles and Processes

>> **ISO/IEC 27050:2018-2021:** Electronic Discovery

TIP

You may notice that all of these standards are pretty dated. It's worth noting that ISO/IEC has reviewed and confirmed them since their initial publications — ISO 27037 was published in 2012, but reviewed and confirmed in 2018; ISO 27041 and 27042 were initially published in 2015, but later confirmed in 2021; ISO 27043 was published in 2015, but reviewed and confirmed in 2020.

Collecting, acquiring, and preserving digital evidence

Generally speaking, the core principles of digital forensics are the same in the cloud as they are in traditional data center environments — you still must collect digital evidence and conduct thorough analysis on it while maintaining its chain of custody. Due to the fundamental differences between cloud environments and traditional data centers, some forensic issues are unique to cloud computing. Among the most important concerns are data ownership and shared responsibility, virtualization, multitenancy, and data location. In the following sections, I cover how to address these concerns as you collect and manage forensic data in the cloud.

Data ownership and shared responsibility

One of the biggest hurdles in cloud computing is the concept of data ownership and understanding how the shared responsibility model impacts it. In the traditional data center model, organizations have no question about data ownership — my building, my servers, my data! Data ownership can get a bit fuzzy when moving to the cloud, and it presents probably the biggest issue for digital forensics. A customer's level of ownership varies based on the cloud service model being leveraged.

For IaaS services, customers have the highest level of ownership and control over their resources and data. As an IaaS customer, you have control over your VMs and everything built on them. Generally speaking, this service model provides a high degree of access to event data and logs to support forensic analysis, but customers are still reliant on the CSP for infrastructure logs and forensic data, if required.

For PaaS and especially SaaS services, customers have noticeably less ownership and control over systems, thus yielding less independent access to data required for forensic investigations. In PaaS and SaaS service models, customers must depend on the provider to capture and appropriately preserve most evidence. Some CSPs have policies that they do not share this type of information with any customers, whereas other providers agree to fully support customers with forensic investigations.

Regardless of your service model, collecting relevant information and maintaining chain of custody requires collaboration between a CSP and their customer. As a CCSP, you should be involved in reviewing all cloud contracts and SLAs to determine whether a given provider can support your digital forensics requirements, if ever needed.

Virtualization

At the heart of cloud computing lies the concept of virtualization — CSPs manage a physical environment that lets customers access and manage logical resources. The use of virtual machines with virtual storage, memory, and networking requires that you not only need to conduct standard forensic activities on your physical hardware, but must also treat your logical environment as if it were physical, too. This requirement means you don't want to shut down VMs before collecting evidence because any valuable information stored in virtual memory would be wiped out. You must pay attention to preserving evidence in your logical infrastructure in order to support your customers' needs for forensic data.

Multitenancy

In traditional data centers and on-premise environments, organizations have complete confidence that their data is physically separate from anyone else's. When conducting forensic activities, they can be certain that evidence is not tainted by another organization's presence.

Cloud providers, however, co-locate multiple customers on the same physical infrastructure, which can cause issues with data collection because the collected data potentially contains information from multiple customers. If customer X has a need to provide forensic records to authorities, it can be a problem if their data is not sufficiently isolated from customers A through W.

To combat this issue, CSPs should enable strong logical controls (like encryption, VPCs, and so on) to isolate tenants from each other. Further, it's important that providers and customers take steps to accurately document where separation does not exist and what data is out of scope.

Data location and jurisdiction

Public cloud environments have data centers and regions around the world. As I'm writing this book, AWS and Google Cloud both have over 32 regions around the globe, and that number is probably even higher as you're reading this. That's great for providing high-performing services just about anywhere on Earth (or Mars, just in case a Mars region has launched by the time you read this).

Benefits aside, geographic dispersion can make collecting and managing forensic data a nightmare. When a customer's virtualized workload is spread across many systems in a data center or even multiple data centers, it can be difficult to thoroughly track down all relevant data during an investigation. Before forensic data collection begins, a CSP must ensure that all locations of data are accounted for.

TIP

Data location is not only a challenge when conducting customer-centric forensics, but also when a CSP needs to collect and preserve evidence for their own forensic investigations. Tracking the location of all provider and/or customer data is a massive task that requires providers to build sophisticated tooling and automated processes.

Aside from the technical challenges associated with data location, jurisdiction often comes into play. When a cybercrime occurs, the laws and regulations that govern the region present challenges. A court order is issued where the impacted data is located (let's say Germany) may not be applicable to the same data stored in the United States. Many CSPs now offer the ability for customers to select or restrict which region(s) their data is located. Cloud customers must understand what laws, regulations, and compliance requirements impact their data and choose CSPs and regions that can appropriately support their needs.

Evidence management

Managing chain of custody from evidence collection to trial is the most important part of any digital forensics investigation. You could have the best tools and the smartest analysts generate the most useful data, but it would all be for naught if you aren't able to protect and prove the integrity of your evidence throughout its entire lifecycle. I cover chain of custody and nonrepudiation in Chapter 6. If you haven't already, you should really check it out for additional background.

Cloud providers must maintain well-documented policies and procedures for evidence management. Policies should establish what types of data to collect and how to properly engage with customers, authorities, and other stakeholders. It's important that a provider understands how cloud-specific factors like multi-tenancy and virtualization impact their collection and preservation of evidence. In some cases, contractual obligations or jurisdictional requirements might mandate that a CSP disclose their collection activities and processes to third parties. In other situations, the investigation may be deemed confidential and require that evidence collection and management processes not be disclosed at all. For either scenario, requirements should be fully documented and understood prior to collecting or handling evidence.

Managing Communication with Relevant Parties

Effective communication is critical in any business. A service provider must be able to accurately, concisely, and timely communicate important facts to customers, vendors, and partners to ensure that business operates smoothly and end-users remain informed and satisfied.

For IT services, and especially cloud providers, communication with regulators is another important facet to consider, as regulations impact not only the provider, but potentially thousands of customers and other stakeholders.

Customers

As a cloud service provider, communicating with customers is among the top of your priorities. Any time you provide a service to someone, it's essential that you understand their needs and wants — an open dialogue between cloud provider and customer is the best way to achieve this goal. Customers are likely to directly engage CSP personnel most during the early stages of procurement, planning, and migration. Depending on the customer, a CSP may designate some combination of sales representatives, technical account managers, and solutions architects to learn a customer's requirements and share the provider's capabilities. Contract and SLA negotiations are pivotal during this time, and it's important that the provider is fully transparent about what they can and cannot do.

Customers have less of a need to communicate directly with a CSP as their cloud journey progresses (at least they hope so!). The bulk of ongoing communications should be updates by the CSP related to service availability, system upgrades, and policy changes that have a customer impact.

TIP

Effective communication isn't solely based on phone calls, meetings, and emails. In fact, both customers and providers benefit from self-service access to information. One great example of this is AWS' Service Health Dashboard (https:// status.aws.amazon.com), which shows the current status for all services in all of their regions. This dashboard is a great example of automated communication that helps providers scale as business grows.

Perhaps the most important ongoing communication between a CSP and its customers involves providing up-to-date documentation. User guides and other product documentation is essential for customers to know best practices when using their cloud services. Even more essential, CSPs must ensure that they accurately communicate what responsibilities they have versus the customer's responsibility. This information is usually documented in a customer responsibility matrix, or similar. These documents are often associated with some sort of regulation or compliance framework and can be used to communicate what security functions a CSP performs and what functions must be performed by the customer.

Vendors

Vendors (or suppliers) are a major part of a CSP's ecosystem; I don't know of a single CSP that doesn't rely on multiple vendors in some form or fashion. Examples include hardware manufacturers, software vendors, outsourced maintenance professionals, and more. Many of these services are mission critical for a CSP; as such, effective communication with vendors is of the utmost importance. Most important CSP-vendor communication is captured within various contracts and agreements; these agreements should detail a vendor's commitments to the CSP from onboarding through termination.

Partners

The type of partners that cloud providers rely on is wide-ranging and can include anything from companies that support go-to-market to organizations that build their SaaS solutions on your IaaS infrastructure. The lines can sometimes blur between partners and vendors or customers, but it's important to evaluate your partner relationships and determine the best method and frequency to communicate with each of them.

Regulators

Just about every cloud provider and cloud customer has regulations to comply with. As a CCSP, it's your job to understand these regulations and help your organization craft ways to satisfy them. Communication with regulators should happen early and often. When a cloud provider is first planning to build their infrastructure or making significant changes to existing infrastructure (like constructing a new region), they should maintain communication with regulators to ensure that all requirements are fully understood. Further, cloud providers generally benefit by having security-minded personnel review and comment on upcoming regulations before they're finalized. Regulatory bodies are often a step or two behind bleeding-edge technology. CSPs that understand the technology and its limitations better than anyone should communicate these factors to regulators in order to help shape realistic policies and requirements.

DATA CENTER FORENSICS

I once had a regulator insist that their forensics unit should be able to come to a cloud data center to conduct forensic activity, should an incident ever occur. This particular regulator was very accustomed to auditing and investigating traditional data centers, where concepts like multitenancy and resource pooling aren't factors. After several conversations, I was able to help the regulator understand that the intent of what they wanted to accomplish (collect evidence to support investigations) could not be achieved by visiting a data center and trying to find which of the 50,000 servers had relevant data. My conversations helped them understand that their legacy policy didn't quite fit the way cloud environments operate, and together we agreed on a way to achieve the same end goal without visiting a data center.

Other stakeholders

Aside from customers, vendors, partners, and regulators, you may find other stakeholders that need to be involved in your communication plans. This need may be based on a particular project or a request from one of the previously discussed parties. In any case, you must evaluate the communication needs of all stakeholders, and determine what, how, and when to communicate with them.

Managing Security Operations

This chapter has a lot of information related to building and deploying security controls to operate and manage the physical and logical components of a cloud environment. It's just as important to consider managing and monitoring those controls to ensure that they're configured properly and functioning as intended. Security operations include all the tools, processes, and personnel required to accomplish that goal.

Security operations center (SOC)

A *security operations center* (*SOC, pronounced "sock"*) is a centralized location where designated information security personnel continuously monitor and analyze an organization's security posture. Rather than focusing on developing security strategies or implementing security controls, a SOC team is responsible for the ongoing, operational aspects of security. SOCs should be staffed 24/7, and its team members are responsible for detecting, reporting, and responding to security incidents using a combination of technology and well-established processes.

TIP

In the olden days, a SOC was strictly considered to be a large room with lots of computers, large monitors, and staff members. That definition still holds true today, but we're seeing the emergence of virtual SOCs. A virtual SOC allows teams in different locations to share resources and communicate in real-time in order to monitor and respond to security issues. This concept is almost a requirement for globally dispersed cloud providers.

REMEMBER

Your organization's incident response (IR) team is likely different from your SOC team, though there may be overlap. Once the SOC identifies a potential incident, it should quickly trigger incident response procedures and work with the IR team to investigate and resolve the matter.

The scope of a cloud provider's SOC should include all their physical and logical assets — all hypervisors, servers, networking devices, storage units, and any other assets under the CSP's control. While tenant's guest operating systems are not generally monitored by a CSP, the SOC should still monitor and identify any malicious activity between a tenant and the CSP or from one tenant to another.

Intelligent monitoring of security controls

On a more tactical level, intelligent monitoring should be in place to assess and validate the effectiveness of your security controls. If you've used a defense-in-depth approach (and I know you have), then you'll need layers of monitoring in place to continuously ensure that your controls remain in place, unmodified, and fully functional.

Monitoring your security controls should begin with documentation that defines the intent of each control and how it is implemented. You should also have documentation that identifies how to monitor each security control, either manually or preferably by automated means. In some cases, vendors provide best practices on how to monitor their security controls. Other scenarios require that your information security team, led by their fearless CCSP, generates the necessary guidance. Make sure that you also maintain complete documentation of all security configuration baselines. I talk about documenting baselines in Chapter 11, and it becomes especially important when it's time to monitor them.

REMEMBER

Enterprise cloud environments include so many platforms, databases, and other resource, each with its own log data that needs to be captured and analyzed. Your SIEM is a critical part of your ability to monitor your security controls, and a good SIEM offers intel-based and even ML-based analysis and alerting. I cover SIEMs in Chapter 6.

Conducting vulnerability assessments and penetration tests are a great way to indirectly assess the effectiveness of your security controls. These tests expose weaknesses in your environment, and penetration tests can even show you the impact of those weaknesses being compromised. Performing these tests can highlight weak areas in your security architecture and help you identify needs for new or modified security controls.

TECHNICAL STUFF

In the spirit of using automation wherever possible, consider automating vulnerability assessments and pentests any time you can. There are vendors that offer ML-based simulated attacks, but you can also build automated functionality in-house, if it makes sense for your business and you have the engineering capacity.

Cloud Security Posture Management (CSPM)

Cloud security posture management (CSPM) is a set of tools and practices that continuously and automatically monitors your cloud environment, identifies misconfigurations and risks, and provides insights to maintain a strong security posture.

An enterprise cloud environment can connect to thousands of networks every day, reflecting the cloud's dynamic nature that's both awesome and challenging to secure. As cloud technologies evolve, companies have a growing list of elements to manage across their vast environments — microservices, containers, serverless functions, the list goes on.

Along with these newer technologies comes the idea of Infrastructure as Code (IaC), which I discuss in Chapter 11. IaC makes it easy to change cloud infrastructure on the fly, but also makes it easy to program in misconfigurations across your entire environment.

TIP

A Gartner report estimates that 95 percent of all security breaches are due to misconfigurations, which cost companies trillions in dollars each year.

Underlying all of these issues is the greatest vulnerability of all: lack of visibility. As cloud environments become increasingly complex, your organization can use CSPM to continuously monitor risk in your cloud through prevention, detection, response, and prediction of where risk may show up next.

Chapter **13**

Domain 6: Legal, Risk, and Compliance, Part 1

I n this chapter, you gain a solid understanding of legal and compliance requirements that impact cloud procurement, usage, and security. You don't have to be a lawyer to benefit from this information — every cloud security professional should be versed in these topics. Domain 6 represents 13 percent of the CCSP certification exam, and this chapter covers the first half of Domain 6.

If you've read any other chapter in this book, there's a good chance you've seen me talk about compliance with legal, regulatory, and contractual requirements. That's because cloud computing, by nature, exposes cloud providers, cloud customers, and other stakeholders to a variety of unique legal and policy challenges (due to global infrastructure, shared responsibilities, and other cloud concepts discussed throughout this book). As a CCSP, it's important that you understand how to approach these challenges. You should have a baseline understanding of relevant security and privacy laws and regulations, and — even if you're not a cloud auditor — you should have a firm grasp of cloud audit processes and methodologies. You learn about these topics in this chapter and the next.

Articulating Legal Requirements and Unique Risks within the Cloud Environment

Cloud environments span numerous regions across multiple jurisdictions and countries. This geographic dispersion not only presents challenges when seeking to understand which legislations apply to the environment, but also creates technical complexities when discovering and collecting data across those regions.

Conflicting international legislation

I use the phrase "security follows the data" throughout this book. For the purposes of this chapter, change that phrase to "regulations follow the data." By this statement, I mean that the laws and regulations that apply to your data are largely impacted by where that data travels and resides. In general, U.S. data centers must adhere to U.S. laws (and applicable state laws), German data centers must adhere to German laws (and applicable EU-wide legislations), and so on — that's the pretty straightforward stuff. Where it can get tricky is when data moves from the United States to Germany to Singapore to India. While having data centers all over the world helps provide broad network access and rapid elasticity, it can be a nightmare to track all the places that specific data resides (or has resided) and understand the impact of that from a legal perspective.

Legal requirements often differ from one country to the next, and in some cases, legislations can directly conflict with one another. While global operations are not unique to cloud companies, the explosion of cloud computing continues to make international legal disputes a growing concern. As a CCSP, you must work with your organization's legal and policy teams to understand how to best treat things like data protection and copyright laws across international boundaries.

ADDRESSING CONFLICTING LAWS

A great example of conflicting international legislation that I see all the time involves limiting administrative access to a specific country's citizens. For example, the International Traffic in Arms Regulations (ITAR) is a set of United States-based rules that requires limiting access to certain controlled data to U.S. persons (which includes U.S. citizens, U.S. permanent residents, and limited others). On the other hand, various EU privacy laws require that data be protected against access by citizens or authorities from non-EU jurisdictions. This requirement directly conflicts with ITAR requirements. Some CSPs take a traditional approach to solving these types of challenges. For example, AWS GovCloud is a cloud offering from AWS that limits data to U.S. soil and U.S. personnel. While this offering addresses ITAR and various other U.S. regulations, the approach does not scale very well. Other CSPs use logical mechanisms (like strong encryption and access controls) to virtually isolate data and control who can access it. While logical separation may scale better than the traditional GovCloud approach, it comes with its own challenges around properly identifying, tagging, and restricting the right data based on the appropriate set of regulations. In a challenging global operating environment, there really is no one-size-fits-all technical solution. Effective management of international legislations comes down to thoroughly understanding all applicable laws and building controls and processes that work best for your given solution.

Evaluating legal risks specific to cloud computing

When your organization owns and manages a data center, you have complete control over the environment and the data within it. This control makes it easy (in theory) to ensure that you're satisfying all of your regulatory and contractual requirements because your fate is in your own hands.

Once you make the move to a cloud environment, you're giving up a lot of that control — instead, you're reliant on the cloud provider to help you meet many of those obligations. (See Chapter 3 for a discussion on the Shared Responsibility Model.) Despite your reliance on the CSP, you (as the cloud customer) are still ultimately accountable for meeting all of your obligations. The cloud provider, in turn, is contractually obligated to support you in doing so.

REMEMBER

Keep in mind, however, that the cloud provider has similar contractual obligations to their other customers. This arrangement poses some legal risks that every CCSP must be aware of. I discuss some of the most common legal risks in the following sections.

Jurisdiction and governing law

Most CSPs have provisions that say they are governed and bound by the laws of the country in which they are incorporated. From a legal perspective, this provision usually means that the laws and regulations of the CSP's home country get the final say whenever disputes or conflicts arise. Customers using cloud services from a CSP outside of their country often want these types of provisions modified to move legal jurisdiction to the customer's home country. While some large, multinational CSPs can accommodate these types of requests, many smaller providers (and some of the large ones) are not able or willing to do so. Some providers opt to remove such provisions from contracts altogether and instead allow case-by-case handling of legal conflicts.

In any event, customers must understand how a prospective CSP treats jurisdictional matters and determine whether any associated risks are acceptable to their business.

Data location

Data location comes up a lot and is worth specific attention here. It should be expected, unless otherwise noted, that a cloud provider permits customer data to be stored and processed at any of their data center locations. In other words, if your SLAs or other contractual agreements don't explicitly prohibit the CSP from maintaining your data across multiple geographic regions, then it is fair game and probably going to happen.

While geographic dispersion is for completely legitimate reasons (redundancy, availability, and overall security), it is a major legal risk for customers who have export control (like ITAR) or other data location requirements.

REMEMBER

If data location is important for you, then make sure it's appropriately addressed in your cloud contract.

Security and privacy

One of the biggest legal risks associated with cloud environments is related to a customer's reliance on the CSP to effectively maintain the security and privacy of their data. The last thing a customer wants is to do everything right on their end and find out that their cloud provider is a weak link.

Many cloud providers agree to provide reasonable or industry standard security measures. While these standards are a good start, it's better to ensure that your CSP agrees to meet independent third-party security standards (ISO 27001, for example). If you're required to maintain HIPAA, PCI, or similar, make sure that you choose a cloud provider that can demonstrate the required compliance.

WARNING

Always confirm that the specific cloud services that you use are covered by your CSP's HIPAA, PCI, FedRAMP, or other compliance attestations. CSPs release new services all the time, and there is often a lag between when a service is launched and when it is included in the CSP's "compliance boundary" that validates security and privacy measures.

Privacy is a huge concern for many customers migrating to the cloud. When moving your data to a trusted third party, you want to feel confident that it's being used and accessed only for intended purposes. To mitigate privacy risks, customers should seek explicit agreement from cloud providers to only use their data in an agreed upon manner (for example, not selling their data without prior consent). Without explicit contractual agreement, meeting privacy expectations can be a challenge.

Data breaches

As an industry, computer security professionals have moved from if a breach occurs to when it occurs. Many countries (and most U.S. states) have data breach disclosure laws that require a cloud provider to inform customers when their data has been compromised. Customers should seek to have the timing and method for communicating such breaches specifically outlined in their SLAs and cloud contracts.

TIP

If and when you deal with your data being breached through one of your third parties (cloud-based or otherwise), you will go through various incident response, business continuity, and risk management processes. Eventually, when the incident is fully resolved, your company's legal team (with your help) should closely evaluate the incident to determine if the third party failed to maintain their required security posture. For example, you may contractually require vendors to patch high-risk vulnerabilities within 30 days, but the root cause of a data breach may have been identified as a seven-month old high-risk vulnerability. Depending on the circumstances, your company may be entitled to legal recourse, and the security team plays a big part in determining that.

Intellectual property and data ownership

Copyright, trademark, and other intellectual property (IP) laws differ from one country to another. Customers who store sensitive IP in the cloud must ensure that their cloud provider protects their IP in accordance with their country's regulations. On a broader level, cloud contracts should explicitly state that a customer's data remains their property even after being moved to the cloud.

IP and data ownership risks can be limited through proactive contractual agreement of important requirements.

Legal framework and guidelines

The number of security and privacy laws and regulations around the world continues to grow every year. As a result, various frameworks and guidelines are now available to help CSPs and other service providers build and manage their security programs in a compliant manner. While many of these guidelines are country-specific, organizations like ISO publish standards and guidelines that are used around the globe.

I cover several standards, frameworks, and guidelines in Chapter 4. In addition to the ones discussed there, the *NIST Cybersecurity Framework* (*NIST CSF*) is worth your attention. Whereas NIST typically issues publications that are heavily relied on by U.S. government agencies and partners, NIST CSF provides security and privacy guidelines that are primarily aimed at private sector companies.

NIST CSF was originally introduced in 2014, but the most recent version as of this writing (v1.1) was finalized in April 2018. The framework is divided into five functions to help organizations assess and build their security capabilities. The five NIST CSF functions (and their unique identifiers) are

>> **Identify (ID):** This function is focused on understanding your organization's assets, systems, data, people, and capabilities.

>> **Protect (PR):** The goal of the controls in this function is to limit or contain the impact of potential security threats and keep your systems functioning.

>> **Detect (DE):** This function includes the set of controls and activities required to discovery security events and incidents in a timely fashion.

>> **Respond (RS):** This function deals with taking appropriate action against detected security incidents.

>> **Recover (RC):** This function is focused on maintaining organizational resilience and restoring all functionality after a security-related incident.

The preceding functions are divided into 23 categories, and these categories are further divided into a total of 108 subcategories, each describing a specific security control or desired outcome. For the list of subcategories and additional guidance on using the NIST Cybersecurity Framework, check out https://nvlpubs.nist.gov/nistpubs/CSWP/NIST.CSWP.04162018.pdf.

TIP

NIST released a draft of the Cybersecurity Framework (CSF) 2.0 on August 2023. As of this writing, it's still out for public comment, and the final CSF 2.0 is expected to be published in early 2024. The most significant change in the draft is the addition of a sixth function, Govern. The CCSP exam won't likely get into great detail on the CSF, but it's worth a quick search to learn more about the latest version, once it's published.

e-Discovery

e-Discovery, or *electronic discovery*, is the process of electronic data being collected, secured, and analyzed as part of civil or criminal legal cases. e-Discovery is commonly associated with lawsuits, government investigations, and other legal proceedings where electronic evidence plays a role in the case.

The *Electronic Discovery Reference Model* (EDRM) provides an overall look at the e-Discovery process. The model is not intended as a step-by-step process, but rather a conceptual view of the typical steps involved in the e-Discovery process. Visit www.edrm.net/ for additional information.

The key steps of the EDRM are

> » **Identification:** Locate and tag potentially relevant digital evidence, based on the details of the e-Discovery request or order.

> » **Preservation:** Place potentially relevant digital evidence in legal hold (see Chapter 6) and ensure that it cannot be modified or destroyed. Preservation occurs before collection to ensure that evidence remains intact throughout the collection process.

> » **Collection:** Gather all potentially relevant digital evidence and prepare for review, processing, and analysis.

> » **Review and analysis:** This step is where your legal counsel typically gets involved with the digital evidence, as they evaluate what you've collected for relevance, completion, and context.

> » **Production:** Digital evidence is delivered to external parties (such as opposing counsel or requesting authority) in the agreed-upon format and via the agreed-upon means.

WARNING

Whenever your organization receives an e-Discovery request, it is likely to be a stressful time for everyone involved. Always remember that e-Discovery is not simply a digital forensics function — it is a legal matter at heart. You, as a CCSP, should know which laws and statutes are applicable to your specific organization and investigation, but do not forget to keep your legal team (and other business stakeholders) deeply involved throughout the entire process.

TIP

If you're interested in diving deeper into the world of U.S. law and evidence collection — or if you're looking for some great bedtime reading — you can check out the Federal Rules of Civil Procedure (FRCP) and Federal Rules of Evidence (FRE). You can find links to both in Appendix B.

e-Discovery is fairly straightforward in traditional data center environments, where an organization owns and controls all systems and processes. Identification and collection of digital evidence is less complex because the organization generally knows which systems perform which tasks, and individual systems can be taken offline for analysis with ease. In cloud environments, single workloads are commonly dispersed across multiple physical servers, data centers, and even jurisdictions. This dispersion adds a great deal of complexity to finding, collecting, and preserving digital evidence as part of an e-Discovery request. Adding further complexity, cloud environments rely on the concept of multitenancy, which means any given physical system likely holds data from other, unrelated tenants. When a formal e-Discovery request is received for or from one customer, cloud providers must be able to thoroughly collect the required data while maintaining the privacy and confidentiality of other tenant's data.

Aside from EDRM, the International Organization for Standards (ISO) and Cloud Security Alliance (CSA) also provide standards and frameworks that offer guidelines relevant to e-Discovery. Those guidelines are discussed in the following sections.

ISO/IEC 27050

Another standard from our friends at ISO, this one was last revised in 2019 and is squarely focused on concepts related to e-Discovery. ISO 27050 attempts to create an internationally accepted standard for electronic discovery terminology and processes. The standard defines the same terms from the EDRM and establishes some common expectations for each step. The document also identifies other relevant standards and discusses how they relate to e-Discovery.

As I mention throughout this chapter, the global nature of cloud providers creates many challenges when navigating multiple jurisdictions, legislations, and regulations. Having an international organization like ISO step up and provide leadership in this space provides a great starting point for CSPs and cloud customers to understand and engage each other consistently on e-Discovery matters.

Cloud Security Alliance (CSA) Guidance

The Cloud Security Alliance (CSA) published CSA Security Guidance v4.0 in 2017; check out the latest version of the publication at https://cloudsecurity alliance.org/research/guidance. Among many other important topics, the publication covers legal issues, contracts, and electronic discovery in Domain 3. The document identifies cloud-specific issues and risks related to e-Discovery and makes recommendations to cloud providers and cloud customers to help ensure that e-Discovery activities are effective and compliant with relevant regulations.

For the sake of this discussion, I first define a couple important terms:

>> **Responding party:** The *responding party* is the person, group, or organization who has received an e-Discovery order and is responsible for providing the digital evidence to the requesting party.

>> **Requesting party:** The *requesting party* is the person, group, or organization who does not own the digital evidence and initiates the request for such evidence from the responding party.

Among the e-Discovery concerns addressed in the CSA Security Guidance, some of the key items include

» **Possession, custody, and control over systems and data:** The United States Federal Rules of Civil Procedure (FRCP) Rule 34(a)(1) specifies that items under the responding party's possession, custody, or control must be produced to the requesting party; certain U.S. states and international jurisdictions make similar statements. This language poses some challenges in a cloud environment, where the responding party (such as the cloud customer) does not physically possess or control the systems or data. Despite not maintaining control over the cloud provider's infrastructure, the cloud customer is not excused from their responsibility to provide the requested information. It is paramount that cloud providers and cloud customers agree upon what data is and is not available to the cloud customer in the event of an e-Discovery order. These agreed-upon terms should be documented in SLAs and contracts and should also include details about the CSP's level of support for such orders.

» **Cooperation and communication between CSP and customer:** Because of the cloud customer's reliance on the CSP to help resolve e-Discovery orders, it's in everyone's best interest that the CSP and customer work together to resolve any such requests. Effective communication begins at the outset of the relationship, and all terms should be clearly documented in the signed SLAs. CSPs should seek to design their systems for ease of discovery and, when possible, should empower customers to collect as much required evidence as securely possible.

» **Responding to subpoenas or search warrants:** If a CSP receives a subpoena or search warrant on behalf of a customer, they should first ensure that the request is legitimate and lawful. If so, it may be natural for a CSP to take swift action in responding to the authorities with the requested information or access. However, the CSP should first give the impacted customer notice of the legal request, giving that customer an opportunity to fight the request. Further, CSPs must be mindful about their environment's shared tenancy and validate that providing the requested evidence won't compromise any other legal or contractual agreements.

REMEMBER

e-Discovery requests are commonly issued against a customer, but may also be issued against the CSP. When this event happens, the request is seeking evidence related to the cloud environment itself and may impact many different cloud customers. Cloud providers must establish clear processes for addressing such requests and be transparent with all customers about how potential e-Discovery orders will be handled.

Forensics requirements

I cover the topic of digital forensics in Chapter 12. Digital forensics is the collection of tools and processes that supports the actual collection of evidence as requested in e-Discovery orders. Conducting forensics activities in the cloud is difficult for all of the reasons highlighted in the e-Discovery section of this chapter. A cloud customer may not have access to the systems or information they require in order to collect forensics data and therefore must work with their CSP to collect such data. Some CSPs refuse to provide forensics data that is not required by a court order — unless otherwise agreed, the CSP is not obligated to do so. Customers should evaluate and understand any prospective CSP's policies for supporting forensics requests before moving their data to the cloud.

Understanding Privacy Issues

Privacy entails limiting access to personal information to authorized parties for authorized uses. In essence, privacy is maintaining the confidentiality of personal information, specifically (rather than just any kind of sensitive data).

As more and more of our personal data moves online, privacy has become arguably the biggest security-related topic for every cloud provider. Every time you shop online, get web-based navigation directions, or download an app to your mobile device, you leave traces of your identity behind. Privacy is all about protecting those traces and keeping your identity as anonymous as possible.

REMEMBER

Privacy is a bit like the missing fourth-leg in the C-I-A security triad; it complements confidentiality, integrity, and availability, but is its own beast that deserves individual attention.

Several prominent privacy laws exist across many countries and jurisdictions. As a CCSP, you should be familiar with these laws and understand how they may impact your organization's security decisions.

Difference between contractual and regulated private data

Private data, such as Personally Identifiable Information (PII), is often subject to some combination of contractual and regulatory requirements. While the source of the requirements may vary, the seriousness with which cloud providers should take these requirements is consistent across the board. Because they're required either by contractual agreement or by the law, CSPs must ensure they have mature auditing capabilities to effectively monitor and report on their compliance with privacy requirements.

Contractual private data

Privacy is a top concern of many customers moving to the cloud. Prudent cloud customers want some level of assurance that PII, PHI, or other private data is protected at least as well as they'd protect it themselves. Cloud customers often gain this assurance by working with their prospective CSP to place specific requirements on the handling and protection of PII. These requirements can range from broad policies (such as who may access private data and what uses of private data are permitted or forbidden) to specific controls that must be in place (a particular method of encryption, for example). Failure to uphold contractual private data requirements can lead to contract penalties (such as the loss of money for the CSP), loss of business, or even civil suits.

Regulated private data

Certain types of private data must be protected by numerous laws and regulations around the world. Regulated private data must be protected even if a customer doesn't specifically request it to be. As discussed in Chapter 6, Protected Health Information (PHI) is a prime example of regulated private data. Various industries (like healthcare and financial services) and many governments around the world have some form of privacy legislation that impacts both cloud providers and their customers. In addition to loss of business, failure to protect regulated private data can lead to steep financial penalties or even criminal charges.

Country-specific legislation related to private data

Global service providers have a whole lotta laws and regulations to keep up with! While the principles of most privacy regulations are often very similar, the specifics of what must and must not be done vary from one jurisdiction to the next. In this section, I cover some of the most prominent regulations from the United States, Canada, the European Union (EU), Brazil, Russia, and China.

United States

It still surprises me, but the United States does not have a single federal law that governs data privacy for all personal information. Instead, multiple federal laws govern privacy for specific types of data and specific industries. Two of the most prevalent U.S. privacy laws are HIPAA and GLBA:

>> **HIPAA:** The *Health Insurance Portability and Accountability Act* (HIPAA) was passed in 1996. The HIPAA Privacy Rule establishes minimum standards for protecting a patient's privacy and regulates the use and disclosure of individuals' health information, referred to as protected health information (PHI).

Under HIPAA, an individual's PHI is permitted to be used for the purposes of performing and billing for health-related services and must be protected against improper disclosure.

>> **GLBA:** The *Gramm-Leach-Bliley Act* (GLBA), also known as the Financial Modernization Act of 1999, is a U.S. federal law that requires financial institutions to safeguard their customer's PII (personally identifiable information). Among the provisions within GLBA, the Financial Privacy Rule requires that financial institutions provide each customer with a written privacy notice that explains what personal information is collected from the customer, how it is used, and how it is protected. The GLBA Safeguards Rule requires organizations to implement proper security controls to protect their customers' personal data. Organizations should consider these provisions and requirements when moving to a cloud provider.

TIP

In addition to federal laws, the United States is seeing an emergence of privacy laws at the state level as well. For example, the California Consumer Privacy Act was passed in 2018 in response to the large and growing economy of the state of California. The Virginia Consumer Data Protection Act went into effect in January 2023, and it aims to provide Virginia residents with certain rights for personal data collected by businesses. As the number of U.S. and individual state laws continues to increase, CSPs and cloud customers must continue to stay on top of their compliance obligations.

Canada

The *Canadian Digital Privacy Act* was published in 2015 and served as a major update to the long-standing Personal Information Protection and Electronic Documents Act (PIPEDA). These regulations apply to the collection, use, and disclosure of personal information throughout the course of all commercial activities in Canada. Among other things, PIPEDA requires that companies protect personal information using appropriate security controls, such as encryption and passwords. Penalties for noncompliance with PIPEDA can include fines of up to $100,000.

European Union (EU) and GDPR

The European Union (EU) and its member countries have some of the strictest privacy laws anywhere on the planet. Many of these regulations prohibit personal information from being sent outside of the physical boundaries of the EU or even outside a specific country. These data localization requirements can be challenging for large public clouds with vast geographical footprints, but can sometimes be waived for CSPs that demonstrate suitable security controls to protect the privacy of EU citizens.

The mother of all privacy regulations was established in 2016 and went into effect in 2018. The *General Data Protection Regulation*, or GDPR, is considered by most to be the world's strongest data privacy law. GDPR replaced the EU's 1995 *Data Protection Directive* with hundreds of pages of regulations that require organizations around the world to protect the privacy of EU citizens. The entire set of regulations includes 11 chapters with a total of 99 articles.

REMEMBER

If you store or process PII of EU citizens or residents, then GDPR applies to you — even if you are not located in the EU.

GDPR Article 5 lays out seven principles for processing personal data:

>> **Lawfulness, fairness, and transparency:** Process personal data in accordance with the laws and inform the customer of how their data will be used.

>> **Purpose limitation:** Personal data may be processed only for legitimate purposes, as specified to the customer. In other words, do what you say you're going to do with the data, and nothing more.

>> **Data minimization:** Collect and process only as much data as is absolutely necessary to provide the agreed-upon services.

>> **Accuracy:** Ensure that personal data is kept accurate and up to date.

>> **Storage limitation:** Personal data may be stored only as long as necessary to provide the agreed-upon services, and no longer.

>> **Integrity and confidentiality:** Ensure the security of the personal data and provide protection against unauthorized access and accidental loss or destruction.

>> **Accountability:** The *data controller* (the person or organization that handles the personal data — usually the cloud customer) must be able to demonstrate compliance with all of these principles.

One of the key rules within GDPR is the right to be forgotten, found in Article 17. This regulation gives the *data subject* (the person whose data is being used) the right to have their personal data deleted if one of several circumstances exists. I won't go into the specifics here, but you should certainly know that this part of the regulation is one of the main requirements that caused many CSPs and their customers to re-examine their data deletion policies and procedures.

GDPR Chapter 4 contains Articles 24 through 43 that focus on requirements related to the data controller and processor. Of particular interest, Article 25 specifically requires data protection by design and by default. This huge mandate codifies what security professionals have been recommending as best practice for over a decade. GDPR requires that *data processors* (the CSP) put data security and privacy front and center. These requirements have caused a shift by many cloud providers toward enabling many security controls (like encryption) by default, rather than merely making it available to customers.

GDPR Article 33 establishes additional rules that directly impact cloud providers. This article requires that data controllers notify authorities within 72 hours of a personal data breach. I've personally experienced this requirement as challenging to enforce simply because the data controller, in the case of cloud environments, does not always have timely insight into potential breaches. Cloud customers must ensure that their CSP is willing and able to commit to notifying them of privacy breaches with enough time for them to then report it to authorities.

TIP

You should be very familiar with GDPR, its requirements, and how it changed privacy throughout the cloud computing industry.

Other countries

North America and Europe are major players in the global privacy landscape, but countries in other parts of the world continue to develop regulations that you, as a CCSP, should stay on top of. The following list is a small sample of key regulations that have been or are in the process of being published, as of this writing. The list is intended to provide further context about the disparate privacy regulations around the world, as is not exhaustive or comprehensive.

>> **Brazil:** The Brazilian General Data Protection Law (LGPD), published in 2018, is modeled after GDPR and establishes standards for managing the privacy of Brazilian citizen personal data. The LGPD defines personal data in a broader manner than GDPR and should be closely reviewed if you do business in Brazil.

>> **China:** Several laws in China control what can and cannot be done with personal information. Among them, the Chinese Cybersecurity Law requires that critical information infrastructure operators store personal information within the territory of the People's Republic of China. The designation of critical information infrastructure operator is a bit vague, but companies operating in China generally offer full data localization options within the region. Because of China's strict requirements, American-based CSPs generally take significantly longer to launch new services and features in their Chinese regions.

>> **Russia:** The Russian Data Localization Law 526-FZ was established in 2015 and mandates that all personal data of Russian citizens be stored and processed on systems that are located within Russia.

Jurisdictional differences in data privacy

New privacy laws are popping up around the world all the time, and they don't always align with each other. Some regulations mandate encryption, while some forbid it. Some laws require data retention, whereas GDPR and other laws focus on timely data deletion.

To make things even trickier, more and more countries want their citizens' data to stay within their own country. CSPs and cloud customers must work together to identify how to satisfy conflicting requirements from one country to the next.

Standard privacy requirements

With all of the differences from one privacy regulation to the next, wouldn't it be nice to have some kind of internationally recognized standard available for guidance? Well, you're in luck — I've got two!

ISO/IEC 27018 fits this bill as an international standard that is specific to privacy in the cloud, and the Privacy Management Framework (PMF) — formerly the Generally Accepted Privacy Principles (GAPP) — provides a broad framework to help you build privacy programs.

REMEMBER

Although each of these standards is valuable in its own way, remember that no single standard or framework replaces your legal obligations.

ISO/IEC 27018

ISO/IEC 27018 was originally published in 2014 and updated in 2019. The document expands on ISO/IEC 27002 to establish a standard code of practice for protecting PII in public cloud environments. According to ISO, the 27018: 2019 standard has the following objectives:

>> Assist the CSP in complying with contractual and regulatory privacy requirements.

>> Enable the CSP to be transparent with its customers about how it handles PII; in turn, enable cloud customers to select CSPs that handle PII in a manner that fits their needs.

>> Assist the CSP and cloud customers in entering contractual agreements by providing a clear framework for discussing and handling privacy concerns.

>> Provide cloud customers with a mechanism for measuring a CSP's compliance with privacy obligations by requiring they undergo periodic independent audits.

Privacy Management Framework (PMF) (formerly the Generally Accepted Privacy Principles)

The Generally Accepted Privacy Principles (GAPP) is a privacy framework that was published in 2009 by a Privacy Task Force created by the American Institute of Certified Public Accountants (AICPA) and the Canadian Institute of Chartered Accountants (CICA). After more than a decade, GAPP was replaced by the Privacy Management Framework (PMF) in 2020. The updated framework was created to respond to significant changes in technologies, laws, and standards.

The GAPP and PMF frameworks were initially created to assist Certified Public Accountants in creating and managing privacy programs, but PMF is also a reliable framework to help the CCSP do the same.

PMF consists of the following nine privacy principles:

>> **Management:** Define, document, and communicate privacy policies and procedures to impacted parties and relevant stakeholders.

>> **Agreement, notice, and communication:** Obtain consent from impacted parties to collect, use, retain, and disclose their PII. Inform impacted parties of how their PII is collected, handled, and protected.

>> **Collection and creation:** Limit PII collection to what has been committed to and consented by impacted parties.

>> **Use, retention, and disposal:** Limit PII use to what has been committed to and consented by impacted parties, retain the PII only for as long as it's absolutely needed, and dispose of the PII when it's no longer needed.

>> **Access:** All affected parties to access their PII to ensure that it's accurate and up to date.

>> **Disclosure to third parties:** Disclose PII to third parties only for purposes identified in the notice and ensure that impacted parties consent to this disclosure.

>> **Security for privacy:** Ensure the confidentiality of PII through the use of logical and physical security controls.

>> **Data integrity and quality:** Maintain the integrity (in other words, accuracy and completeness) of PII for the purposes identified in the notice.

>> **Monitoring and enforcement:** Audit systems and processes to ensure that privacy policies and procedures are effective. Ensure that there are means to find, report, and remediate privacy gaps.

Privacy impact assessments (PIAs)

A *privacy impact assessment* (PIA) is an evaluation process that organizations undertake to identify, assess, and mitigate the potential privacy risks and implications associated with a particular system, project, or initiative. The primary goal of a PIA is to ensure that personal data is handled in a responsible and compliant manner, protecting individuals' privacy rights and adhering to relevant data protection regulations.

There are many ways to approach a PIA, but the following are some common steps and considerations:

>> **Data mapping:** Identify the types of personal data that will be collected, processed, stored, or transmitted throughout the project or system.

>> **Risk identification:** Evaluate potential privacy risks and concerns that could arise from the collection and processing of personal data. This includes assessing the likelihood of unauthorized access, data breaches, unintended data sharing, or other privacy breaches.

>> **Assessment of legal and regulatory compliance:** Ensure that the project aligns with relevant data protection laws and regulations, such as GDPR, HIPAA, and CCPA, depending on the jurisdiction and the nature of the data being processed.

>> **Mitigation strategies:** Develop strategies to mitigate the identified privacy risks. This could involve implementing privacy safeguards, enhancing data security measures, or obtaining informed consent from individuals.

TIP

You should conduct a privacy impact assessment any time you launch a new product, build a new system, or make a significant change that might impact personal data. It's important that you continuously monitor and reassess privacy impacts throughout a product's (or system's) lifecycle — especially as the product (or system) evolves or new data practices are introduced.

Chapter **14**

Domain 6: Legal, Risk and Compliance, Part 2

n this chapter, you dive into the risk management and auditing of cloud systems. Domain 6 represents 13 percent of the CCSP certification exam, and this chapter covers the second half of Domain 6.

The area of Governance, Risk, and Compliance (GRC) focuses on the oversight of your security program. I introduce various legal, regulatory, and other compliance requirements in Chapter 13 and throughout this book. In the following sections, I discuss more of the governance and risk side of things. Even if you're not a cloud auditor, you should have a solid understanding of cloud audit processes and methodologies. You learn about these topics in the rest of this chapter, and I also cover the topic of risk management, as it pertains to the cloud.

Understanding the Audit Process, Methodologies, and Required Adaptations for a Cloud Environment

As I highlight throughout this book, the uniqueness and complexity of cloud environments requires that you make certain adaptations to the traditional data center processes and methodologies — audit is no exception. If you've done any auditing of noncloud IT systems, then many of the terms, concepts, and requirements discussed in this section are going to be very familiar. Having said that, every CCSP must be familiar with the unique considerations, processes, and controls that are required to effectively audit cloud environments.

Unfortunately for us cloud folks, there are many requirements, certifications, and attestations out there that were created for legacy IT environments, and still very few cloud-specific auditing frameworks to help us. Fortunately for us cloud folks, however, the Cloud Security Alliance has developed the Cloud Controls Matrix (CCM), which the CSA describes as the only meta-framework of cloud-specific security controls, mapped to leading standards, best practices, and regulations. As of this writing, the latest version of CSA's CCM is v4, and it was released in early 2021. Check out Appendix B for the download link.

TIP

The CSA CCM does a great job of identifying cloud-specific control requirements, identifying their applicability to each cloud service category (IaaS, PaaS, and SaaS), and mapping to numerous other standards and frameworks (like ISO/IEC 27001, PCI, HIPAA, FedRAMP, and many others). It's a great place to start for organizations that have no semblance of a cloud auditing framework or for organizations that need additional structure around their current audit process.

Internal and external audit controls

Any environment or application that stores or processes sensitive data should be subject to both internal and external audits, each with its own assortment of controls and audit requirements. Most of the audit and compliance information I speak about in this book is focused on external audits. These audits are the ones typically performed by an independent third party that comes in and assesses your system's security. These independent external audits are necessary to provide customers and regulators assurance that a CSP is meeting all of its regulatory and contractual security and privacy obligations. As daunting as it can be to have a perfect stranger come audit your security posture, you can imagine why it makes sense to conduct regular internal audits, as well.

Most organizations, and just about every cloud provider, should have an internal audit department. Internal audit acts as an organization's third (and final) line of defense against security threats and can be used to catch potential security or compliance gaps before an external auditor does. In addition to proactively identifying security and privacy gaps, internal audits can help an organization ensure that its policies and procedures are operating effectively and efficiently. In many cases, an internal audit report can identify potential cost savings or operating efficiencies that an external audit would not detect.

TIP

The concept of lines of defense is common at many enterprise organizations; I first heard it used in the banking industry, but have since heard it increasingly used in other industries (including by cloud providers). Within this model, the first line of defense includes the Information Security department and the actual business units that own the cyber risks and controls. The second line of defense is your organization's risk management function that looks at aggregate risk at an enterprise level. The third line of defense is your internal audit function. The three lines of defense model is effectively the organizational equivalent of "defense in depth," and it helps provide multiple layers of oversight of an information security program.

Impact of audit requirements

Audit requirements can have a major impact on any organization, system, or application. Certain features of cloud environments lead to some additional considerations and impacts when conducting audits. Many traditional audits require that an auditor physically visit each data center — imagine how hard this would be to manage for a globally dispersed CSP.

Additionally, the shared responsibility between the CSP and the customer requires that all parties fully understand their security responsibilities and properly prepare for their specific audit requirements.

All in all, the unique nature of cloud environments provides some challenges for those seeking to validate compliance. CCSPs (and cloud auditors, specifically) must consider these challenges and come up with new ways to audit cloud environments.

Identifying assurance challenges of virtualization and cloud

Hypervisors, virtual machines, and other virtualization technologies create massive challenges to auditing cloud environments. Audits of traditional data center environments usually start with a well-known inventory of all assets, and these auditors often expect to physically inspect the data center and those assets. It's easy to see how physical data center inspections can be a challenge for a large public cloud environment that includes hundreds of thousands (or even millions) of assets across dozens of data centers around the world. The notion of sampling is paramount in addressing this challenge. *Sampling* is the process of randomly selecting and auditing a subset of all systems. Some forms of sampling are as simple as randomly auditing 10 percent (for example) of all systems, but I have personally seen (and used) some pretty complex sampling methodologies that scale up or down depending on the size of the total asset population.

Sampling can help address challenges associated with the size and scope of an asset inventory, but what about the whole physical inspection ordeal? Well, data centers can be sampled, too. Although CSPs don't open their data center doors to the public, and in many cases not even to their customers, most CSPs have a process for specific external auditors to visit their data centers to audit physical and environmental controls. For large public clouds, rotating sampling of all the data centers across all regions is typical. Audit sampling reduces the audit burden on both the external auditor and the CSP, but ensures that every data center is physically inspected at least every few years.

REMEMBER

As great as this sampling stuff is, it fails to address the major challenges associated with virtualization. Auditors need to be able to audit the security of both physical and virtual resources, and the latter can be really . . . really challenging. It's incredibly important that a cloud auditor has a strong understanding of a CSP's virtualization architecture. The auditor gaining this understanding requires a lot of transparency from the cloud provider, but is critical to successfully provide assurance of a CSP's virtualized infrastructure.

In order for cloud auditors to effectively develop an audit plan, they must have access to full and complete documentation that describes the architecture and functioning of the cloud infrastructure or application. While no CSP is willing to disclose this information directly to their customers, most CSPs provide external auditors (under NDA) some level of access to architecture documentation and diagrams to do their jobs. Cloud auditors must pay close attention to hypervisor security and ensure that hypervisors and the virtualization infrastructure are implemented and configured properly. In doing so, the auditor can provide some level of assurance that the underlying virtualized components are secure and compliant with relevant regulations and best practices.

Types of audit reports

An *audit report* is a set of documents and artifacts that describe the findings from an audit and explain the audit's opinion of the system that was examined. These reports have been standardized by various entities over the years, each tailored to a specific industry or audience.

Despite their individual differences, the audit reports described in the following sections all serve the same general purpose of representing a system's security (or other organizational aspects) to interested stakeholders. SSAE, SOC, and ISAE are three of the most widely used audit report frameworks.

Statement on Standards for Attestation Engagements (SSAE)

SSAE stands for Statement on Standards for Attestation Engagements. SSAE 18 is a standard published by the AICPA in 2017 that is focused on audit methods. SSAE 18 imposes requirements on organizations to evaluate and report on their third-party vendors' security and risk profile.

In other words, in the cloud world, the SSAE 18 standard requires that CSPs evaluate their organizational controls to ensure that they meet a certain bar for managing risk.

SSAE 18 is intended to protect cloud customers from unknowingly exposing their business and data to risk by partnering with vendors (like cloud providers) that lack appropriate risk management practices. The standards outlined in SSAE 18 require organizations to create and issue SOC reports, which I introduce in Chapter 4 and discuss in the next section.

Service Organization Control (SOC)

SOC reports come in three types, and each has its own specific use.

SOC 1 is a control report that focuses strictly on an organization's financial statements and a service organization's controls that can impact a customer's financial statements. SOC 1 reports are considered *restricted use reports*, meaning that they are restricted to a limited scope of controls and restricted to a limited audience (including the service organization's management, controller, and auditors).

The two types of SOC 1 reports are

>> **Type I reports** focus on a description of the service organization's system, and the effectiveness of its policies and procedures at a specific point in time (a specific date).

>> **Type II reports** focus on the effectiveness of the same policies and procedures of Type I reports, but evaluate over a period of time instead of a single point in time. Type II reports must include an evaluation of a service organization's controls over a period of at least six consecutive months. Most organizations and users prefer (or even require) Type II reports because the evaluation over time provides a more comprehensive view than a single point in time.

SOC 2 audits and reports evaluate an organization based on AICPA's five Trust Services principles:

>> **Security:** The system is protected (both physically and logically) against unauthorized access and unauthorized disclosure of information.

>> **Availability:** The system is available for operation and data is available for use as committed and agreed upon in SLAs or contracts.

>> **Processing integrity:** System processing is complete, accurate, valid, and authorized.

>> **Confidentiality:** The system safeguards information designated as confidential or sensitive in accordance with laws, regulations, and best practice.

>> **Privacy:** The system collects, uses, and stores PII in accordance with the organization's stated privacy policy, and all relevant laws and regulations.

REMEMBER

SOC 2 reports can include some or all of the five trust services principles. The security principle must always be included, but the other four are optional, depending on the product/service provided by the organization. SOC 2 reports for cloud providers generally include all five principles, as all are applicable to the type of services they provide.

As you can see, SOC 2 reports cover a lot more than just financial risks; instead, they provide a comprehensive evaluation of the products/services that a CSP provides. There are two types of SOC 2 reports. Type I reports affirm that controls are in place, while Type II reports attest to the controls being in place and working effectively over a period of time. So, you guessed it: SOC 2 Type II reports are the ones you want to see to determine whether a CSP is adequately managing and protecting your data. As such, they are often relied upon by regulators and customers performing due diligence.

WARNING

Because of their names, many people mistakenly believe that a SOC 2 report is simply the next level up from a SOC 1 report. They are apples and oranges!

SOC 3 reports are closely related to SOC 2 reports — they share a common scope and cover the same principles. However, SOC 3 reports remove many of the details that SOC 2 reports include. They're intended to be publicly available reports that indicate whether an organization has demonstrated each of the five trust services principles, without disclosing anything sensitive or proprietary. SOC 3 reports are commonly used for marketing purposes, and you may also use them as an initial due diligence check of a potential cloud provider.

International Standard on Assurance Engagements (ISAE)

The International Standard on Assurance Engagements 3402 (ISAE 3402) is an international assurance standard that closely mirrors SSAE 18 (and its predecessor, SSAE 16). There are a few subtle differences between ISAE 3402 and SSAE 18, most of which are technical in nature. These differences are outside the scope of this book, but you should at least know that ISAE 3402 is mostly used outside of the United States, whereas SSAE 18 (and its SOC reports) are primarily used within the United States.

Restrictions of audit scope statements

Before a cloud provider (or any organization, for that matter) undergoes an audit, they generate a set of *audit scope restrictions* that set restrictions on what an auditor may and may not audit. The audit scope statements are important mechanisms that an organization uses to inform an auditor's creation of their audit plan and the eventual execution of the actual audit.

The specific list of scope restrictions that an organization sets is entirely up to the organization's management. Cloud providers must be careful not to overly restrict the auditor's ability to perform a thorough assessment that meets the provider's compliance objectives and customer obligations. In my experience, however, a good auditor has no issue telling a CSP when they are being too restrictive.

In general, audit scope restrictions should seek to limit operational impact by meeting the following objectives:

>> **Identify assets that are out of scope:** CSPs need to restrict certain physical or logical assets from the audit scope for various reasons. Certain assets may contain data that should not be included in the particular audit (for privacy reasons, for example). In other cases, the CSP may need to restrict technical testing (like vulnerability scanning) of their production environment or specific critical assets to maintain service availability and integrity.

>> **Identify blackout periods:** CSPs should identify times of week that are off limits for technical testing. These blackout periods may include times when the CSP expects to be unable to support the auditor's inquiries or periods when patch updates are planned for deployment, for example.

>> **Identify unacceptable tests:** Some CSPs give auditors free reign to choose their testing methods, but many restrict certain types of tests, particularly destructive tests that may cause outages or loss of data.

Gap analysis

A *gap analysis* is a comparison of actual results with desired results. In the audit world, a gap analysis is performed at the end of an audit and compares the results of the information that has been gathered and reviewed against relevant industry standards, regulations, and laws. Any deviation between what was discovered during the audit and the requirements in those standards/regulations/laws is known as a *gap*.

Gap analysis is one of the single most important components of an audit because it identifies room for improvement. An effective gap analysis should include input from reviews of documentation, system configurations, system scans and tests, and interviews with key personnel. By examining all these components, an auditor can identify gaps between what an organization says they do (in documentation and interviews) and what they actually do, as well as gaps between what the organizations does and what they should be doing (by law, for example).

Gaps are often called *findings* once they make it to an audit report. While findings are considered bad, let me tell you that it is rare to find an audit report without one (if not several).

Audit planning

A successful audit is largely dependent on having a solid, well-thought-out audit plan. *Audit planning* is conducted at the beginning of the audit process and includes all the steps necessary to ensure the audit is conducted thoroughly, effectively, and in a timely fashion.

You can use several methodologies to structure audit planning, but just about every audit includes the following steps or phases:

1. **Define the objectives of your audit.**
2. **Define your audit scope.**
3. **Complete the audit.**
4. **Review the results of your audit and identify lessons learned.**

TIP

A helpful reference for audit planning is ISO/IEC 19011:2018. This standard offers guidance on the steps to follow when you audit an information management system and can be a helpful resource when forming an audit program.

Defining your audit objectives

The first part of your audit plan nearly always deals with defining the audit objectives. You need to clearly outline what you want your audit to accomplish and identify how that will happen. Your audit objectives lay the groundwork for defining your audit scope (in the next step).

In general, you should accomplish the following during this phase of audit planning:

>> Identify and document the specific goals and objectives you hope to achieve.

>> Define the format of the audit.

>> Determine the desired outputs of the audit.

>> Establish roles and responsibilities for the audit, including number of auditors, and what personnel is required to support the audit.

>> Define an audit review process.

Defining your audit scope

An *audit scope* is a set of statements that identifies the focus, boundary, and extent of an audit. Your audit scope defines the physical and virtual locations of the audit, the resources that will be audited, and the time period that will be covered (for example, point in time audit versus one that covers six months). Defining a clear audit scope is the most important part of the entire audit plan, and having as much detail as possible helps ensure that the actual audit is straightforward to complete.

Many different types of audits exist, and scope can vary greatly from one audit to the next. The following list identifies some considerations that generally apply to the majority of audits:

>> **Previous audits:** One of the first things that an auditor must consider is the output of previously conducted audits. Specifically, new audits should validate that any previously identified critical or high audit findings have been remediated and closed by the CSP. If you're under audit, you want to demonstrate improvement from one audit to the next — having repeat findings not only shows lack of progress, but it is very frowned upon by auditors and regulators.

>> **Audit procedures:** Auditors should document the stages, steps, and procedures that they intend to follow during the audit. This documentation should include a broad description of the types of assessments that are planned and a rough sequencing of planned events.

» **Audit criteria:** The audit plan must identify and document what criteria the CSP is being audited against and the metrics that they'll be measured against. This documentation should include specifying any relevant standards or regulations and identifying the control sets that will be tested.

» **Time:** The audit scope should include a project timeline that identifies all key milestones and the timing of each stage. In addition, any blackout periods (or timeframes where testing is not permitted) should be specified up front.

» **Communications:** This is one of the most critical parts of the audit plan. The CSP, auditor, and (if applicable) the cloud customer must establish a list of all points of contact that will assist during the audit. On the CSP side, these contacts usually include members of the CSP's compliance team and SOC, among other stakeholders. In addition to a list of people, the audit plan should also include agreed-upon methods and frequency of communication, as well as a clearly defined escalation path for emergency situations.

» **Physical location:** When it comes to audit scope, physical location has two components. First, the audit scope must identify the physical location of all data centers, systems, and personnel that will be audited. This information must be clearly documented so that the CSP can ensure the right resources are available for review and testing. Secondly, the audit scope should identify the location from which any technical testing is to be conducted. Some CSPs require auditors to perform all testing on-site (like at the CSP's offices, on their corporate network), while others permit auditors to perform tests from remote locations. Remote audits are far more common in the post-pandemic world.

» **Included (and excluded) components:** When auditors talk about something being in scope, they are most often talking about which components are actually being audited. The audit scope should specify which data centers (including the specific hardware and software), documentation, and personnel will be evaluated. Audits that include technical testing generally begin with an established inventory of hardware and software components that will be tested. As I describe in the "Restrictions of audit scope statements" section, it's also important that the audit scope identifies any relevant restrictions, such as devices that should not be tested (in other words, out of scope).

REMEMBER

Which components are included in an audit is greatly dependent on the service model being tested. IaaS audits cover a broader scope and tend to include far more components than PaaS and SaaS environments.

» **Reporting:** Your audit plan should clearly set expectations around the delivery of the final audit report and any interim reporting milestones. Report format should be defined and documented, and the method of delivery should be identified up front. In addition, the target audience of the report should be specified — some reports are sent to the CSP, while others may be delivered to a regulator.

Completing your audit

Once you have a fully developed and approved audit plan, you can kick off the actual audit. While you conduct the audit, you should monitor to ensure that you remain in line with your audit objectives, assumptions, and defined schedule. In addition, you should continue to reassess the completeness of your defined scope; you should be constantly searching for unknown unknowns — or things that you did not plan to audit that add value to the overall engagement. For audits that include scanning or other potentially intrusive tests, you should continuously monitor for unintended impact to systems or users.

Identifying your lessons learned

Once you're done being audited, you can sleep for the first time in weeks. Aside from getting some much needed rest, you should also take time to identify any lessons learned from your audit.

Start with a thorough review of the audit report and focus on the critical, high and medium findings — try to identify any themes that that give you an indication of broad areas that need to be addressed. For example, maybe you have multiple findings that are related to CSP employees potentially accessing customer data; these findings would indicate an insider risk theme and may suggest that you might need to evaluate how your company protects customer data from disgruntled employees or user error. Also, keep an eye out for any findings that are easy fixes and make note of them for future audits. If this audit was your first, then the audit report is a great way to identify the types of things auditors look for — which can help you avoid those easy mistakes in the future.

Many cloud providers undergo multiple audits every year. In fact, the largest CSPs are continuously under some kind of audit all year around. After every audit, you should take a look at what was done and see whether you have room to consolidate multiple audits into one. Maybe your ISO auditor is capable of performing SOC 2 audits, and you can build a semi-annual schedule to perform both at once. Or, perhaps you can identify similarities in the types of evidence that each audit requires and potentially streamline efforts across the various audits.

Finally, step back and examine the overall audit process and think about what worked. More importantly, try to identify things that didn't work and find ways to improve them. Maybe the auditor knocked out a critical system — next time, you might have that system on the restricted list. Perhaps your staff was so bombarded by audit requests that they couldn't perform their day jobs — consider extending the timeline next time (or start collecting evidence before the audit even starts). The key is to learn something from every audit that makes future audits less painful.

Internal information security management system (ISMS)

An *information security management system* (ISMS) is a set of policies, procedures, and systems for systematically managing the security of an information system, like a cloud service offering. The main objectives of an ISMS are to manage risks to organizational and customer data, ensure business continuity, and protect the organization's reputation.

TIP

An effective ISMS must be built on three pillars: people, process, and technology. A large collection of security tools is useless without meaningful policies and effectively trained personnel to implement and use them.

As a CCSP, you should design and implement your organization's ISMS using one or more widely accepted standards. While various industry standards can fit the bill, the most widely accepted international standard is ISO 27001 (which I reference throughout this book and cover in Chapter 4). The latest version, ISO 27001:2022, was published in late 2022. ISO 27001 is the standard that most organizations refer to for ISMS best practices and compliance requirements. While ISO 27001 provides the ISMS specification, ISO 27002 offers guidance and recommendations that can be used to enforce the specification.

An ISO 27001-compliant ISMS begins with a complete set of security policies that govern the organization's implementation, management, and use of security controls. While these policies should already be in place, an ISMS requires that they receive upper-level management support that establishes information security as a priority for the organization. Once the policies are fully in place, the next step is to perform a risk assessment. I discuss risk assessments in the "Understanding the Implications of Cloud to Enterprise Risk Management" section of this chapter, but for now, it's important to understand that ISO 27001 requires an ISMS to use a risk assessment to guide an organization's selection of controls. In other words, you should understand the threats and risks associated with your particular system, application, or data, and use that to determine the best set of security controls to protect your information system.

TIP

Aside from the ISO 27000 family of standards, the ITIL and COBIT frameworks offer standards and guidance on implementing and managing an ISMS. I introduce ITIL in Chapter 12, and you can research COBIT if you're interested in learning more.

Whether you rely on ISO 27001 or another established standard, a well-structured ISMS offers several benefits. Among other things, an ISMS helps you

>> Protect the confidentiality, integrity, and availability of your data — in all forms, in all locations; this includes on-premise and cloud data.

>> Assess and reduce the threat of constantly evolving security risks and respond to security threats more effectively.

>> Reduce costs associated with information security by applying a risk-based approach to selecting and implementing security controls.

>> Build a company-wide culture of security that starts with executive management and makes its way down throughout the organization.

Internal information security controls system

As part of establishing your information security management system, you should identify a set of security controls by which you'll manage your information security. You have several options here, and your selection often depends on your company's industry. Companies that operate in the healthcare space usually rely on control sets for HIPAA, financial institutions often default to PCI, and U.S. federal agencies are very fond of NIST and FedRAMP controls.

Because cloud providers tend to have customers that span multiple industries, a broad international standard is a good place to start. That's right, you guessed it — ISO/IEC 27001 has its own control domains, each with a set of controls. If you've already read Chapter 4, then you know the 14 domains inside and out. If you haven't, then you should definitely go check them out before taking the exam!

TIP

Aside from providing you with a structure for managing your information system, information security controls systems are also very useful frameworks to help you prepare for an audit.

Policies

Policies are the cornerstone of every ISMS and are central resources that shape your organization's security culture. A *policy* formally documents a desired or required standard for a system or an organization — they are the overarching tenants that drive your organization. Policies set the bar for what an organization deems acceptable in a wide variety of areas and guide the organization's and its employees' operations and activities. Most organizations, especially large ones, manage a vast number of policies. Together, these policies form a holistic structure to govern the organization's people, processes, and systems. Policies are generally classified as organizational or functional.

WARNING

Do not confuse policies with procedures. I often hear these two terms used interchangeably, and though they are closely related, they are not the same! A policy is a guiding principle or standard, while a *procedure* is a series of steps that should be followed to accomplish a particular result. Policies generally focus on what should be done, while procedures are more focused on how to do it.

Organizational

Organizational policies govern how an organization is structured and guides the organization in running systematically and efficiently. Organizational policies are all of the higher-level policies that don't govern specific functions within an organization.

Some prime examples of organizational policies include

>> Code of ethics

>> Acceptable use policy

>> Vacation and sick leave policy

Functional

Functional policies are a bit more specific than organizational policies, and they set guiding principles for individual business functions or activities.

Some of the most common functional IT policies include

>> Information security policy

>> Access control policy

>> Physical security policy

>> Incident response policy

>> Backup and recovery policy

>> Email use policy

>> Password policy

>> Remote access policy

>> Disaster Recovery (DR) policy

>> Portable media policy

>> BYOD policy

Cloud computing

Cloud computing changes the policy game for customers and cloud providers, alike. When migrating to the cloud, customers must reassess their policies and make changes that accommodate the shift toward a shared environment with different risks and unique considerations. Customers must also review and understand their potential CSP's policies around encryption, data retention, and so on and determine whether those policies align with their own needs and compliance obligations.

On the other hand, a CSP must develop and maintain policies that meet or exceed their customer's requirements. A cloud provider must be sensitive to its customer's regulatory obligations in order to establish compliant policies and manage compliant systems.

Whenever a cloud provider cannot satisfy certain components of a customer's policies, those components must be identified and documented as policy gaps. The customer is then responsible for finding and implementing suitable compensating controls to reduce any risk associated with those gaps.

Identification and involvement of relevant stakeholders

Identification and involvement of relevant stakeholders throughout all security and compliance discussions is critical to ensure a highly compliant system and smooth audit planning. With a complete list of all stakeholders, you can better ensure that discussions include all needed inputs and communications are shared with all appropriate parties.

This phase is important for any organization or system, but is especially important in cloud environments. And, as always, the cloud presents its own unique considerations here. While your company must always search through its organization to identify the right people to involve in audits, you must now add your cloud provider to the mix. You should do so because the CSP (depending on your service model) may be responsible for much of your IT infrastructure and/or services. If you're using an IaaS offering, the cloud provider has access, control, and responsibilities that directly impact your ability to be secure and compliant — and you need their input anytime you face an IT audit. Mature CSPs have well-established processes for sharing pertinent audit information with their customers, but it is up to the customer to ensure they request and collect all the information they need for their given audit.

A few teams and business units routinely need to be involved in audits, on both the customer and provider sides. Expect to involve the following, at a minimum:

>> Compliance

>> Risk management

>> Legal

>> Operations

>> IT

>> InfoSec

Specialized compliance requirements for highly regulated industries

I've spent a great deal of my career focused on security and compliance for highly regulated industries. Healthcare, financial services, and government organizations tend to have very specific, often very stringent, security requirements. For example, FedRAMP/NIST requires CSPs to implement FIPS 140-3 validated encryption modules if they want to host U.S. government data — that's pretty darn specific, and it's only the tip of the iceberg. So, in addition to managing tons of jurisdictional security requirements, CSPs must be mindful of the type of data their customers have and any specialized requirements that come with that.

The most common compliance frameworks for highly regulated industries are HIPAA for healthcare and PCI for financial services. In addition, several countries have their own unique requirements for hosting government data — FedRAMP (and others) in the United States, IRAP in Australia, and so on. It's important to understand your data (and your customer's data) and recognize the associated compliance requirements.

TECHNICAL
STUFF

In addition to the compliance programs I mention throughout this book, NERC/CIP is another regulatory requirement to keep an eye on. The North American Electric Reliability Corporation (NERC) is a nonprofit regulatory body that oversees the bulk power system in North America. NERC enforces a set of reliability standards known as the NERC Critical Infrastructure Protection standards. Although cloud providers are not directly subject to NERC/CIP standards, customers in the energy space who own or operate power systems must consider these standards when using cloud providers. Some public cloud providers help their regulated energy customers by mapping NERC/CIP requirements to FedRAMP or other highly regulated compliance regimes.

Impact of distributed Information Technology (IT) model

Whereas legacy IT systems and applications usually rely on a traditional client-server model — with a handful of data layers in between — modern environments (like clouds) break this trend with highly complex, distributed architectures. By migrating your infrastructure or data to the cloud, you are thrust into a *distributed IT model* — one where components of your information systems are shared among multiple computers and locations to improve performance and efficiency. As you learn throughout this book, the nature of cloud comes with numerous challenges that must be evaluated before, during, and after any cloud migration.

With distributed systems, you must keep in mind the impact that diverse geographic locations can have on your systems and processes. In the traditional data center model, you're in full control of selecting the locations of your resources. You're able to research locations and their associated jurisdictional regulations, and you can choose locations that work best for your organization. In a distributed cloud environment, you're less in control of where your assets reside. A cloud provider can (and almost always does) move your data from one region to the next, in order to load balance and provide optimal performance. As a cloud customer, you must consider the needs of your data and determine whether this geographic distribution poses any compliance risk to your organization.

Understanding the Implications of Cloud to Enterprise Risk Management

As with any other IT product or service that your organization uses, using cloud services has an impact on your business' risk posture, which adds yet another consideration for potential users of the cloud. It's essential that you understand the implications that using the cloud has on your organization's enterprise risk management program.

Assessing providers' risk management programs

Any time you use a third party to host or manage your data, you must understand the vendor's risk management programs. When your data is hosted in the cloud, it is essential that you evaluate the provider's risk policies and methodologies and determine how they align with your own risk management objectives. You're really seeking to ensure that a CSP treats your data at least as well as you treat it.

Seeking this assurance is where audits and certifications come in handy; they can inform you about the information security controls that a CSP uses and the gaps and risks that they have accepted.

Difference between data owner/controller versus data custodian/processor

One of the key factors in determining the risk to your data is identifying the parties that access or control your data and understanding their roles and responsibilities. Many regulations and certifications require that organizations identify specific individuals or groups of individuals as data owner and data custodian. These meanings of these titles can vary slightly between regulations or from one organization to the next. In general, their definitions are as follows:

>> **Data owner:** A *data owner* is the individual who holds the responsibility for dictating how and why data is used, as well as determining how the data must be secured. In some cases, the data owner uses, handles, or otherwise processes the data. In other cases — like the cloud — the data owner outsources that to a third party. Even when outsourcing happens, the data owner does not lose control of the data (or the associated responsibilities). No matter who processes the data, the data owner is always responsible for specifying how the data is used, processed, and secured. In the privacy world, the data owner may be referred to as the data controller. The *data controller* determines the purposes and means for processing personal data.

>> **Data custodian:** A *data custodian,* simply put, is an individual who handles data on behalf of the data owner, under the oversight of the data owner. The data custodian is responsible for adhering to the data owner's established requirements for using and securing the data, and must handle or process the data in accordance with the data owner's established purposes.

Data processor is the privacy parallel to data custodian. A *data processor* is the person or entity who processes personal data on behalf of the data controller. In cloud environments, the CSP is typically considered the data processor.

TIP

The terms data controller and data processor have been around for some time, but really became popular with cloud providers when GDPR hit the scene. GDPR takes a strong focus on establishing roles and responsibilities for data ownership and processing, and it is the first global regulation that establishes legal implications to defining and assigning these roles.

Regulatory transparency requirements

Because of the shared responsibility between data owners (cloud customers) and data processors (cloud providers), many regulations have placed an increasing focus on transparency requirements for CSPs. Without a CSP sharing important risk information, cloud customers would be kept in the dark about their own risk profile, which would make it very difficult for them to ensure the security of the data that they own and control. Regulations like GDPR and Sarbanes-Oxley (SOX) include requirements for a cloud service provider to share relevant security and risk information with their customers.

TIP

One of the most common regulatory transparency requirements focuses on data breaches. Under regulations like HIPAA and ITAR, a CSP is formally required to notify all impacted customers if it discovers a breach of its systems or data.

Risk tolerance and risk profile

Together, the data owner and business management must establish an organization's risk appetite. *Risk appetite* (sometimes called *risk tolerance*) is the level of risk that an organization is willing to accept in its course of business. A high risk appetite means that your organization is prepared to accept a large amount of risk in favor of cost savings, innovation, or other factors. Companies with a low risk appetite have a conservative approach to risk management and often take extra levels of precautions to reduce threats to the business and its data.

Once your organization has established its risk appetite, you should conduct period risk assessments to determine and monitor your risk profile. A *risk profile* is an analysis of the existing threats posed to an organization and its assets (including its data). By comparing your risk profile against your established risk appetite, you're able to determine when changes to your security controls are necessary.

REMEMBER

Be sure to evaluate your cloud provider's risk profile as part of your organization's self-assessment. Understanding third-party risk is an important component of the overall risk view.

Risk assessment

A *security risk assessment* is a set of activities that seek to understand the information system and its environment and identify security risks by collecting and analyzing information, such as security policies, system configurations, network policies, and so on. Various regulations — like GDPR, HIPAA, FedRAMP, and others — require organizations to conduct risk assessments in order to verify that appropriate security controls are in place to safeguard against risks to the system.

You can use multiple different methodologies to conduct risk assessments, and I highlight some common risk frameworks in the "Different risk frameworks" section of this chapter. Generally speaking, four broad steps are involved in risk assessments:

1. **Identification.**

   The first step is to identify all critical assets within your organization and classify all your sensitive data. This step is all about finding the systems, applications, and information that need protecting. After identifying those systems, applications, and information, identify and describe the vulnerabilities, threats, and risks to all those assets.

2. **Analysis.**

   This phase focuses on evaluating the likelihood of identified threats exploiting weaknesses in your environment and determining the impact to your assets if that happens.

3. **Evaluation.**

   In this step, you compare the results of your risk analysis to your organization's established risk profile/tolerance. This comparison leads you to determining the best course of action for each of your identified risks.

4. **Treatment.**

   This final step is where you determine what to do with each of the identified risks. You have several options here, which I cover in the next section.

REMEMBER

Every risk assessment should begin with a vulnerability assessment and threat assessment. Once you have this information, risks are identified by assessing impact and likelihood. *Impact* essentially defines how disastrous something would be if it were to happen, while *likelihood* describes the probability that an event will actually occur.

Risk treatment

A comprehensive risk assessment should evaluate an organization's vulnerabilities (weaknesses), identify the threats that might exploit those vulnerabilities, and determine the likelihood and impact of successful exploits. Risk is the intersection of threat and likelihood. As Figure 14-1 shows, risk is really the intersection of likelihood and impact.

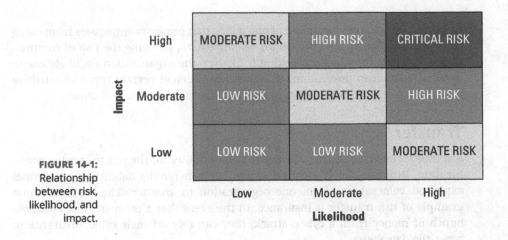

	Low	Moderate	High
High	MODERATE RISK	HIGH RISK	CRITICAL RISK
Moderate	LOW RISK	MODERATE RISK	HIGH RISK
Low	LOW RISK	LOW RISK	MODERATE RISK

Impact (vertical axis) — **Likelihood** (horizontal axis)

FIGURE 14-1: Relationship between risk, likelihood, and impact.

Once you identify and assess your organization's risks, the next step is to determine the best way to treat each of those risks. The four main categories for risk treatment are

>> Avoid

>> Mitigate

>> Transfer

>> Accept

Avoid

Risk avoidance is all about eliminating the identified risk by removing the activity or technology that causes the risk in the first place. Organizations use risk avoidance when a particular risk exceeds their acceptable risk tolerance. For example, an organization may use vulnerable SSL to encrypt certain internal communications. A risk assessment may determine that this risk is an easily exploitable vulnerability (high likelihood) that could cause highly sensitive data to be stolen (high impact). An example of risk avoidance would be deprecating the use of SSL within the organization and replacing it with TLS 1.3 encryption.

Mitigate

Risk mitigation (also called *risk reduction* or modification) is a strategy that involves lessening the potential impact that a threat can have on the organization. When an organization cannot avoid a risk, they can implement processes and technologies to reduce the harm that the risk might cause. For example, if an organization is using vulnerable SSL for internal communications, the organization might not be able to completely deprecate SSL because of technical dependencies. In this case, the organization can implement a policy that prevents employees from using the SSL communications channel for sensitive data, reducing the risk of compromised sensitive information. Taking it further, the organization could choose to use DLP (data loss prevention) technologies to detect certain types of sensitive information and prevent it from being sent across the insecure channel.

Transfer

Risk transfer involves shifting the entire responsibility for the risk to another organization. Risk transfer is most often used to transfer the liability of a potential exploited vulnerability from one organization to another. The most common example of risk transfer is insurance. In the event that a company loses a whole bunch of money from a cyber-attack, they can rely on their cyber insurance to cover the damages.

WARNING

Outsourcing functions like Help Desk or Security Operations Centers does not transfer risk. Although these functions transfer the day-to-day operation of certain tasks, the risk and responsibility ultimately falls on the data owner.

TIP

Many people refer to risk transfer as *risk sharing* and argue that risk can never be fully transferred, but only shared between parties. For example, even insurance plans come with premiums that the insured party must pay.

Accept

Risk acceptance involves, well, accepting a particular risk if it is completely within an organization's risk tolerance. Risk acceptance is the way to go if mitigating, transferring, or avoiding the risk would cost more than the costs associated with an exploit of the associated vulnerability. For example, an organization that uses insecure SSL to encrypt internal communications may opt to do nothing at all if the risk assessment determines that not enough compensating controls are in place to make up for use of the weak encryption algorithm.

WARNING

Risk acceptance must not be taken lightly! Deciding to take no action on a known vulnerability can have huge financial and reputational impacts. You also run the risk of legal trouble, if it's determined that you were negligent in protecting sensitive information. There's certainly a time and place to accept risks, but the decision must be backed by solid evaluation of your company's environment, threats, controls, and external obligations.

Different risk frameworks

Numerous risk frameworks exist in the IT world. Our friends at ISO and NIST have a couple noteworthy frameworks that pertain to cloud computing.

ISO 31000

The ISO 31000 standard provides organizations with risk management guidelines, including a framework and process for managing risk. Although this particular ISO standard cannot be used to achieve a particular certification, it is useful in helping organizations align their risk management practices with a globally accepted benchmark.

As of this writing, the current version of this standard is ISO 31000:2018. The standard defines a framework with five phases:

1. Design

2. Implementation

3. Evaluation

4. Improvement

5. Integration

ISO 31000:2018 also identifies the following eight principles that identify the essential characteristics of an effective and efficient risk management program:

» Integrated

» Structured and comprehensive

» Customized

» Inclusive

» Dynamic

» Best available information

» Human and cultural factors

» Continual improvement

NIST

Many of the best practices I share throughout this book are based on principles in one or more NIST standards. As part of the Federal Information Security Management Act (FISMA), the U.S. federal government requires that all U.S. government agencies conduct risk assessments that align with the NIST Risk Management Framework (RMF). NIST 800-37 revision 2 was published in 2018 and provides guidelines for establishing a risk management framework for information systems and organizations. Though it's only required by U.S. government agencies, it's a very helpful reference for cloud providers and other organizations.

Metrics for risk management

As I mention in a previous section, risks are measured in terms of the likelihood of an exploit occurring and the impact of successful exploit. In addition to impact and likelihood, you should be familiar with two specific risk metrics:

>> **Inherent risk** is the level of risk that exists prior to any actions being taken; it is the worst-case scenario that a risk poses. I'll use an everyday example to describe this risk. Any time you leave your home, you are taking the risk of being hurt — by a texting teenage driver, your neighbor's dog, or a falling piano. The likelihood of each of these risks probably varies from moderate to insanely low, but an inherent risk is there.

>> **Residual risk** is the level of risk remaining after you take preventative measures. You could (and should!) wear your seatbelt when you're in the car. This precaution reduces the potential impact of getting hurt in an accident, but some level of residual risk remains.

Assessing the risk environment

Thorough assessment of your risk environment involves assessing risks associated with your own infrastructure, as well as all vendors and services used to store, manage, or process your data. As a cloud customer, you should ensure that your cloud provider and its infrastructure have gone through a complete risk assessment and determine how the results of that risk assessment align with your organization's risk tolerance.

Understanding Outsourcing and Cloud Contract Design

Back in the Stone Age, understanding outsourcing and its impact on contract design was solely the responsibility of procurement and legal teams. As companies began outsourcing some of their data hosting responsibilities to *colocation data centers* (shared data centers that lease out equipment and bandwidth to companies), contract design got a little more technically involved and required additional input from IT teams. Though companies may lease space in a data center, they are still in full control of their systems and operations.

When outsourcing to the cloud, however, the equation changes — companies lose some of that control and must figure out how to address this in their cloud contracts. In addition, characteristics like on-demand self-service and rapid elasticity introduce additional complexities around cloud contracting: fixed-fee contracts don't typically work because of the fluid nature of cloud environments. Companies must understand their business requirements and the potential contractual implications of outsourcing to the cloud.

Business requirements

Before you enter into a contractual agreement with a cloud provider, your organization must consider the needs and requirements of your business and determine how a cloud provider can help meet those requirements. You should start by assessing your current infrastructure and applications and evaluating how your systems interact with each other and the outside world. This process can help you identify the business (and technical) requirements that your cloud provider needs to replicate (or at least come close to). As a CSSP, you should work closely with your organization's procurement team to identify gaps between a potential CSP's offering and the requirements that your organization has generated.

Finally, you should perform a risk assessment of the identified gaps to determine whether the CSP's risk posture fits within your organization's overall risk tolerance. Before entering into a contract with a cloud provider, you should identify all gaps and risks and determine whether each one can be accepted, mitigated, or transferred. If there are any unacceptable risks (like the CSP lacking HIPAA compliance to support your PHI), then risk avoidance means you'd need to move on to another option.

As with any vendor contract, your cloud contract should include various SLAs that codify expectations around your business requirements — things like system availability, performance, response times, and minimum level of security should be identified in your SLA. Equally as important, your SLA should also identify penalties on the CSP for any noncompliance or failure to meet the agreed-upon SLA.

Vendor management

The rise of cloud computing has caused Information Technology leaders to shift their attention from managing internal technologies to managing their cloud vendors. Instead of monitoring their company's home-grown infrastructure and applications, these IT leaders are increasingly focused on interacting with cloud vendors and monitoring their performance.

Vendor management is the process by which an organization manages risks related to vendors and ensures effective service delivery by that vendor. Vendor management is a new concept for many IT professionals, who have grown accustomed to being responsible for technology that they fully own and control. When this control is handed over to a cloud provider, it requires IT leaders to consider factors that they may not have considered in the past:

>> **Contract negotiation:** IT leaders should have a front-row seat for any cloud-related contract negotiations. As a CCSP, you are uniquely equipped to understand your organization's business requirements, cloud strategy, and risk profile. You are best suited to advise management about appropriate SLAs related to uptime, service availability, compliance, and so forth. And here's a free tip: You have more power in the negotiation phase than you do after you sign the contract.

>> **SLA monitoring:** As a CCSP, you should be involved in monitoring your cloud vendors' compliance with agreed-upon SLAs. You should have a technical POC at the cloud provider that you can communicate with on a day-to-day basis and should meet with the CSP regularly to review their SLA performance.

>> **Communications:** Managing a cloud vendor involves a whole new level of communications — internally and externally. IT leaders must ensure they are effectively communicating their needs and requirements to their vendors, while also appropriately setting expectations with internal management and cloud users. As a CCSP, you are the conduit between your organization and your cloud provider.

Contract management

Contract management is the process of managing contract negotiation, creation, and execution to reduce risk and maximize performance. When managing cloud contracts, you should consider several things. The following list is a great place to start, but should not be considered exhaustive:

>> **Definitions:** Every contract should include a list of terms used in the contract, along with their definitions. It's important that a cloud customer and provider reach agreement on what key terms mean before money changes hands. Failure to do so can lead to misunderstood commitments and difficult conversations down the road.

>> **Metrics:** Your contract should identify what metrics will be used to measure the vendor's performance and fulfillment of the contract and SLAs. The contract should specify the required criteria and define how they will be measured and quantified.

>> **Access to data:** How you (as a customer) access your data should be front of mind at all times, especially during contract management. Your contract should

include details about the methods and requirements related to you accessing your data in the cloud. You should also seek clear terms as to whether (and under what conditions) your cloud provider can access your data.

» **Performance:** Your SLA (which is part of your contract) should absolutely, positively include agreed-upon performance requirements. These performance requirements often include service availability and response times.

» **Security:** If you require any specific security requirements, then they should be included in your contract. Contractual security clauses can include technical requirements (like encryption of data-at-rest) or an operational requirement (like background checks for any cloud employees who can access your data).

» **Legal and regulatory compliance:** This point is a big one! If you have any specific legal or regulatory requirements, they should definitely be mentioned in your cloud contract. For example, if your cloud workload will include PHI, you should make sure that your CSP is committed to providing a HIPAA-compliant service. Remember, as data owner, it is your responsibility to satisfy your compliance obligations. Contractual commitment from your CSP can provide peace of mind, but you should also validate compliance by requesting relevant certifications and compliance reports.

» **Right to audit:** In true trust, but verify fashion, many customers want a right-to-audit clause in the cloud contracts, granting them permission to personally inspect a cloud provider's processes and even data centers, upon request. Most CSPs push back on this clause, as it can be insanely challenging to manage at scale — just imagine 2,000 customers individually asking to audit you. If you're a cloud customer seeking audit rights, you should have a really strong reason and prepare for a potential battle.

» **Litigation:** The contract between cloud customer and cloud provider should document the responsibilities of each party if either party should face legal action.

» **Termination:** They say all good things must come to an end. Your contract must clearly define the terms under which the contract may be terminated by either the provider or the customer. It should not only include the reasons for potential termination (for example, failure to meet SLAs), but should also identify any penalties associated with contract termination.

Supply-chain management

As technology systems grow increasingly complex, infrastructures and applications are becoming increasingly reliant on external components for functionality. When using a cloud environment, you are using all of the cloud provider's technologies as well as any external technologies that they are leveraging, and so on, creating a long chain of dependencies known as the *supply chain*.

Supply-chain management involves looking beyond your own technologies and evaluating the security and compliance of technologies that your organization depends on. As a CCSP, you should identify and document all components in your supply chain and fully assess the risk that each poses to your systems, applications, and data. You should evaluate your cloud provider and seek to understand what products and services they incorporate into their services that may present a risk to your organization. With this assessment, you'll be better able to design your own systems to compensate for any downstream supply-chain risk.

ISO/IEC 27036 is an international standard that offers guidelines for security of supplier relationships. Part 4 of this standard focuses specifically on cloud services and offers guidance on evaluating security risks related to cloud services and managing those risks effectively.

Supply-chain management is a critical topic that is increasingly gaining attention across most industries and within governments around the world. In addition to standards like ISO/IEC 27036 and NIST 800-161 ("Supply Chain Risk Management Practices for Federal Information Systems and Organizations"), the U.S. Department of Defense (DoD) recently established the Cybersecurity Maturity Model Certification (CMMC), which provides guidance for all suppliers that handle Controlled Unclassified Information (CUI). Regulations like the CMMC not only impact federal agencies, but also private sector companies (including cloud providers) who fall anywhere within the DoD's supply chain.

WARNING

Supply chain management doesn't only apply to standard hardware and software products. As generative AI (GenAI) gains popularity, organizations need to be increasingly focused on the supply chain implications of using AI models. It's important that you understand and monitor how the AI models that you use have been trained — a compromise to the underlying models can lead to unexpected behavior in your AI applications.

3

The Part of Tens

Identify and remember keys to preparing for your exam.

Set yourself up for success on exam day.

Chapter **15**

Ten (or So) Tips to Help You Prepare for the CCSP Exam

There's more to successfully passing the CCSP than reading an awesome book like this one! In this chapter, I share some tips to help you prepare for the exam — from the start of your journey until test day.

Brush Up on the Prerequisites

Cloud Computing and Information Security are two topics that involve a great deal of knowledge from different fields within Information Technology. It stands to reason, then, that mastering the field of Cloud Security requires knowledge about lots of technical (and even nontechnical) topics.

Before studying for the CCSP exam, you should make sure you have a grasp of the fundamental prerequisites. Chapter 2 provides an introduction to information security, which is absolutely critical.

In addition, you should brush up on networking (TCP/IP, routing, switching, etc.) and consider exploring the fundamentals of some of the bigger cloud providers (like Amazon Web Services, Google Cloud Platform, and Microsoft Azure).

Register for the Exam

It may sound trivial, but registering for the CCSP exam is one of the best things you can do to prepare for the exam. By selecting and committing to an exam date early on, you give yourself a fixed target to keep in mind as you study. Having this date marked on your calendar as soon as possible helps prevent procrastination and also supports you in establishing a realistic study plan and goals.

TIP

When registering for the exam, make sure that you first assess how much of the exam material you know and how much you need to learn. Consider your obligations between now and the potential exam day and make sure that the date you pick is realistic for your schedule.

In addition to giving you strong motivation (like $599 worth!) to study hard, registering for the exam early is a good idea to ensure that you get the date and time that works best for you. While Pearson VUE generally has multiple test centers and several time slots to choose from, availability can vary from city to city and based on the time of year.

Once you're sure that you want to take the CCSP, go online and head to `https://www.isc2.com/register-for-exam` to find your nearest test center and get registered.

Create a Study Plan

TIP

Create a study plan and commit to sticking to it. Depending on your knowledge level and amount of professional experience with the CCSP domains, I usually recommend between a 90- and 120-day study plan; anything shorter is likely to be too aggressive, while anything greater than 120 days often tends to lead to less intensive studying than required.

When creating your study plan, be sure to take into account your work schedule, holidays, travel plans, and anything else that may get in the way of intensive studying. The most important factor of a good study plan is that it is realistic — otherwise, you're setting yourself up for failure.

How granular you get with your study plan is up to you and depends on your need for more or fewer milestones. In general, I recommend breaking study plans up into weekly objectives, but some people prefer daily targets to more regularly hold themselves accountable. Whatever you choose, make sure to allocate enough time to get through all exam material before your exam date. For some, enough time may mean two hours of studying per day, while it's perfectly normal for CCSP candidates to spend four to six hours per day studying.

Find a Study Buddy

Having someone to study with can make the task of preparing for the exam much easier. Maybe you know someone who's already studying for the CCSP, or perhaps you have friends or colleagues who would benefit from the exam. If you're able to pair up for some of your study sessions, you should do it.

REMEMBER

If a traditional study partner isn't available, finding an accountability partner is a solid alternative. The objective here is to have someone you trust to check in during your CCSP journey and another ear to vent to when the going gets tough.

Take Practice Exams

One of the best ways to prepare for the CCSP exam is to practice with questions and exams that have similar questions. While no practice exams completely mirror the CCSP exam, several resources are available for you to practice and assess your CCSP readiness. To get you started, this book comes with two online practice exams (see the Introduction for more information).

WARNING

Stay clear of so-called exam dumps or brain dumps, which are actual CCSP exam questions that have been posted on the Internet. Not only does this method violate (ISC)² terms, but these dumps are often either out of date or just plain wrong. Stick to trusted sources for your practice questions and exams.

Get Hands-On

Experience really is the best teacher. To qualify for the CCSP cybersecurity certification, you must pass the exam and have at least five years of cumulative paid work experience in information technology, of which three years must be in information security and one year in one or more of the six domains of the (ISC)² CCSP Common Body of Knowledge (CBK). Aside from being a requirement to get certified, this hands-on experience is the best way to gain practical, real-life experience that translates to the concepts on the exam.

Getting started with cloud environments is simple and requires little more than an Internet connection and a credit card. Try setting up your own cloud environment and exploring the security features they offer. You may be surprised how quickly concepts stick when you see them in action.

Attend a CCSP Training Seminar

Depending on your learning style, you may benefit from taking an official (ISC)² CCSP Training Seminar or Bootcamp. These trainings are instructor-led and offered in-person and online. In-person options are five-day courses that cover all six domains within the CCSP exam, while the online training allows more flexible scheduling. These seminars are very rigorous and give you the option to ask questions from a CCSP trainer in real-time. You can find training schedules, costs, and other information at www.isc2.org.

Plan Your Exam Strategy

It's a good idea to give some thought to how you'll approach the exam on your big day. You have four hours to answer 150 questions, which comes out to just over 90 seconds per question. You'll know the answer to many questions in a fraction of that time, but you should plan ahead for how you'll approach questions that you don't immediately know the answers.

One strategy is to answer all the easier questions and flag the harder ones for review and answer at the end. The drawback to this approach is you can be left with quite a few challenging questions to answer in a relatively short period of time.

Another approach is to use the process of elimination to narrow things down to the two most probable answers; if you can get the toughest questions down to 50/50 chances, you're likely in good shape.

Aside from knowing when to skip questions and when to make educated guesses, you should have a strategy for taking breaks. If you don't build breaks into your exam strategy, you may forget to take them when the heat is on.

Get Some Rest and Relaxation

I've seen people still studying for certification exams as they're walking into the examination center. While it's good to double- or triple-check your knowledge, at some point you either know the information or you don't.

TIP

As a general rule, I recommend using the day before the test as your cutoff point and setting your study materials aside 24 hours before the exam. Find something you enjoy doing that doesn't involve reading technical reference materials or cramming for an exam. Catch up on shows you've missed while studying, go out for a bike ride, or hang out with friends and family that probably feel neglected by now! Whatever you do, remain confident in the study plan you created and followed and find as many ways to relax as possible.

Chapter **16**

Ten Keys to Success on Exam Day

I t's here, the day you've been waiting for . . . exam day! You've studied for months, practiced what you've learned, and now it's time to show that test who's boss! In this chapter, I provide some key tips to keep you focused and sharp during the examination. Good luck!

Make Sure You Wake Up

There's nothing worse than waking up late and rushing to a test center when you're already a little anxious. Set an alarm . . . set two alarms . . . have a friend call to make sure you're up on time. Do whatever you must do to make sure you get up with enough time to fully prepare for the day.

REMEMBER

It's important that you wake up in time to not only take the test, but also give your brain time to get up and running. It takes the human brain some time to fully boot up, so best practice is to wake up at least two hours before your exam.

Dress for the Occasion

Keep in mind that you're sitting for a four hour exam, and you'll want to make sure you wear comfortable clothes. Test centers can be warm or chilly, so it's a good idea to dress in layers (or pack a light jacket). Oh, and don't forget your lucky socks!

Eat a Great Meal

I've sat for lengthy exams and had my stomach growling halfway through. Don't be that guy (or gal)! Eating a well-rounded meal before you head to the test center is so important and goes a long way to helping you operate at a high level.

TIP

Focus on brain foods like fruits, nuts, and healthy fats (like fish or avocado) and stay away from food and drink that will have you crashing halfway through the exam.

Warm Up Your Brain

It's a good idea to help your brain reach optimal performance before walking into the test center. Starting your day off with a tall glass of water is a great idea to getting your brain and body up and running, and eating a great meal (see previous section) is crucial.

Some other things you can do include yoga, meditation, listening to classical music, and reading the newspaper. All of these activities have the secondary benefit of taking your mind off the exam, which is great if you're worried about getting nervous.

Bring Snacks and Drinks

Even after eating a healthy and hearty breakfast, you should pack a small bag of snacks to get you through the four hours. Start with a large bottle of water to keep you hydrated, but also consider packing a sandwich, trail mix, energy bars, or fruits and veggies to munch on while you test.

TIP

It's a good idea to first check with your test center to see whether they allow food or drinks on-site. Your registration confirmation email may have this information, or you can check www.pearsonvue.com/isc2 for the rules.

Plan Your Route

Whether your test center is five minutes or an hour away, you should map out your route from home ahead of time so that you know where to go and are prepared for any traffic or road closures that day.

Arrive Early

Plan to arrive at the testing center roughly 30 minutes before your scheduled exam time. An early arrival gives you a chance to make yourself at home before hopping on a computer and jumping right into the test. Arriving early allows you to find the restrooms, water fountains, and a good place to stretch your legs whenever you decide to take a breather.

Take Breaks

The CCSP exam is four hours long, and that's a long time to sit still in front of a computer. Plan ahead to take periodic breaks and make sure that you actually take them! You should think about how often you need breaks as you create your exam-taking strategy. Perhaps a break after every hour works best for you, or maybe taking a break after every 50 questions makes the most sense.

TIP

I recommend taking short breaks — just enough time to give your brain a break and your body an opportunity to relax. Get up, stretch, use the restroom, or just rest your eyes for a moment.

Aside from planned breaks, you should take a break anytime you hit a mental roadblock or feel like you're losing focus. Staring at a computer for too long can lead to loss of focus, which may contribute to careless mistakes as you take the exam. If you feel like your mind is starting to shut down, take a quick break before continuing.

Stay Calm

No matter how much you study, you will encounter questions that you just don't know the answer to — and that's fine! Keep this point in mind when you come across a difficult question. Take a deep breath. Close your eyes for a second. Stand up and stretch. Do whatever you must do to remain calm (within the rules of the testing center).

Remember Your Strategy

When things get challenging, neglecting your training and forgetting your strategy are easy things to do. You've studied for months, brushed up on all your weak areas, and you've developed an exam strategy that caters to your strengths. Remember everything you've learned and all the tips in this chapter (as well as in Chapter 15) and stay focused on your strategy.

4

Appendixes

Master key terms with the glossary.

Discover additional resources to help you learn and study.

Appendix A

Glossary

access control: the sum of all the technologies, processes, and personnel that are responsible for controlling access to resources

account deprovisioning: the process of removing access and disabling an account when a user no longer requires access to cloud resources

account hijacking: an occurrence when an unauthorized party gains access to and takes over a privileged account

account provisioning: the process of creating user accounts and enabling access to cloud resources

address allocation: the process of assigning one or multiple IP addresses to a cloud resource; this can be done either statically or dynamically

adverse event: an event that comes with negative consequences

aggregate risk: the combined risk of multiple individual security flaws or vulnerabilities

agile: an SDLC methodology in which development and testing activities occur simultaneously, cyclically, and iteratively

anonymization: the process of removing information that can be used to identify a specific individual from a dataset

application programming interface (API): a software-to-software communication link that allows two applications, such as a client and a server, to interact with one another over the Internet

application virtualization: the process of encapsulating (or bundling) an application into a self-contained package that is isolated from the underlying operating system on which it is executed

applistructure: includes the applications that are deployed in the cloud and the underlying services used to build them

artificial intelligence (AI): the field devoted to helping machines process things in a smart manner; AI involves giving machines the ability to imitate intelligent human behavior

asymmetric-key (public-key) encryption: a form of encryption that operates by using two keys — one public and one private

audit planning: conducted at the very beginning of the audit process and includes all the steps necessary to ensure the audit is conducted thoroughly, effectively, and in a timely fashion

audit report: a set of documents and artifacts that describe the findings from an audit and explain the audit's opinion of the system that was examined

audit scope restrictions: a set restrictions on what an auditor may and may not audit

audit scope: a set of statements that identifies the focus, boundary, and extent of an audit

authentication: the process of validating a user's identity

authenticator: things used to verify a user's identity

authorization: the process of granting access to a user based on their authenticated identity and the policies you've set for them

availability management: the process of ensuring that the appropriate people, processes, and systems are in place in order to sustain sufficient service availability

availability: security principle focused on ensuring that authorized users can access required data when and where they need it

bandwidth allocation: the process of sharing network resources fairly between multiple users who share the cloud network

bastion host: a system that runs outside your security zone that is generally designed to serve a single purpose (such as connecting to the management zone) and has been extremely hardened for enhanced security

black box testing: a software testing method in which the internal design of the component being tested is not known by the tester

blockchain: a string of digital information that is chained together by cryptography; each block of information contains a cryptographic hash of the previous block, transaction data, and a timestamp

breakout attack: a hypervisor security flaw that can allow one guest to break out of their virtual machine and manipulate the hypervisor in order to gain access to other cloud tenants

broad network access: the cloud characteristic that suggests that cloud computing should make resources and data ubiquitous and easily accessed when and where they're required

broken authentication: a vulnerability that allows an attacker to capture or bypass an application's authentication mechanisms; broken authentication allows the attacker to assume the identity of the attacked user, thus granting the attacker the same privileges as that user

building management system (BMS): a hardware and software control system that is used to control and monitor a building's electrical, mechanical, and HVAC systems

business continuity (BC): the policies, procedures, and tools you put in place to ensure critical business functions continue during and after a disaster or crisis

Canadian digital privacy act: a 2015 Canadian regulation that served as a major update to the long-standing Personal Information Protection and Electronic Documents Act (PIPEDA)

capacity management: the process of ensuring that the required resource capacity exists, at all times, to meet or exceed business and customer needs, as defined in SLAs

cardholder data: a specific subset of PII that is related to holders of credit or debit cards

chain of custody: the process of maintaining and documenting the chronological sequence of possession and control of physical or electronic evidence, from creation until its final use (often presentation in court)

change management: an IT discipline focused on ensuring that organizations employ standardized processes and procedures to make changes to their systems and services

checksum: a value derived from a piece of data that uniquely identifies that data and is used to detect changes that might have been introduced during storage or transmission

CIA triad: the three primary security principles: confidentiality, integrity, and availability

client-side kms: a key management service that is provided by the CSP, but the customer generates, holds, and manages the keys

cloud access security broker (CASB): a software application that sits between cloud users and cloud services and applications, while actively monitoring all cloud usage and implementing centralized controls to enforce security

cloud application: an application that is accessed remotely (via the Internet or secure network path) rather than installed and accessed locally

cloud auditor: a cloud service partner who is responsible for conducting an audit of the use of cloud services; the audit may be for general security hygiene, but is often for legal or compliance purposes

cloud controls matrix (CCM): a meta-framework of cloud-specific security controls, mapped to leading standards, best practices and regulations; published by the Cloud Security Alliance

cloud data portability: the ability to easily move data from one cloud provider to another

cloud deployment model: the way in which cloud services are made available through specific configurations that control the sharing of cloud resources with cloud users; the cloud deployment models are public, private, community, and hybrid

cloud resources: compute, storage, and networking capabilities that a cloud provider shares with a cloud user

cloud security posture management (CSPM): a set of tools and practices that continuously and automatically monitors your cloud environment, identifies misconfigurations and risks, and provides insights to maintain a strong security posture

cloud service broker: a cloud service partner who negotiates relationships between cloud service providers and cloud service customers

cloud service category: a collection of cloud services that share a common set of features or qualities; cloud service categories are labelled XaaS (where "X" can be anything, and "aaS" stands for "as a Service"); the most common cloud service categories are IaaS, PaaS, and SaaS

cloud service customer data: any data objects under the control of the cloud service customer that were input to the cloud service by the cloud customer or generated by the cloud service on behalf of the cloud customer

cloud service customer: a person or group that is in a business relationship to provision and use cloud services from a cloud service provider

cloud service derived data: any data objects under the control of the cloud service provider that were derived by interaction of the cloud customer with the cloud service; may include access logs, utilization information, and other forms of metadata (data about data)

cloud service partner: a person or group that supports the provision, use, or other activities of the cloud service provider, the cloud service customer, or both

cloud service provider (CSP): an entity making cloud services available for use

cloud service provider data: any data objects related to the operation of the cloud service that are fully under the control of the cloud service provider; may include cloud service operational data, information generated by the cloud service provider to provide services, and similar data not owned or related to any specific cloud customer

cloud service user: a person or entity (which may be a device, for example) that uses cloud services on behalf of the cloud service customer

cloud service: capabilities made available to a cloud user by a cloud provider through a published interface (a management console or command line, for example)

co-location data center: a shared data center that leases out equipment and bandwidth to companies

common criteria: a set of guidelines that establishes processes for products to be evaluated by independent laboratories to determine their level of security

community cloud: a cloud deployment model where cloud services are provided to a group of cloud service customers with similar requirements; it is common for at least one member of the community to control the cloud resources for the group

confidential computing: a cloud-based technology focused on protecting sensitive data by isolating it in a protected central processing unit (CPU) during processing

confidentiality: security principle that entails limiting access to data to authorized users and systems; in other words, confidentiality prevents exposure of information to anyone who is not an intended party

configuration management: the process of tracking and controlling configuration changes to systems and software

containers: a cloud technology that involves logically decoupling an application from its environment so that the containerized application can be developed, deployed, and run consistently in different environments (public cloud, private cloud, or even a personal laptop)

continual service improvement management: a lifecycle of constantly improving the performance and effectiveness of IT services by collecting data and learning from the past

continuity management: the process of ensuring that a CSP can recover and continue providing service to its customers, even amid security incidents or during times of crisis

contract management: the process of managing contract negotiation, creation, and execution to reduce risk and maximize performance

control plane: the part of the cloud environment that carries information necessary to establish and control the flow of data through the cloud; enables management of the cloud's infrastructure and data security

cross-site scripting (XSS): a specific variant of an injection attack that targets web applications by injecting malicious code

crypto-shredding: the process of encrypting data and then destroying the keys so that the data cannot be recovered

cryptographic module: any hardware, software, and/or firmware combination that performs encryption, decryption, or other cryptographic functions

cryptography: the science of encrypting and decrypting information to protect its confidentiality and/or integrity

cryptojacking: a form of malware that steals computing resources and uses them to mine for Bitcoin or other cryptocurrencies

cryptoprocessor: a dedicated chip that carries out cryptographic operations

dashboard: a single graphical view of multiple alerts and datapoints

data archiving: the process of removing information from production systems and transferring it to other, longer-term storage systems

data breach: an incident that occurs when an unauthorized party gains access to confidential or protected data; this access can include any type of data, with the key factor being the fact that it is viewed, retrieved, or otherwise accessed by someone who shouldn't have access

data classification: the process of categorizing and organizing data based on level of sensitivity or other characteristics

data custodian (data processor): an individual who processes the data on behalf of the data owner; the data custodian is responsible for adhering to the data owner's established requirements for using and securing the data and must process the data in accordance with the data owner's established purposes

data de-identification: the process of removing information that can be used to identify a specific individual from a dataset

data discovery: the process of finding and identifying sensitive information in your environment

data dispersion: the process of replicating data throughout a distributed storage infrastructure that can span several regions, cities, or even countries around the world

data localization law 526-fz: a Russian law established in 2015 that mandates that all personal data of Russian citizens be stored and processed on systems that are located within Russia

data loss prevention (DLP): a set of technologies and practices used to identify and classify sensitive data, while ensuring that sensitive data is not lost or accessed by unauthorized parties

data obfuscation: the process of disguising data to protect its confidentiality; examples include tokenization, masking, and de-identification

data owner (data controller): the individual who holds the responsibility for dictating how and why data is used, as well as determining how the data must be secured

data portability: The ability to easily move data from one system to another, without needing to re-enter the data

data retention policy: an organization's established set of rules around holding on to information

data science: a multidisciplinary approach to studying large and complex datasets and extracting meaningful insights using machine learning and various statistical techniques

data subject: the person whose data is being used

data tampering: an attack on the integrity of data by intentionally and maliciously manipulating data

data-at-rest: data that is stored on a system or device and not actively being read, written to, transmitted, or processed

data-in-transit (data-in-motion): data that is actively being transmitted across a network or between multiple networks

data-in-use: information that is actively being processed by an application

decryption: the process of using an algorithm (or cipher) to convert ciphertext into plaintext (or the original information)

defense-in-depth: applying multiple, distinct layers of security technologies and strategies for greater overall protection

degaussing: a data erasure method that involves using strong magnets to destroy data on magnetic media, like hard drives

deserialization: reconstructing a series of bytes into its original format (like a file)

DevSecOps: a software development practice aimed at combining security and IT operations into every stage of the software development lifecycle (SDLC)

digital forensics: a branch of forensic science that deals with the recovery, preservation, and analysis of digital evidence associated with cybercrimes and computer incidents

digital rights management (DRM): processes focused on protecting intellectual property throughout its distribution lifecycle

digital signature: a piece of information that asserts or proves the identity of a user using public-key encryption

direct identifiers: pieces of information that can be used on their own to identify an individual; an SSN is a perfect example of this, because there is a 1:1 assignment of Social Security Number to human being

directory service: a relational hierarchy of cloud identities that manages the storage and processing of information and acts as the single point through which cloud users can locate and access cloud resources

disaster recovery (DR): a subset of business continuity focusing on recovering your IT systems that are lost or damaged during a disaster

Distributed Denial of Service (DDoS): a coordinated attack by multiple compromised machines causing disruption to a system's availability

distributed IT model: a computing model in which components of your information systems are shared among multiple computers and locations to improve performance and efficiency

distributed resource scheduling (DRS): a feature that enables clustered environments to automatically distribute workloads across physical hosts in the cluster

domain name system (DNS): a decentralized naming system that translates domain names (like websites) to their IP addresses and back

domain name system security extensions (DNSSEC): a set of security extensions to standard DNS that support the validation of the integrity of DNS data; DNSSEC can help prevent DNS hijacking, DNS spoofing, and man-in-the-middle attacks

durability: the concept of using data redundancy to ensure that data is not lost, compromised, or corrupted

dynamic application security testing (DAST): also known as dynamic code analysis, this form of testing involves assessing the security of code during its execution

dynamic host configuration protocol (DHCP): a protocol that assigns and manages IP addresses, subnet masks, and other network parameters to each device on a network

dynamic masking: the process of masking sensitive data as it is used in real-time, rather than creating a separate masked copy of the data

dynamic optimization (DO): the automated process of constantly reallocating cloud resources to ensure that no physical host or its resources become overutilized while other resources are available or underutilized

e-discovery (electronic discovery): the process of electronic data being collected, secured, and analyzed as part of civil or criminal legal cases

edge computing: a form of computing that involves capturing, processing, and analyzing data at its source

electronic discovery reference model (EDRM): a model that provides an overall look at the e-Discovery process

encryption: the process of using an algorithm (or cipher) to convert plaintext (or the original information) into ciphertext

ephemeral storage: temporary storage that accompanies more permanent storage

evaluation assurance level (EAL): a numeric score that is assigned to a product to describe how thoroughly it was tested during the Common Criteria process

event: an observable occurrence in a system or network

factor: an individual method that can be used to authenticate an identity

federated identity: the act of linking a user's (or system's) identity on one system with their identity on one or more other systems

federation: the process of linking an entity's identity across multiple separate identity management systems, like on-prem and cloud systems

field-level encryption: a form of encryption that lets you encrypt individual fields as opposed to entire files or databases; field-level encryption offers more granular protection over your most sensitive information

filtering: the process of selectively allowing or denying traffic or access to cloud resources

FIPS 140-2: a U.S. government standard and program that assesses and validates the security of cryptographic modules

firewall: a hardware or software system that monitors and controls inbound and outbound network traffic

full-scale test: a business continuity/disaster recovery test that involves shutting down all operations at the primary location and shifting them to the BCDR site; the only type of test that provides a complete view of what would happen during a disaster

functional policies: policies that set guiding principles for individual business functions or activities

functional testing: a type of software testing that evaluates individual functions, features, or components of an application rather than the complete application as a whole

gap analysis: a comparison of actual results with desired results

gap: any deviation between what was discovered during the audit and the requirements in those standards/regulations/laws

general data protection law (LGPD): a Brazilian law that was published in 2018 and modeled after GDPR; it establishes standards for managing the privacy of Brazilian citizen personal data

general data protection regulation (GDPR): considered by most to be the world's strongest data privacy law; replaced the EU's 1995 Data Protection Directive with hundreds of pages of regulations that require organizations around the world to protect the privacy of EU citizens

generally accepted privacy principles (GAPP): a privacy framework that was published in 2009 by a Privacy Task Force created by the American Institute of Certified Public Accountants (AICPA) and the Canadian Institute of Chartered Accountants (CICA)

governance: the policies, procedures, roles, and responsibilities in place to ensure security, privacy, resiliency, and performance

Gramm-Leach-Bliley Act (GLBA): also known as the Financial Modernization Act of 1999, a U.S. federal law that requires financial institutions to safeguard their customer's PII

hardware security module (HSM): a specialized hardware device designed to act as a secure environment for generating, storing, and managing cryptographic keys, as well as for performing cryptographic operations (encryption and decryption)

hashing: the process of taking an arbitrary piece of data and generating a unique string or number of fixed-length from it

health insurance portability and accountability act (HIPAA): a law passed in 1996 that establishes minimum standards for protecting a patient's privacy, and regulates the use and disclosure of individuals' health information, referred to as Protected Health Information (PHI)

honeypot: a decoy system that mimics a sensitive system in order to lure attackers away from the legitimate target

host cluster: a group of hosts that are physically or logically connected in such a way that they work together and function as a single host

host-based DLP: data loss prevention that involves installation of a DLP application on a workstation or other endpoint device

hybrid cloud: a cloud deployment model that uses a combination of at least two different cloud deployment models (public, private, or community)

hypertext transfer protocol secure (HTTPS): TLS over HTTP — the gold standard for protecting web communications

hypervisor: a computing layer that allows multiple operating systems to run simultaneously on the same piece of hardware, with each operating system seeing the machine's resources as its own dedicated resources

identification: the process by which you associate a system or user with a unique identity or name, such as a username or email address

identity and access management (IAM): the sum of all the technologies, processes, and personnel that are responsible for controlling access to resources

identity provider: a trusted third-party organization that stores user identities and authenticates your credentials to prove your identity to other services and applications

IEC: International Electrotechnical Commission

impact: a metric that defines how disastrous something would be if it were to happen

incident handling: the process of preparing for, addressing, and recovering from security incidents

incident management: the process of monitoring for, responding to, and minimizing the impact of incidents

incident response plan: a set of policies and procedures that identifies steps to follow when an incident occurs, as well as roles and responsibilities of all stakeholders

incident: a violation or imminent threat of violation of computer security policies, acceptable use policies, or standard security practices

indirect identifiers: information that can help narrow down a set of individuals, but cannot be used to identify a single individual on its own; examples of indirect identifiers include birthdates, race, gender, and the other identifiers that apply to multiple people

information rights management (IRM): a data security technology that protects data (typically files, but also emails, web pages, and other information) from unauthorized access by limiting who can view, copy, forward, delete, or otherwise modify information

information security management system: a set of people, processes, and technologies that manages the overall security of a company's systems and data

information security management: codifies the protection of your environment's confidentiality, integrity, and availability as part of your overall IT management objectives

information security: the practice of protecting information by maintaining its confidentiality, integrity, and availability

infrastructure application security testing (IAST): an approach to security testing that identifies an application's vulnerabilities during runtime (like DAST), but does so from within an application code

infrastructure as a service (IaaS): the cloud service category that provides infrastructure capabilities to the cloud service customer

infrastructure as code (IaC): a tool that allows developers to view and manipulate their IT environments directly from lines of code using a programming or configuration language

injection attack: a broad class of attacks in which a malicious actor sends untrusted commands or input to an application

input validation: the process of ensuring that all input fields are properly checked and approved by the application prior to processing the input; requires locking down your application code to only allow expected input types and values, and filtering any suspicious or untrusted inputs

insecure deserialization: an occurrence when an application or API takes an untrusted stream of bytes and reconstructs it into a potentially malicious file

insider threat: the potential for someone who has (or has had) legitimate system or data access to intentionally or unintentionally compromise a system, data, or organization

interaction identifier: a mechanism used to link all relevant events to a single user interaction

integrity: the security principle that involves maintaining the accuracy, validity, and completeness of information and systems; ensures that data is not tampered with by anyone other than an authorized party for an authorized purpose

International Information System Security Certification Consortium (ISC)[2]**: International Standard on Assurance Engagements 3402 (ISAE 3402):** an international assurance standard that closely mirrors SSAE 18 (and its predecessor, SSAE 16)

Internet of things (IoT): a term used to describes everyday devices, such as smart home devices, that are connected to the Internet

Internet Small Computer Systems Interface (iSCSI): an IP-based storage standard that enables the use of SCSI over TCP/IP networks

interoperability: the ability for two or more systems to seamlessly work together by sharing information and using that information as necessary

intrusion detective system (IDS): a hardware appliance or software application that monitors networks and systems and alerts designated personnel of any malicious or unauthorized activity

intrusion prevention system (IPS): a hardware appliance or software application that is designed to actually block suspected attacks, in addition to alert on them

ISO: International Standards Organization

Kubernetes: an open-source platform for managing containerized workloads

KVM switch (KVM): an input/output device that allows users to access and control multiple computers from a single keyboard, video display, and mouse

layered security: *see defense-in-depth*

least privilege: the security practice that asserts that access to information should only be granted on a need-to-know basis

legal hold: the process of preserving any data that is, will, or might be relevant during a legal investigation

lift-and-shift: the process of taking applications and workloads from one environment and seamlessly placing them in another, usually cloud-based, environment

likelihood: a metric that describes the probability that an event will actually occur

limit: acts as the opposite of a reservation and sets a maximum amount cloud compute resources that can be used

log injection attack: an occurrence when an attacker creates false log entries or injects malicious content into logs through unvalidated input

log management infrastructure: the hardware, software, networks, and media used to generate, transmit, store, analyze, and dispose of log data

logical unit number (LUN): a unique identifier that's used to label each individual chunk; can represent a single disk, a partition of a disk, or an array of disks, depending on how much storage space a cloud tenant provisions

machine learning (ML): a subset of AI that focuses on allowing machines to alter themselves as they are exposed to additional data

maintenance mode: allows a provider to gracefully move a tenant's workloads to another physical host while maintenance is being performed

management plane: the interface and set of functions that supports and enables control of a cloud environment and the hosts within it

masking: the process of partially or completely replacing sensitive data with random characters or other nonsensitive data

measured service: delivery of cloud services in such a way that its usage can be monitored, accurately reported, and precisely billed

metadata: filenames, file headers, or other information that provides valuable insight about the data and its contents; often referred to as data about data

metastructure: the set of mechanisms that connects the infrastructure layer to the applications and data being used

multifactor authentication (MFA): a control that requires more than one form of authentication be used for user authentication in order to reduce the risk of granting access to someone impersonating someone else

multitenancy: allocation of cloud resources such that multiple tenants and their data reside on the same physical hardware and share the same physical resources

network controller: a centralized point of control used to configure, manage, and monitor a physical and virtual network infrastructure

network security group: a feature popularized by Microsoft that effectively combines the concepts of security groups with network ACLs; network security groups allow you to control traffic to and from either an OS or an entire network

network-based DLP: data loss prevention that involves monitoring outbound traffic near the network perimeter

nonrepudiation: the ability to ensure that the origin or author of data cannot be disputed

North American Electric Reliability Corporation (NERC): a nonprofit regulatory body that oversees the bulk power system in North America; NERC enforces a set of reliability standards known as the NERC Critical Infrastructure Protection standards

OAuth: an open standard that applications can use to provide clients with secure access delegation

object: file storage that can be accessed directly through an API or web interface, without being attached to an operating system

on-demand self-service: a characteristic of cloud that allows a cloud service customer to provision cloud resources and capabilities with little or no interaction with the cloud service provider

open web application security project (OWASP): an online community that is dedicated to providing organizations around the world with free, practical resources to support application security

OpenID: an open standard and a decentralized authentication protocol that allows users to authenticate to participating applications (known as relying parties)

orchestration (application or service): the process of bundling and integrating two or more applications or services to automate a process

organizational policies: policies that govern how an organization is structured and guide the organization in running systematically and efficiently; higher level policies that don't govern specific functions within an organization

parallel test: a type of business continuity/disaster recovery test that involves bringing the secondary site up to full operational capacity, while maintaining all operations in the primary site

patch management: the part of configuration management that includes all processes for finding, testing, and applying software patches (or code changes) to your systems

PCI-DSS: Payment Card Industry Data Security Standard (PCI-DSS) is a proprietary security standard established by Visa, MasterCard, American Express, Discover, and JCB International in 2004

penetration testing: the process of conducting a simulated attack on a system or application in order to discover exploitable vulnerabilities (also called pentesting)

performance monitoring: routine collection and analysis of performance metrics for key components of the cloud environment; key components that should be monitored include network, compute, and disk, and memory

personal information protection and electronic documents act (PIPEDA): a Canadian regulation that applies to the collection, use, and disclosure of personal information throughout the course of all commercial activities in Canada; this was replaced by the Canadian Digital Privacy Act in 2015

personally identifiable information (PII): personal information, such as birthdates, addresses, and Social Security numbers, that can be used to identify an individual

platform as a service (PaaS): the cloud service category that provides platform capabilities so that the cloud customer can run code and develop applications using programming libraries that are managed and controlled by the cloud service provider

policy: formal documentation of a desired or required standard for a system or an organization

portability: the ease with which a party can move or reuse application or service components

privacy impact assessment (PIA): an evaluation process that organizations undertake to identify, assess, and mitigate the potential privacy risks and implications associated with a particular system, project, or initiative

privacy: entails limiting access to personal information to authorized parties for authorized uses; in essence, privacy is maintaining the confidentiality of personal information, specifically (rather than just any kind of sensitive data)

private cloud: a cloud deployment model where cloud services are provided to a single cloud service customer who controls their own cloud resources

private key: the key in public-key encryption that remains a secret of the owner and is required to decrypt messages that come in from anyone else

privilege escalation: an occurrence when an unprivileged (or regular) application user can upgrade their privileges to those of a privileged user (like an administrator)

privileged access management: all technologies and processes involved in managing the entire lifecycle of accounts with the highest privileges

problem management: the process of managing any and all problems that happen or could happen to your IT service

procedure: a series of steps that should be followed to accomplish a particular result

process for attack simulation and threat analysis (PASTA): a risk-based threat model, developed in 2012, that supports dynamic threat analysis

protected health information (PHI): information related to the past, present, or future health status of an individual that was created, used, or obtained in the course of providing healthcare services, including payment for such services

protection profiles: a set of security standards unique to a specific type of product, such as operating systems, firewalls, antivirus, and so on

public cloud: the cloud deployment model where cloud resources are controlled by the cloud service provider, and cloud services are made available to any cloud service customer

public key: the key in public-key encryption that is made publicly available for anyone to encrypt messages

quality assurance (QA): the process of ensuring software quality through validation and verification activities

rapid elasticity: the cloud characteristic that allows a cloud customer to quickly obtain additional cloud resources as the user's needs require

rate limiting: the process of controlling the amount of traffic into or out of the cloud network

raw-disk storage: storage that allows data to be accessed directly at the byte level, rather than through a filesystem

recovery point objective (RPO): the maximum amount of data loss that's tolerable to your organization

recovery service level (RSL): the percentage of total computing power, performance, or functionality needed during business continuity

recovery time objective (RTO): the amount of time within which business processes must be restored in order to avoid significant consequences associated with the disaster

regulatory compliance: the requirement for an organization to meet or satisfy regulations, guidelines, policies, and laws relevant to its business

release and deployment management: planning, scheduling, and managing software releases through different phases, including testing in development environments and deployment to a production environment, while maintaining the integrity and security of the production environment

remote KMS: a key management service that is owned, operated, and maintained on-premises by the customer

repudiation: the ability of a party to deny that they are responsible for performing some action

requesting party: the person, group, or organization who does not own the digital evidence and initiates the request for such evidence from the responding party in an e-Discovery request

reservation: a feature that guarantees a cloud customer to have access to a minimum amount of cloud compute resources, either CPU or RAM

resiliency: a metric that measures the ability of a cloud provider to continue providing fully functioning services in the event of disruption

resource contention: an occurrence insomuch that there are too many requests and not enough resources available to supply all of those requests

resource pooling: aggregation of a cloud service provider's resources to provide cloud service to one or more cloud service customers

responding party: the person, group, or organization who has received an e-Discovery order and is responsible for providing the digital evidence to the requesting party

reversibility: the capability for a cloud service customer to retrieve their cloud service customer data and for the cloud service provider to delete this data after a specified period or upon request

risk acceptance: accepting a particular risk if it is completely within an organization's risk tolerance

risk appetite (risk tolerance): the level of risk that an organization is willing to accept in its course of business

risk avoidance: elimination of an identified risk by removing the activity or technology that causes the risk in the first place

risk management: the field that deals with identifying threats and vulnerabilities and quantifying and addressing the risk associated with them

risk mitigation (risk reduction or modification): a strategy that involves lessening the potential impact that a threat can have on the organization

risk profile: an analysis of the existing threats posed to an organization and its assets (including its data)

risk transfer (risk sharing): involves shifting or sharing the entire responsibility for risk to another organization

risk: the intersection of threat and vulnerability that defines the likelihood of a vulnerability being exploited and the impact should that exploit occur

sampling: the process of randomly selecting and auditing a subset of all systems

sandboxing: the process of isolating an application from other applications and resources by placing it in a separate environment (the sandbox)

scheduling: the process of taking customer resource requests and prioritizing those requests (or tasks) in such a way that available resources are assigned and utilized most efficiently

scrambling: an obfuscation technique that mimics the look of real data, but simply jumbles the characters into a random order

secure sockets layer (SSL): a deprecated network traffic encryption protocol that was replaced by TLS

security and information event management (SIEM): a software product or service that collects, aggregates, and indexes logs from multiple sources and makes those logs easily searched and analyzed

security assertion markup language (SAML): an XML-based open standard used to share authentication and authorization information between identity providers and service providers

security event management (SEM): refers to real-time monitoring and correlation of events

security group: a network ACL that operates that the VM level rather than the network level

security information management (SIM): products and services that provide long-term storage, analysis, and reporting of log information

security operations center (SOC): a centralized location where designated information security personnel continuously monitor and analyze an organization's security posture

security risk assessment: a set of activities that seek to understand the information system and its environment, and identify security risks by collecting and analyzing information, such as security policies, system configurations, and network policies

serialization: the process of breaking down an object (like a file) into a stream of bytes (0s and 1s) for storage or transmission

serverless computing: a cloud computing model that allows developers to run their code without needing to provision or manage servers

serverless function: a small piece of code that is executed in response to an event or trigger

service-level agreement (SLA): an agreement between a cloud service provider and cloud customer that identifies the minimum level of service that must be maintained

service-level management: the process of negotiating, developing, and managing all CSP SLAs

shadow IT: the use of unsanctioned or unauthorized technology (such as cloud services) within an IT environment, which may lead to unauthorized sharing of information with unapproved third parties

share: a technical feature that is used to mediate resource allocation contentions

simulation exercise: an enhanced version of a tabletop exercise that leverages a predefined incident scenario

single sign-on (SSO): an access control property that allows a single user authentication to be used to sign on to multiple separate, but related, applications

snapshot: a copy of a virtual machine, its virtual disks, and any settings and configurations associated with the VM; saved to disk as a simple file

software as a service (SaaS): the cloud service category that provides software/application capabilities to the cloud service customer

software development lifecycle (SDLC): the series of steps followed to build, modify, and maintain computing software

software-defined networking (SDN): an approach to network management that enables a network to be centrally controlled (or programmed), providing consistent and holistic management across various applications and technologies

spoofing: an attack during which a malicious actor assumes the identity of another user (or system) by falsifying information

statements on standards for attestation engagements (SSAE): a standard published by the AICPA in 2017 that is focused on audit methods

static application security testing (SAST): a security testing technique that involves assessing the security of application code without executing it; SAST is a white box test that involves examining source code or application binaries to detect structural vulnerabilities within the application

static masking: the process of duplicating the original data with sensitive components masked in the new copy

storage clusters: the logical or physical connection of multiple storage systems in a way that allows them to operate as a single storage unit

storage controller (disk array controller): a device that manages and controls storage arrays

structured data: information that is highly organized, categorized, and normalized

substitution: an obfuscation technique that mimics the look of real data, but replaces (or appends) it with some unrelated value

supply chain: the list of hardware and software dependencies that a system or application is built with

symmetric-key (secret key) encryption: a form of encryption that uses the same key (called a secret key) for both encryption and decryption

tabletop exercise: a formal walkthrough of the BCDR Plan by representatives of each business unit involved in BCDR activities

tenant: one or more cloud service users sharing access to a set of cloud resources the nonprofit organization behind the CCSP, CISSP, and other information security certifications

threat actor: the entity that poses a threat to a system, application, or data

threat modeling: a technique by which you can identify potential threats to your application and identify suitable countermeasures for defense

threat: anything capable of intentionally or accidentally compromising an asset's security

token: a reference to sensitive data that has no meaning or sensitivity on its own

tokenization: the process of substituting a sensitive piece of data with a non-sensitive replacement, called a token

transport layer security (TLS): the standard technology used to encrypt traffic over a network, it creates an encrypted link ensuring all traffic between two points remains private

trust zone: a network segment that includes systems and assets that share the same level of trust

trusted platform module: a microcontroller (computer chip) that is designed to provide hardware-based security functions to a system

unified extensible firmware interface (UEFI): a backward-compatible specification that improves on legacy BIOS functionality and security

unsanctioned SaaS: a form of modern shadow IT that refers to employees using SaaS applications without proper approval or oversight

unstructured data: information that cannot be easily organized and formatted for use in a rigid data structure, such as a database

vendor lock-in: occurs when something prevents a customer from moving from one cloud provider to another

vendor management: the process by which an organization manages risks related to vendors and ensures effective service delivery by that vendor

versioning: the process of creating and managing multiple releases of an application, each with the same general function but incrementally improved or otherwise updated

virtual local area network (VLAN): a set of servers and other devices within a LAN that are logically segmented to communicate with each other as if they were physically isolated on a separate LAN

virtual machine (VM): technology that emulates the functionality of physical hardware and allows cloud customers to run operating systems (OS) in a virtualized environment

virtual private cloud (VPC): a logically isolated network within a shared cloud environment; a VPC simulates private cloud functionality within a public cloud

virtual private network (VPN): technology that allows a private network to be securely extended over a public network (like the Internet) by creating a point-to-point connection between the private network and a device that sits outside that network

virtual TPM (vTPM): provided by the hypervisor and brings the security goodness of physical TPMs to virtual machines and guest operating systems

virtualization management tools: interface with virtualized components as well as the underlying physical hardware to oversee and manage the operations of the virtualized environment

virtualization: the act of creating virtual (for example, not actual) resources like servers, desktops, operating systems, and so on

VM sprawl: the uncontrolled growth of VMs to the point where the cloud administrator can no longer effectively manage and secure them

volume: a virtual hard drive that can be attached to a virtual machine (VM) and utilized similar to a physical hard drive

vulnerability management: the process of identifying, classifying, and fixing vulnerabilities that exist in your system

vulnerability scanning: the process of assessing an application or system for known weaknesses

vulnerability: a weakness or gap existing in a system

waterfall: an SDLC methodology in which you complete each phase in sequential order, flowing through each step of the cycle from beginning to end

web application firewall (WAF): a security appliance or application that monitors and filters HTTP traffic to and from a web application

white box testing: the opposite method of black box testing, it involves granting the tester complete knowledge of the tested component's inner workings

XML external entity (XXE) attack: an attack that occurs when XML input containing a reference to an external entity is processed by an application without thorough parsing

zero day vulnerability: a security flaw that is so new that the software developer has yet to create a patch to fix it

zero trust architecture (ZTA): a security model that's built on the idea that no entity inside or outside of an organization's security perimeter should be trusted

Appendix B
Helpful Resources

CISSP For Dummies, 7th Edition, by Lawrence Miller and Peter Gregory, is a fantastic book from the Wiley collection that covers all the information you need to learn the Information Security prerequisites — and pass the CISSP exam (the CCSP's older brother). In addition, check out the other helpful resources I list in this chapter.

(ISC)² and CCSP Exam Resources

Make sure that you check out the following exam resources:

>> **(ISC)² Non-Disclosure Agreement:** www.isc2.org/exams/non-disclosure-agreement

>> **(ISC)² certification reference materials:** www.isc2.org/certifications/References

>> **(ISC)² training resources:** www.isc2.org/training

>> **CCSP experience requirements:** www.isc2.org/Certifications/CCSP/experience-requirements

>> **CCSP exam outline:** www.isc2.org/CCSP-Exam-Outline

Standards and Guidelines

This section includes some of the most essential standards and guidelines provided by organizations like NIST and ISO. These are great references to understand best practices (or even requirements) for public sector and commercial organizations.

NIST:

>> **NIST 800-145: The NIST Definition of Cloud Computing:** https://csrc.nist.gov/publications/detail/sp/800-145/final

- » **NIST 800-53 (Revision 5): Security and Privacy Controls for Information Systems and Organizations:** https://csrc.nist.gov/pubs/sp/800/53/r5/upd1/final

- » **NIST 800-37 (Revision 2): Risk Management Framework for Information Systems and Organizations: A System Life Cycle Approach for Security and Privacy:** https://csrc.nist.gov/pubs/sp/800/53/r5/upd1/final

- » **NIST 800-88: Guidelines for Media Sanitization:** https://csrc.nist.gov/publications/detail/sp/800-88/rev-1/final

- » **NIST Cybersecurity Framework (CSF):** www.nist.gov/cyberframework

- » **Federal Risk and Authorization Management Program (FedRAMP):** www.fedramp.gov

ISO/IEC:

- » **ISO/IEC 27001:2022 Information Security Management:** www.iso.org/standard/27001

- » **ISO/IEC 27002:2022: Code of Practice for Information Security Controls:** www.iso.org/standard/75652.html

- » **ISO 27017:2015: Code of Practice for Information Security Controls based on ISO/IEC 27002 for Cloud Services:** www.iso.org/standard/43757.html

- » **ISO/IEC 27018:2019: Code of Practice for Protection of Personally Identifiable Information (PII) in Public Clouds Acting as PII Processors:** www.iso.org/standard/76559.html

- » **ISO/IEC 17788:2014: Cloud Computing — Overview and Vocabulary:** www.iso.org/standard/60544.html

- » **ISO 19011:2018: Guidelines for Auditing Management Systems:** www.iso.org/standard/70017.html

- » **ISO/IEC 20000-1:2018: Service Management System Requirements:** www.iso.org/standard/70636.html

- » **ISO/IEC 27037:2012: Guidelines for Identification, Collection, Acquisition and Preservation of Digital Evidence:** www.iso.org/standard/44381.html

- » **ISO/IEC 27041:2015: Guidance on Assuring Suitability and Adequacy of Incident Investigative Method:** www.iso.org/standard/44405.html

- » **ISO/IEC 27042:2015: Guidelines for the Analysis and Interpretation of Digital Evidence:** www.iso.org/standard/44406.html

- » **ISO/IEC 27043:2015: Incident Investigation Principles and Processes:** www.iso.org/standard/44407.html

- » **ISO/IEC 27050-1:2019: Electronic Discovery Overview and Concepts:** www.iso.org/standard/78647.html

- » **ISO 31000:2018: Risk Management Guidelines:** www.iso.org/standard/65694.html

Others:

- » **GDPR:** https://gdpr-info.eu/

- » **Common Criteria:** www.commoncriteriaportal.org/

- » **SSAE 18:** www.aicpa.org/content/dam/aicpa/research/standards/auditattest/downloadabledocuments/ssae-no-18.pdf

- » **Federal Rules of Civil Procedure:** www.uscourts.gov/sites/default/files/cv_rules_eff._dec._1_2018_0.pdf

- » **Federal Rules of Evidence:** www.uscourts.gov/sites/default/files/Rules of Evidence

Technical References

This section includes some great technical references:

- » **OWASP Top 10:** https://owasp.org/www-project-top-ten/

- » **OWASP Logging Cheat Sheet:** www.owasp.org/index.php/Logging_Cheat_Sheet

- » **Shared Responsibility Model (as described by AWS):** https://aws.amazon.com/compliance/shared-responsibility-model/

- » **CSA Top Threats to Cloud Computing: Pandemic Eleven:** https://cloudsecurityalliance.org/artifacts/top-threats-to-cloud-computing-pandemic-eleven/

- » **CSA Cloud Controls Matrix (CCM):** https://cloudsecurityalliance.org/research/cloud-controls-matrix/

- » **SANS Top 25 Most Dangerous Software Errors:** www.sans.org/top25-software-errors/

- » **Verizon Data Breach Investigations Report (DBIR):** www.verizon.com/dbir

- » **Electronic Discovery Reference Model (EDRM):** www.edrm.net/

Index

F

FaaS (Function as a service), 59–60

factors, authentication, 31, 238, 356

Federal Information Processing Standard (FIPS) 140-2, 103–104, 356

Federal Information Security Management Act (FISMA), 68, 141

Federal Risk and Authorization Management Program (FedRAMP), 68, 101

Federal Rules of Civil Procedure (FRCP), 295

Federal Rules of Evidence (FRE), 295

federated identity, 181–182, 234–235, 356

federation process, 181, 356

FedRAMP (Federal Risk and Authorization Management Program), 68, 101

field-level encryption, 74–75, 356

filtering, 150, 356

Financial Modernization Act of 1999, 141, 300, 357

FIPS (Federal Information Processing Standard) 140-2, 103–104, 356

firewalls, 231, 258, 356

FISMA (Federal Information Security Management Act), 68, 141

FRCP (Federal Rules of Civil Procedure), 295

FRE (Federal Rules of Evidence), 295

full-scale test, 194, 356

Function as a service (FaaS), 59–60

functional policies, 320, 357

functional security requirements, 93

functional testing, 224, 357

G

gap analysis, 314, 357

GAPP (generally accepted privacy principles), 303–304, 357

gaps, 314, 357

General Data Protection Regulation (GDPR), 126, 301, 357

generally accepted privacy principles (GAPP), 303–304, 357

geofencing, 80

GLBA (Gramm-Leach-Bliley Act), 141, 300, 357

governance, 67, 357

Gramm-Leach-Bliley Act (GLBA), 141, 300, 357

guest operating systems, 251–252, 267–268

H

hackers, 88

hardware monitoring, 268–269

Hardware Security Module (HSM), 115, 246–247, 357

hashing, 116–117, 357

Health Insurance Portability and Accountability Act (HIPAA), 68, 129, 141, 299–300, 357

HIDS (Host IDS), 259

high availability, 267

honeypots, 260, 357

host cluster, 266, 357

Host IDS (HIDS), 259

host-based DLP, 119, 357

HSM (Hardware Security Module), 115, 246–247, 357

hybrid cloud deployment, 49, 63–64, 357

Hypertext Transfer Protocol Secure (HTTPS), 34, 358

hypervisors, 81, 94, 155–156, 170–171, 358

I

IaaS (Infrastructure as a service), 49, 57–58, 94, 138–139, 359

IaC (Infrastructure as Code), 222, 264–265, 287, 359

IAM (Identity and Access Management), 16, 31–32, 77–79, 83, 234–241, 358

IAST (interactive application security testing), 225–226, 358

identification, 31, 181–182, 358

Identity and Access Management (IAM), 16, 31–32, 77–79, 83, 234–241, 358

identity attribution, 139–140

identity providers (IdPs), 236–237, 358

IDS (intrusion detective system), 258–259, 359

impact, 326, 358

incident handling, 39–43, 358

incident management, 277, 358

Incident Response (IR) lifecycle, 39–43

incident response plan, 358

incidents, defined, 358

indirect identifiers, 128, 358

information disclosure, 218

Information Rights Management (IRM), 129–132, 358

information security, 25–43, 358

information security management, 358

Information Security Management System (ISMS), 97, 276, 358

infrastructure application security testing (IAST), 225–226, 358

Infrastructure as a service (IaaS), 49, 57–58, 94, 138–139, 359

Infrastructure as Code (IaC), 222, 264–265, 287, 359

infrastructure service capability, 56

injection attacks, 210–211, 359

About the Author

Arthur J. Deane, CCSP, CISSP, is the chief information security officer (CISO) of Amazon Health Services. He is a seasoned information security professional with nearly two decades of experience building security programs and teams at multiple global organizations. Prior to Amazon, Arthur held security leadership roles at Google, Capital One, and PricewaterhouseCoopers, as well as security engineering roles at various U.S. Government agencies.

Arthur is an adjunct professor at American University and a member of the Computer Science Advisory Board at Howard University. He holds a bachelor's degree in electrical engineering from Rochester Institute of Technology (RIT) and a master's degree in information security from the University of Maryland. Arthur holds numerous industry certifications and is also the co-author of *The Official (ISC)2 CISSP CBK Reference, 6th Edition*.

Dedication

To one of the most inspiring people I know: my mother, Deserrie. Thank you for being such a special person to so many people. I wouldn't be who I am today without you. This book is for you!

Author's Acknowledgments

I'd like to thank the Wiley team for the opportunity to create and maintain this important book. I especially want to call out Lindsay Lefevere and Kezia Endsley for being amazing editors throughout this project — you really made my job easy. A special thanks to my brilliant friend, Pat Saint-Tulias, for agreeing to lend his expertise as the technical editor for this book.

Thanks to my family, friends, and loved ones for the encouragement during those long nights. Marcus, thank you for your support along the way.

There are also many other people and organizations — seen and unseen — that helped make this book possible. Thank you, all!

Publisher's Acknowledgments

Acquisitions Editor: Lindsay Lefevere

Managing Editor: Kristie Pyles

Project Editor: Kezia Endsley

Technical Editor: Patrick Saint-Tulias

Production Editor: Pradesh Kumar

Project Manager: Elizabeth McKee

Cover Image: © alice_photo/Adobe Stock Photos